MW01280017

THE
HAUNTED
SOUTHWEST

THE
HAUNTED
SOUTHWEST

Towards an Ethics of Place in
Borderlands Literature

CORDELIA E. BARRERA

TEXAS TECH UNIVERSITY PRESS

This book is typeset in EB Garamond. The paper used in this book meets the minimum requirements of ANSI/NISO Z39.48-1992 (R1997). ♾

Designed by Hannah Gaskamp

Library of Congress Cataloging-in-Publication Data
Names: Barrera, Cordelia E., 1966– author.

Title: The Haunted Southwest: Towards an Ethics of Place in Borderlands Literature / Cordelia E. Barrera. Description: [Lubbock, Texas]: Texas Tech University Press, [2022] | Includes bibliographical references and index. | Summary: "Literary criticism situated within the Southwest borderlands, exploring embodiment and ethics, place and landscape, memory and haunting."—Provided by publisher.

Identifiers: LCCN 2021036728 (print) | LCCN 2021036729 (ebook) | ISBN 978-1-68283-125-0 (cloth) | ISBN 978-1-68283-132-8 (ebook)

Subjects: LCSH: Literature—History and criticism. | Borderlands—Southwestern states. | Collective memory—Southwestern states.

Classification: LCC PN98.M67 B37 2021 (print) | LCC PN98.M67 (ebook) | DDC 810.9/979—dc23
LC record available at https://lccn.loc.gov/2021036728
LC ebook record available at https://lccn.loc.gov/2021036729

Printed in the United States of America
22 23 24 25 26 27 28 29 / 9 8 7 6 5 4 3 2 1

Texas Tech University Press
Box 41037
Lubbock, Texas 79409-1037 USA
800.832.4042
ttup@ttu.edu
www.ttupress.org

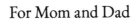
For Mom and Dad

CONTENTS

Contents

ILLUSTRATIONS

PROLOGUE

A letter to my father from the Spanish Archives division of the General Land Office in Austin, Texas, dated May 5, 1977, reads: "Our records show that Manuel Barrera is the original grantee of the tract La Tinaja de Lara which comprised 25,684 acres located in Jim Wells County. On September 28, 1836, the grantee was put in possession of the tract, he having occupied it in 1833. It was patented to the original grantee on May 8, 1899" (see appendix).

I remember early conversations about my family's history and my great-great-great-grandfather, Manuel Barrera. We held these talks around the dinner table during my high school years in the 1980s. Often these conversations focused on the fact that my father, as purported heir to the descendants of original owners of the Spanish and Mexican land grants, now called the Texas land grants, petitioned, in association with the Asociación de Reclamantes, that he was eligible to claim certain monies that Mexico accepted responsibility for owing due to an exchange of debts with a treaty signed by the US and Mexico on November 18, 1941.

What did it mean that my great-great-great-grandfather was presumably the original grantee of the tract La Tinaja de Lara, which comprised all that land in Jim Wells County? Why was my family now in Laredo, and why were we not rich landowners? Could anybody really *own* the land, and what of the people or structures that occupied the area now? For that matter . . . what did it mean that I had Spanish, and Mexican and Indian blood and lived on what was once Mexican soil but was now the United States?

My father, whose family lineage traces to Old Spain, remained haunted to his death by this history of dispossession. After years of pushing through the proper channels in Austin, he gave up the ghost that was La Tinaja de Lara. In the end, he acceded that any land our family had once had a legal claim to had been so permanently altered by Anglo dispossession, commercial farming and agribusiness, and rampant growth that "no amount of radical idealism [could] get it back" (Comer 1999, 222). At the legislative level, the whole project seems to have just fizzled out. I don't think he ever believed he'd actually get the land back, if there indeed was an actual *porción* to be "reclaimed." But my father was a storyteller like his father before him, and it was the story that was important. The story was moons away, at the threshold of a landscape first stolen and then denied, but it oriented his bones and spoke to his desires *to matter*. Stories, Norma Cantú (2015) reminds us, "mirror how we live life in our memories" (xxviii). The stories he told us were ours, he said. As a child, I was too young to make sense of plots and details, but I remember the names: Sor Juana Inés, La Adelita, Pancho Villa . . . La Llorona. His stories were full of battles, curses, *curanderas*, and rain gods, and the settings—Mexico, Old and New Spain, the Río Bravo—internalized our family's border origins. There were answers and lessons here in the psychic terrain of memory, but it would be decades until I formulated the question I now realize drove his desire to synthesize a past not dead, but reshaped, revised, and silenced. The question was: What is lost when people, and entire cultures for that matter, are not given the opportunity to read the stories of their lives meaningfully and correctly?

I now see that my father embodied a kind of exile and isolation, as throughout his life he remained oriented by a future that was only possible by recalling a reality bound by experiences in which his familial history had not been denied. It was as though he needed to release those memories, unnaturally and unjustly confined to the past, in order to feel genuinely and with a measure of certainty rooted in the present. He sought to undo the colonial logics that severed the familial traces he *felt* remained in the landscape, in the soil beneath his feet. The stories he told his children continually disturbed the present in that they spoke to an alternative hermeneutics attuned to bodies of knowledge and internal narratives generally dismissed or destroyed by colonizing Euro Americans. He wanted us to treasure and learn from the ghosts of our ancestors, those phantoms nourished by other places and times and attuned to other worlds but nonetheless integral to our culture. Haunted by spectral pains and hopes perpetually disappointed, his memories of what La Tinaja meant to his father might never be resolved

Figure 1: My father, Ramiro Barrera Jr., jogs along undeveloped E. Del Mar Blvd. in Laredo, Texas, on December 11, 1989. Courtesy of *The Laredo Times*.

or accounted for, he said. The place signified by La Tinaja was real only in memory now, drained of the history and cultural allegiance that once oriented generations and, like my grandfather, citizens for whom land manifested a shared cultural past, a kind of soul. As a child, such feelings of dispossession and loss were incomprehensible to me. Why was my father so haunted by the meaning behind a place, a plot of land he never set foot on? The answer, it seemed, lay in the gaps among memory, history, and the complex, unassimilable, *felt* forces of modernism that dissolve a necessary and interrelated continuity with the past.

My father taught life sciences and kinesiology for over forty years, mostly at Laredo Community College, where he was also a basketball coach. A while back, I found an unpublished essay he wrote titled "On Middle-Age Running: 'And Miles to Go Before I Sleep,'" which was written in 1985, when he was forty-four years old. In this piece, he discusses the "running boom" and the pleasures of competitive sport. But what I found most fascinating was the way he described the simple contact with the earth beneath his feet as a "privilege." He wrote that a "bonus" to being an old runner was the presence of "the old earth itself. Becoming ever more intimately acquainted with the surface of the earth is probably the most powerful pleasure of my running in middle age. The sense of contact must have always been there; however, now I love it"[1] (figure 1).

My father (and his father before him) was desperate for his children to never lose sight of a cultural landscape eternally haunted by the threat of extinction and the absence of foundations. His stories veered from an abstract faith in modern values and the immediate promise of power and profit—values of little worth to him—towards preconquest and native modes of production and being in the world. A naturalist to the core and a marathoner well before it was trendy and fashionable, he was infatuated with the Tarahumara of Chihuahua, who he reminded his children relied on their aboriginal knowledge of the land, water, and agriculture for their survival. Such were the shapes that filled the empty space of what La Tinaja de Lara signified.

PREFACE

I am a product of the South Texas *monte*. Indoor games meant little for me and my friends growing up in Laredo in the 1970s and 1980s. As kids in the newly developing suburbs of north Laredo, we spent our summers exploring the open terrain a mere two blocks from our homes. Our north side neighborhood dissolved into thickets of native chaparral, and we lived to explore monolithic plateaus of sticky brush where we built endless forts from mesquite limbs broken by families of wild javelina. The land stretched forever, it seemed, and we built forts and waded to our knees in natural ponds where we fished for crawdaddies. We prowled the *senderos* and explored miles of untamed *monte* fed by natural creeks and reservoirs.

Today, the wild landscape of my childhood home has been overtaken by malls, expanding suburbs, and endless strip centers. In fact, with the passage of the North American Free Trade Agreement (NAFTA) in 1994, Laredo was poised to burst its small-town seams, which it now seems to have done in earnest, as evidenced by a nearly doubled population between 1990 and 2010. In the twenty-first century, initial 2020 census reports indicate a population of 265,761; but this does not include the Laredo–Nuevo Laredo metropolitan area, which has an estimated population of over 636,000, a number that may or may not include those who live and work in the area without official residency papers. Although the city is recognized as the largest and most important inland port on the US–Mexico border, Laredo's infrastructure is notoriously disorganized, and the new wealth and substructures created by NAFTA have wrought havoc on the ecological limits of this once sleepy border place of overwhelmingly Mexican and Hispanic origin.

Laredo's wild spaces, like those of South Texas and the greater Southwest, are vanishing. In *Adios to the Brushlands*, Arturo Longoria bemoans the systematic clearing of native chaparral in South Texas by large-scale ranching and dry farming practices that exploded in earnest in the 1970s and 1980s.[1] But this was only the beginning. Today, the devastation of the chaparral in the name of oil and gas exploration and unbridled corporate interests is choking the lifeblood of the *monte verde* that is our sacred heritage as *tejanas/os*. With the impending possibility of an expanded border wall, unceasing immigration debates, and a spillover of Mexican *narco* violence along this desiccated stretch of earth, it remains to be seen how this unique biosphere will fare. Finally, the dark shadow of an ever-increasing military presence and additional threats wrought by the building of detention centers to house asylum seekers and refugees in the Borderlands comprises another layer in the complex matrix of what I call the "Bordered frontier," a term I use to unpack what I argue are the intrinsic connections between the frontier and the border in the American Southwest.[2] I conceptualize the Bordered frontier as a kind of container that entwines both systems; like the two sides of a coin, the Bordered frontier signifies an obverse relationship between border and frontier imaginaries. Reading with the Bordered frontier in mind necessitates shifting the lens between a discursive mixture of registers from American literary forms—such as the Gothic—alongside conceptions that speak to Indigeneity, Aztec and Mayan mythologies, and preconquest ways of living in the world.

A brief example illustrates my point. Larry McMurtry's *Dead Man's Walk* (1995), chronologically the first installment of the *Lonesome Dove* tetralogy and the third published, details the earliest exploits of fictional Texas Rangers Augustus McCrae and Woodrow Call.[3] The year is 1842 and the young rangers are on an expedition to capture and annex Santa Fe, New Mexico for Texas—an enterprise doomed to catastrophic failure. In fact, the novel can be read as a series of failures during which the Rangers' various missions are brutally and continually thwarted by Comanche warriors and Mexican officials. These failures resonate for Woodrow Call as aspects of landscape. Significantly, Call will remain supremely stubborn and steadfast in his unwavering commitment to serve the Republic and later the State of Texas throughout the tetralogy. Yet, after an initial encounter with Comanche fighters led by the warrior Buffalo Hump that leaves two Rangers killed and the others stupefied as to the stealth, skill, and ease with which the "wild Indians" thwart their efforts, a disconcerted Call muses: "The land before him, which looked so empty, wasn't. A people were there who knew the emptiness better than he did; better than [Rangers] Bigfoot or Shadrack. They knew it and they claimed it. They were the people of the emptiness" (81, 83). Later, Call once more thinks to himself how he "had a sense of trespass, as he rode. He felt that he was in a country that wasn't his. . . . [I]t was the Comanches he trespassed on. Watching them move across the face of the canyon, on a trail so narrow that he couldn't see it, had shown him again that the Comanches were the masters of their country to a degree no Ranger could ever be" (261).

As a Texas Ranger, Woodrow Call wholly embodies the "myth of the frontier," a decidedly American story that translates landscape to symbol and is entrenched in the idea of vast spaces to be filled and a process of finite expansion. The sentiment Call manifests, however, has no basis in a frontier mythology, as it speaks not to processes and signifiers of settlement central to Manifest Destiny and American exceptionalism but to aspects of *place* that subvert a frontier mythogenesis. What Call registers is a nascent structure of feeling tethered to an alternative hermeneutics that underscores what Pierre Nora (1989) calls *milieux de mémoire*, "real environments of memory" (7). This break in Call's reasoning, a rationale that signals the incongruity of his colonial violation, is more than a rupture in his equilibrium. Rather, it is the ephemeral nature of the landscape itself that disturbs the currency of the frontier vision, for the landscape has revealed itself as a place rife with history and a cultural legacy of its own. As I discuss herein, Call's collapse of memory speaks to a dialectic that indexes the complexities social and cultural geographers theorize in terms of space and place.

The Bordered frontier allows us to theorize intrinsic relationships between the mythic space of the American frontier imaginary in the Southwest alongside *and in conversation with* the US–Mexico Borderlands as a place rife with a history and culture of its own. In her pioneering work of cultural studies, *Borderlands/La Frontera*, Gloria Anzaldúa (2012) reminds readers of the ancient, continuous story that Indigenous cultures and *mestiza/os* must recover on the path towards a historical accounting that insists upon a moral and ethical reckoning with ancestral places and originary sites of collective belief. With this in mind, *The Haunted Southwest* makes manifest the dialogic nature of complex ideologies that entwine the intrinsic connections between border and frontier paradigms in the Southwest. The goal is to deconstruct ideologies based in the historical prioritizing of vast, open spaces, for it is the imperatives bound within the myth of the frontier that stagnated, silenced, and erased the histories and stories of those othered by official US policy. This path requires us to read the landscape as a palimpsest, a system of related colonial and contemporary geographies, as does Saldaña-Portillo (2016) in her study of national spaces and racialized notions of citizens on the US–Mexico Borderlands.[4] José David Saldívar (1997) reads the landscape similarly. He uses the term "topospatial" (75) to configure the US–Mexico Borderlands as palimpsest, as a space worked upon, etched over in terms of history and modernist practices that occluded or erased earlier customs, conventions, and belief systems. It is upon this palimpsest that American ideologies and Indigenous and other ways of knowing contend for legitimacy.

A primary goal of *The Haunted Southwest* is to re-situate the histories and ruling mythologies of cultures and people—literary and otherwise—men and women like my father whose stories, and thus memories, have been effectively silenced by official doctrines and policies in the American Southwest. A question *Haunted* seeks to answer is whether there is an ethical component to affirming the American Southwest as something akin to a cultural heritage site, a signifier of history for Mexican Americans, *tejanas/os* and *mestizas/os*. This brings to mind the legendary Aztlán and the historical speculation of its location in the American Southwest. The naming of Aztlán as a Chican@ homeland in the 1960s announced a shift in terms of a new consciousness seated in the myths and legends of the Mexica, a move that consciously and publicly recognized Native American and Indigenous heritage. To date, although it has lost much of its cultural currency, Aztlán remains a powerful signifier of the lingering grief that resulted from the annexation of Mexican territories by the US as a result of the Mexican–American War of 1846–1848. The ethics surrounding the naming of Aztlán, however, remain problematic, as the mapping of Aztlán necessitated the appropriation and incorporation of Indigenous territory from Texas to Colorado and Utah and all along the Pacific Coast.[5] It is beyond the scope of *Haunted* to trace specifics regarding Indigenous peoples and issues of survivance in the American Southwest that resulted from the Treaty of Guadalupe Hidalgo.[6] What is clear, however, is a trajectory of erasure that begins in earnest following the signing of this treaty and which I argue coalesces with the language and metaphorical thrust of Frederick Jackson Turner's frontier thesis at the turn of the twentieth century. The resultant disidentification and alienation from landscape and Indigenous origins for formerly Mexican citizens (now Americans or Mexican Americans) and Native Americans with tribal affiliations to Comanche, Lipan, Yaqui, Kickapoo, and countless others are complex and perhaps unsurprising, given that, in Turner's historiography Indigenous peoples "eventually cede ground and vanish from the landscape in the face of white settlement's superior order" (Saldaña-Portillo 2016, 9). But I am concerned with traces, with what Lauret Savoy (2016) so beautifully describes as "unvoiced lives," which carve "sharp-felt" absences that insist we remember how landscapes hold memories, and how reaching *beyond* memory can move us towards "some origin, to some direction" (29, 17) that extends one's individual and immediate consciousness beyond the boundaries of our communities and to the landscape itself.

Throughout *The Haunted Southwest*, I seek to trace the evidence of counternarratives such as those registered by Woodrow Call that suggest spectral forms and absences continuing to mark the Southwestern landscape, what Anne McClintock (2014) has called policies of "administered national forgettings" or topographies where unresolved forms of imperial violence push through (819). I draw from Avery Gordon's (2008) language to make contact with haunted spaces and citizens, and to move beyond an acknowledgement of the material effects they produce to establish what Gordon describes as "a reckoning with the instrumentality of hauntings" (18). By means of social and cultural geography, and in concert with Raymond Williams's (1977) "structures of feeling," I establish place and place-making as a primary way memories—private and public—are constituted. In this way, I show how conceptualizing landscape as both charged and permeated with memory and mythical and historical meaning anchors locality and historical context to disturb modernity's machinery, revealing beneath the surface a silenced subtext that begs for attention.

Anzaldúa assesses counterevidence in US–Mexico Borderland narratives and ideologies that have left material and spectral traces on *mestiza/o* bodies to evoke a Borderlands consciousness that is, arguably, nothing short of utopic. Using primal metaphors tied to Indigenous and embodied knowledge, she unearths deep and unexplored hidden transcripts with the goal of decoding a secret language that speaks of what is "other" to compel individuals and, indeed, entire cultures, beyond fragmentation towards forms of remembrance and coherence. Evoking myths and stories that yet haunt an American genocidal past, she labors to excavate Indigenous stories buried but not forgotten to rewrite a *new* reality where Borderlands subjects can embrace history as a process linked to humanistic desires beyond the tangle of administered forgettings.

The textual and literary discussions that frame *The Haunted Southwest* encompass stories in which characters like Woodrow Call and the "haunted cowboys" of chapter 4 signify aspects of space. Conversely, in classic works by Chicanos like Rudolfo Anaya, Arturo Islas, and Américo Paredes, as well as in the Chicana feminist theories of Gloria Anzaldúa, Cherríe Moraga, and Emma Pérez, individuals have to "home in" or return to very specific places of origin to find a basis of belief as well as to move forward. I discuss this pattern of return in conversation with scholars like Jelena Šesnić and Stuart Cochran to link ideas that speak to the ways that rootedness to a cultural landscape within postmodern narratives connects a vision of communal ethics to memories of lost places or ways of being. Following from the work of Latin@ and Chican@ theorists like Mary Pat Brady, José David Saldívar, Walter Mignolo, and others, I contend that characters—literary and otherwise—who are haunted by place or elements of landscape speak to the maintenance of a moral connection or a moral obligation *beyond* both the self and the present.

INTRODUCTION

I. Space: The Frontier as Origin Myth in the American Southwest

The story of the US–Mexico border has its origins in a frontier of exclusion, a frontier that existed solely in the interest of Euro American settlers.[1] At the Chicago World's Fair in 1893, Frederick Jackson Turner first presented his now famous address, "The Significance of the Frontier in American History," in which he confirmed the closing of the first period of American history: the end of the frontier. For Turner (1962), the so-called opening of the western landscape was a specifically white movement westward predicated on an "idealistic conception of the vacant lands as an opportunity for a new order of things" that could be found only in a vast, unsettled wilderness terrain (43). Turner lamented the vanished "free lands" of early, hearty pioneers, largely immigrants from Old World European countries such as Germany and Scandinavia who imagined a modern world, a "new order of society" (42, 44). He wrote:

> [T]he fact is that here is a new product that is American. At first, the frontier was the Atlantic coast. It was the frontier of Europe in a very real sense. Moving westward, the frontier became more and more American. . . . [T]he advance of the frontier has meant a steady movement from the influence of Europe, a steady growth of independence on American lines (5).

In the Turnerian model, Euro Americans moved west with a mind towards what he called freedom of opportunity, liberty, social advancement, and "a resistance to the domination of class which infused a vitality and power into the individual atoms of this democratic mass" (43–44). For Turner, the country's most effective social values were epitomized by a westward movement associated with democratic values. Turner, however, spoke only for whites—specifically white, middle-class men. More problematic is the fact that Turner based the "closing of the frontier" on 1890 census data that reflected a western population where most frontier land was comprised of individually owned property. He continues: "Up to our day, American history has been in a large degree the history of the colonization of the Great West. The existence of an area of free land, its continuous recession, and the advance of American settlement westward explain American development" (1966[1893], 79). Because Turner's language harmonized well with the faith in American exceptionalism, his conservative myth-making that this one causal force—the frontier—could *explain* American development as well as historical consciousness held sway for some time. Turner gave the frontier a national significance by adopting a certain terminology and point of view. This point of view, however, was entirely ethnocentric, as it viewed an intergroup contact situation from the vantage point of only one of the interested parties: Euro Americans. For Turner, the "most significant thing about the American frontier is that it lies at the hither edge of free land . . . the meeting point between savagery and civilization" (4).

By the twentieth century, New Western scholars like Richard White, Richard Slotkin, and Patricia Nelson Limerick explored the myth of the frontier, tracing its origins and evolution in terms of its narrative thrust and as a vehicle of cultural ideology. Limerick (1987), in her influential *Legacy of Conquest*, situates Turner's frontier thesis as the "origin myth" of white America (322). The "burden" of Western American history, she contends, lies with a mythology that ignores some very basic facts about Western history. Most notable is the fact that the myth, this "tale . . . bears little resemblance to the events of the Western past" (323). The myth transforms the landscape as well as Europeans, now Americans:

> *Europe was crowded; North America was not. Land in Europe was claimed, owned and utilized; land in North America was available for the taking. . . . Europeans moved from crowded space to open space, where free land restored opportunity and offered a route to independence. Generation by generation, hardy pioneers, bringing civilization to displace savagery, took on a zone of wilderness, struggled until nature was mastered, and then moved on to the next zone. . . . [T]he result was a new nation and a new national character: the European transmuted into the American. Thrown on their own resources, pioneers recreated the social contract from scratch. . . . At the completion of the conquest, that chapter of history was closed. The frontier ended, but the hardiness*

and independence of the frontier survived in [the] American character (322–23, italics in original).

Limerick's West is vast and far-reaching and includes the present-day states of California, Oregon, Washington, Idaho, Utah, Nevada, Arizona, New Mexico, Colorado, Kansas, Nebraska, Oklahoma, Texas, Montana, Wyoming, and North and South Dakota. The West—this space that has historically undergone conquest and, in fact, yet grapples with the consequences of conquest—nonetheless begs a certain fluidity.[2] Although the Turner thesis is the basis upon which much of early Western history rests, Turner's model, as the origin myth of white Americans, obviously erases a significant portion of the players—most notably Native Americans and Mexicans who occupied vast expanses of the Western frontier prior to Euro American movement westward.

In writing about myth and historical memory, Slotkin (1985) argues that "a constellation of stories, fables, and images" (16) have organized historical memory in the American West. Slotkin's *Fatal Environment* outlines an American historical narrative that takes place between 1800 and 1890, and so lies just outside the scope of the present study. I turn to Slotkin here for his focus on the metaphorical language and formal qualities and structures of myths as symbolizing functions key to understanding the culture that produces them. Slotkin, who continues his study of the frontier myth in *Gunfighter Nation: The Myth of the Frontier in Twentieth-Century America,* writes:

> The myth of the Frontier is our oldest and most characteristic myth, expressed in a body of literature, folklore, ritual, historiography, and polemics produced over a period of three centuries. According to this myth-historiography, the conquest of the wilderness and the subjugation or displacement of the Native Americans who originally inhabited it have been the means to our achievement of a national identity, a democratic polity, an ever-expanding economy, and a phenomenally dynamic and "progressive" civilization (1992, 10).

Fatal Environment begins with the idea that a story, a frontier myth positioned to explain American identity and ideology, is firmly entrenched within an expansive Western landscape. He states that the "mythic space called the Frontier" is patterned by a historical sequence suffused with meaning in the form of a story that transforms landscape to symbol and historical temporality into "'doom'—a fable of necessary and fated actions" (11). In this story, white settlers enlist and then index Native Americans

xxiv   Introduction

across a broad spectrum of omnipresent danger, making the landscape "a place of great hazard and disarray which they have been heroic enough to have brought into order" (R. White 1991, 618). Accordingly, *The Haunted Southwest* breaks open the meanings behind the fated actions that have shaped the stories and landscapes that pattern the frontier. More direct to my purpose in situating the frontier myth as a function of Euro American expansionist aims and storytelling in the Southwest, Slotkin, like Limerick, lays a firm foundation for deciphering Turner's language, specifically Turner's use of the frontier from the mid-1890s and onward. Slotkin (1985) argues that the myth of the frontier "was developed by and for an America that was a colonial offshoot of Europe, agrarian in economy, localistic in politics, tentative as to nationality, and relatively homogenous in ethnicity, language, and religion" (15). Further, Slotkin expands our understanding of how the myth further shaped early Euro Americans' response to Western industrialization and imperial expansion.

In *Frontier Gothic*, the myth is described as a "creation myth" that crafts a "Golden Age out of a vexed and complex heritage, artificially dislocating the present from the past" by viewing it with a time-fracturing nostalgia (1992, 19). As regards Turner's paradigm, editors Mogen, Sanders, and Karpinski consider how the myth serves as a nexus that guides the means by which Americans both romanticize their heritage and distance themselves from it. The moral failings that result from such distancing are evident in the fiction of Arturo Islas, Cormac McCarthy, Américo Paredes, and Larry McMurtry, as described herein. In Limerick's (1987) careful examination, the West's "moral burden" is comparable to that of the South, as is evidenced by the lingering injustice that an invading and conquering people did and still impose on a native population. This moral failure is a result of competition for land and natural resources as well as a struggle for cultural dominance (27). I turn to Limerick here because she writes from a decidedly ecological and multicultural point of view to show how historians have failed to understand the environmental limits of the land itself. Additionally, she situates her rewriting of Western history with an eye towards place and place-making that deemphasizes Turner's "migratory, abstract" (26) frontier as process, as well as history based on a "frontier of exclusion" (226). Accordingly, Limerick contrasts a Euro American vision with a Spanish vision, theorizing that, along the Borderlands, "the Spanish might well have had a 'frontier of inclusion'" that more readily and easily incorporated Indians into colonial society and economy (226).

Limerick, following David J. Weber (1998), further speaks to Turner's imprecise and shifting use of the term "frontier." Historian Kerwin Lee Klein (1997) concurs, commenting at length about "Turner's professed disinterest in precise definition" (15). Sometimes, states Weber, Turner used the frontier "to represent a place, sometimes a process, and sometimes a condition" (34). Weber further recognizes that frontier zones impact cultures, institutions, and peoples quite differently, acknowledging that we must take into account motives on "both sides of a frontier" (41) This reminds us how Spanish Americans, as comparative historians tell us, attempted to assimilate Indigenous Americans rather than push them back or annihilate them as the English more generally did. Besides, in the American Southwest, even after 1848, writes Limerick, the Borderlands were "an ecological whole; northeastern Mexican desert blended into southwestern American desert with no prefigurings of nationalism. The one line that nature did provide— the Rio Grande—was a river that ran through but did not really divide continuous terrain" (222). Whereas the Spanish northern Borderlands of New Mexico served as a line of defense holding off Indian raiders as well as a strategic response to English and French imperial rivalry, Spanish colonization of Texas was a counter "chessboard" move against a French presence in the Mississippi Valley. Russian and English interest in California similarly provoked a Spanish countermove "extending the unwieldy unit of the borderlands" ever southward (227).[3] This brief foray into the metaphoric thrust of the shape of the frontier as origin myth shapes a complex mythology rooted in history, symbols, and cultural values. Similarly, the "Southwest" refers not simply to geographical lines on a map but to a landscape that can be conceptualized in terms of space, place, and time in the historical as well as modern imagination.

In terms of the American Southwest as a distinct region, Eric Gary Anderson's (1999) *American Indian Literature and the Southwest* makes clear "the need for a critical resituating of the Southwest" (195). Just as "southwestering narratives" cannot be bounded by any one single thesis (3), neither can we "bound" the peoples of the Southwest by a border or even a frontier for that matter. The Southwest is a region in constant motion, argues Anderson, and it is constantly moved through. Additionally, the Southwest as region functions as an active and complicated "convergence point that proves difficult to contain inside any one disciplinary or critical sphere" (4). For Anderson, the Southwest is a restless place of paradox where "alien, migratory cultures" have been encountering each other in competition for generations (3). Because the moves these "alien, migratory" peoples make are physical as well as metaphorical and metaphysical, his Southwestern boundary remains fluid and portable. Further, because historically and figuratively the Southwest is in constant motion, it must be defined from multiple, shifting points of view. In this light, the Southwest is a "complicated convergence point" where Euro American and American Indian cultures have, for generations, been migrating *"against"* each other (4, 5, italics in original).

I argue that critical regionalism is necessary to identify the forces that shape the frontier myth. This stratagem is described by José E. Limón (2008) as a theory and methodology by which to recognize, examine, and finally, foster localized identities in their cultural and socioeconomic fullness, especially as such stand antagonistically with burgeoning aspects of capitalism and later patterns of globalization. I discuss critical regionalism in conversation with a century-old performance in Laredo in chapter 2. I introduce the concept here as one way to inculcate the American Southwest as a distinct region that patterns a basic paradox entwined within the dualities of tradition (the past/place) and progress (the future/space)—a contradiction that plays out spatially, along a geographical axis, and temporally, in terms of historical processes.

Thus, the Southwest in which Anderson's "alien" bodies are both produced by and reflected in time and space is the same Southwest that Anzaldúa (2012) reminds readers became the "homeland" of 100,000 Mexican citizens annexed by conquest upon the signing of the Treaty of Guadalupe Hidalgo on February 2, 1848. Home—Mexico—was ripped, swindled away from the Native Mexican Texan; from one day to the next the US–Mexican border, the *"herida abierta*, where the Third World grates against the first and bleeds,"* was conceived (25). The geopolitical border, that line that separates the US from Mexico, metaphorically announces a physical border that tears through her body, her flesh, as can be seen in the following verse from *El otro México*, which opens *Borderlands/La Frontera*:

> 1,950-mile-long open wound
> dividing a *pueblo*, a culture
> running down the length of my body,
> staking fence rods in my flesh,
> splits me splits me
> *me raja me raja* (24)

For Anzaldúa, as for those who reside there, the Southwestern borderline is not merely a physical presence. A great river that snakes through a vast desert landscape marks the borderline. The river, like a living being, is a repository of struggles and memories. History, at least in the late-nineteenth and early-twentieth centuries, however, has tended to undervalue the nature of the Rio Grande, once known as the Río Bravo. But waters, like the migrations of peoples, recede only to surge and roil. If the stories of the people who associate natural ecological systems like bodies of water with a homeland become silenced, they will, as we witness in Alex Rivera's *Sleep Dealer* (2008), which comprises the final chapter of *Haunted*, spill forth. Accordingly, John Sayles's classic Borderlands thriller, *Lone Star* (1996), which I discuss in chapter 1, further reveals how control of water figures into the racial and ecological power dynamics of the Borderlands.

II. Place: The US–Mexico Border

Turner and those who followed in his footsteps envisioned an imaginary line that ran from north to south across the United States, a line predicated upon an east–west migration that signaled the boundary of a decidedly westward movement and the subsequent advance of "civilization" by Euro Americans. Inherent in the Southwest is this East/West paradigm of early settler movement as well as a North/South paradigm of US–Mexico race relations and racial politics. Border crossings in the twenty-first century continue to be colored by these historically constructed imaginings of place, space, and geography. With this in mind, José David Saldívar (1997) situates the "histories and myths of the American West and Southwest in a new perspective" to re-vision stories that have challenged and endeavored to deterritorialize cultural forms within what he calls a "*Transfrontera* contact zone"—that two-thousand-mile–long border that ostensibly separates the US and Mexico (ix, 13). Because, writes Saldívar, "U.S.–Mexico border writing is a continuous encounter between two or more reference codes and tropes" (14), it is both productive and essential that we understand the historically constructed spaces that complicate previously held Eurocentric linear views of migration and immigration. In Saldívar's view, only when we reorient discourses of citizenship, identity politics, and nation-building can we begin to effectively intervene and work to "undo the militarized frontier 'field-imaginary,'" an idea gleaned from the writings of Donald Pease. As a result, we can reconfigure this field-imaginary within an emerging US–Mexico *frontera* imaginary (xii) with the purpose of remapping American studies so as to make space for alternative narratives of "ethno-racialized cultures of displacement" (7). The Borderlands and the American frontier field-imaginary that are enmeshed in the historical experience of this region, then, are also entwined in the political and social underpinnings of space and place.

The most compelling scholarship on the US–Mexico Borderlands reinforces a need to conceptualize the dialectical narratives that shape the Borderlands. Saldívar maps a discourse of the US–Mexico border "as a paradigm of crossing, resistance, and circulation" to critique "the great discontinuity between the American frontier and *la frontera*" (xiii–xiv). Similarly, Mary Pat Brady's (2002) study of spatial transformations in the Southwest brings together cultural geography, Chicana feminism, and literary theory to read the US–Mexico border as a "complex system with multiple and diverse nodes of production and reproduction" functioning within a "swirl of histories, temporalities, and narratives" (48, 49). Drawing on the work of Henri Lefebvre and Neil Brenner, Brady emphasizes the disjuncture between space and time in border crossings in terms of crossing from one temporality to another (50). Although Brady's is a useful way to view any border crossing, it is especially productive to the approach I take here, as it accounts for the ways that geography and history shape US–Mexico border imaginaries wherein each nation functions within its own geopolitical and socio-imaginary "aesthetic project" (52).

Brady's work is indebted to insights of space put forward by Lefebvre (1992) and Edward Soja (1993, 1999), both of whom broadly theorize how the production of space never simply refers to the built environment—buildings, or transportation and communication networks and such—but also the regulation and management of these products, an administration that further shapes how such are experienced and understood *as produced*. The production of space, for these writers, Brady adds, greatly affects subject formation in that it is "highly affective," shaping "feelings and experiences" (8). As such, imagining space as background or setting—as does the frontier myth—obscures temporality and the narrative qualities that shape and conceptualize the "traditions, myths, and meanings ascribed to space, including how places are discussed or named and the grammatical structures that regulate their production" (8). The historical and contemporary accounts and narratives I examine within *The Haunted Southwest* support the need to conceptualize the US–Mexico Borderlands as a landscape where groups of people—spatially connected—mediate the demands of nation-making, cultural identity, and community.

I too am indebted to Lefebvre (1992), whose widely known triad of social space defines space as *conceived, perceived,* and *lived,* which is to say that it comprises material forms as well as lived and imagined spaces.[4] Lived spaces are of foremost importance to Lefebvre, as are actual, physical bodies, what he terms *spatial bodies.* He writes: "[T]he body's material character derives from space, from the energy that is deployed and put to use there" (195). Because physical bodies are materially inscribed in space, relationships between bodies and space help shape the constitution of the self. Where re-presentations of space signal overriding discourses of space that connect to the "dominant 'order' of any society, and hence to its codes, signs, and knowledge," lived spaces reference and bring into being "alternative imaginations of space," including "symbolic values" and "conflicting rhythms" of everyday experience (Simonson 2016, 6–7). The present study seeks to expose what remains *as absence* between re-presentations of space and lived space on the Borderlands, for it is the distance between this gap that marks the Bordered frontier. If adherence to a frontier mythology re-presents space, and the Borderlands organize knowledge quite differently, not on a linear but a cyclical bearing that more comfortably accounts for place-making and "contradictory and ambivalent historical narratives, family memories, desires, and national(ist) frameworks" (Brady 2002, 83), a question remains. How have conflicting Native American, Chican@, and Mexican American cultures resisted, negotiated, and otherwise subverted ideologies and ways of living in the Borderlands that move against or beyond the re-presentations of space, those rupturing spaces of modernism that focus primarily on use and exchange values, that—like the frontier myth itself—sweep humans along an axis of artificiality, unsustainable productivity, and appropriation?

In his reading of David Harvey, Tim Cresswell (2015) reminds us that places embed "discursive and symbolic meaning" beyond that of mere location (91). In working through theorizations of place by Doreen Massey and David Harvey, he concludes that relationships to the past and specific localities bring complexity to an understanding of place in terms of globalizing practices. Although the works and performances discussed throughout *Haunted* do not necessarily speak to broad-based globalizing systems, they are conversant with postmodern practices that illuminate issues of boundaries, rootedness, and connections across time and space. Cresswell's reading of Harvey is especially apt to our current discussion due to Harvey's focus on the "political economy of place construction under capitalism" (92), a presumption I discuss in terms of the annual George Washington's

Birthday Celebration held in Laredo, Texas, each year since 1898 as well as the aforementioned films, *Lone Star* and *Sleep Dealer*.

In a classic description of the Mexican landscape evinced by Malcolm Lowry, Octavio Paz (1961) describes the terrain as a living thing that takes a thousand different forms. Both symbolic and stretching beyond the symbolic, the landscape is "a voice entering into the dialogue, and in the end the principal character in the story" (33). The Mexican landscape does not simply describe the surface of things: it reveals what lies behind visible appearances. A landscape does not refer to the thing itself, he writes. Rather, "it always points to something else, to something beyond itself" (15). In the American Southwest, we must similarly look *beyond* the material and external so as to break open traditional categories and cartographies of the Southwest, the frontier, and the US–Mexico border. This stance allows us to illuminate ideologies and metaphors that yet shape reality in the region.

In 1923, D. H. Lawrence (1971) wrote about "the spirit of place" that pervades the American West, where the "ghosts" of Indian nations yet persist (40). For Lawrence, Indian nations, though "dead," remain "unappeased." He writes, "Do not imagine him in his Happy Hunting Ground. No. Only those that die in belief die happy. Those that are pushed out of life in chagrin come back unappeased, for revenge" (40). Lawrence's language is overtly psychoanalytic, outmoded in its phraseology, and his premise that certain American writers are spiritually starved is problematic in that it tends towards over-generalization. Arguably, his standpoint embeds a retreat into a romantic sense of place. However, the precedence he places upon the Western landscape is quite telling. Writing from Lobo, New Mexico, he examines the work of Cooper, Poe, Hawthorne, Melville, and Whitman, to conclude that these American authors tell "lovely half-lies" (71), because they tell only half-truths as a result of their obligatory dodging of "old ghosts" that yet occupy the landscape they dwell upon. These American artists, who greatly inform the canon, are caught between "the old master . . . like a parent . . . over in Europe" (10). They inhabit a homeland where they have "physically and psychically denied the claim on the land and its spirit held by those prior Americans, the Indians" (Sanders 1993, 56). Although these writers have all pushed toward a new American consciousness, Lawrence refers to this as a "false dawn" (11). According to Lawrence, "men [*sic*] are free when they are obeying some deep, inward voice of religious belief—obeying from within. Men are free when they belong to a living, organic, *believing* community, active in fulfilling some unfulfilled, perhaps unrealized purpose. Men are freest when they are most unconscious of freedom" (12). His point is that the power of the American landscape is imbued with vengeful spirits that must not simply be appeased but somehow *integrated* within the psyche of the artist. For Lawrence, the west is a place of timelessness where the writer must permeate the features of the earth in order to speak truth.

Following political geographer John Agnew, who focuses on three fundamental aspects of place in terms of location, locale, and sense of place, Cresswell (2015) underscores the definition of place as "a meaningful location" (12) that speaks to the means by which people and cultures shape material settings in terms of wider social relations. The subject of place and place-making, however, is complex and can be approached in many ways. Perhaps this is the reason place itself remains a contested concept. Place-making can be apprehended in terms of cultural geography, ecology, architecture and urban planning, and a focus on the built environment, as well as philosophy and a host of other disciplines. For my purposes in *Haunted*, I approach place as a concept that draws largely from philosophy and cultural geography. I align myself with Cresswell for ways that he links place to spatial politics and "arguments over who gets to define the meaning of a place" (19).

A key figure in critical geography is Yi-Fu Tuan (1997), who proposes that place signifies security and attachment, whereas space corresponds to movement and freedom. As humans, however, we require both, as they are poles by which we organize behaviors, thoughts, and experiences. Tuan writes that in human experience,

> the meaning of space often merges with that of place. . . . The ideas "space" and "place" require each other for definition. From the security and stability of place we are aware of the openness, freedom, and threat of space, and vice versa. Furthermore, if we think of space as that which allows movement, then place is pause; each pause in movement makes it possible for location to be transformed into place (6).

What Henri Lefebvre (1992) calls "social space" is very near to Yi-Fu Tuan's definition of place. Lefebvre distinguishes between abstract space, which he calls absolute space, and social spaces, which signify lived, or experiential and meaningful, spaces. Cresswell pushes Lefebvre's ideas regarding social space to interrogate not just how humans continue to make the world meaningful by the ways we shape places but how place is also "space invested with meaning in the context of power" (19).

Armando C. Alonzo (1998) collapses the Southwest as region to focus on South Texas as a linchpin of identity for Mexican Americans and Chican@s. In *Tejano Legacy*, he argues that South Texas was historically viewed as a space, largely unoccupied and vacant in the "Anglo mythic history" (6–13). In his reconstructive history of *tejana/o* land tenure in the Lower Rio Grande Valley of Texas, he shows how in South Texas, as in other Southwestern regions, "later Anglo arrivals have appropriated the history of the pioneer effort for themselves" (6). In his account, which begins in the early eighteenth century with the origins of Spanish and Mexican society and moves through the early twentieth century, he argues that *tejanas/os*, in spite of setbacks in the form of illegal barbed wire fencing and Euro American dispossession (some illegal, some not), nonetheless asserted control over a vast territory:

> Despite fifty years of settlement by newcomers from Europe and the United States, south Texas remained a virtual Mexican homeland until the 1910s and 1920s, when large numbers of midwestern and southern farmers, businessmen and professionals migrated to the region with the inception of intensive irrigated farming (111).

According to Alonzo, *tejanas/os* "identified with their place. To them, the land has always possessed meaningful cultural and economic values. It is their home, a special place" (10). This is in sharp contrast to Euro Americans who "saw the lands in the Lower Valley as a frontier instead of a settled place occupied by *mejicanos*" (6).

In *Postmodern Geographies*, Soja (2011) describes the production of space as both a physical construct and a social process. Human patterns of being in the world exist simultaneously and dialectically in time and space and are necessary to understanding power struggles that extend through time and along geographical space. Soja's writing speaks to ways that break open geographical landscape to discover relationships between people— indeed, whole cultures—with regard to the landscapes upon which they daily toil and dwell. These ideas help us understand how the frontier in the Southwest, as an imagined mythology, was historically contingent upon a bordered space. The methodologies of critical and social geography allow us to explode a main goal of Alonzo's: the failure of writers and scholars of the Southwest "to see the inherent contradiction of a 'no-man's land' existing in a place previously occupied by Spanish and Mexican settlers" (7). Much like Alonzo, Daniel Arreola, in *Tejano South Texas* (2002), reminds us that places create bonds among inhabitants who reside there, and those bonds are what give a place its distinctiveness. He foregrounds his study of what he calls "Mexican South Texas" in an analysis of the physical details of the landscape as it is inextricably linked to the inhabitants, human or otherwise, who shape that landscape into a place that must be viewed as a product of transformation, experience, and, ultimately, translation.

III. Space and Place in the Southwest: The Bordered Frontier

Any understanding of the frontier in the American West, and in the present study, the Southwest in particular, must begin with a consideration of the language Turner first used to describe the frontier, for it is his use of the term that stuck among academicians, scholars, and even laypeople. By the 1950s or so, other ways of imagining the American West and specifically Southwestern frontiers appeared contemporaneously with the emergence of Chicano, and later Chicana, historicisms. A precursor to this movement was the work of Herbert Eugene Bolton, a graduate student of Turner's. Bolton's narrative revised Turner's and steered the knowledge that "for borderlands scholars[,] natives could not be swept as easily into the wilderness as they were for 'mainstream' historians" (Klein 1997, 262). For Bolton, just as for Mexicans, Native Americans, and later Chican@s, the Southwest border and frontier necessarily bled into each other.[5] This is the case historically as well as in the present day. Early frontier writings, however, render invisible any contact situation between and among entire societies, cultures, and groups of people; consequently, nineteenth and early twentieth century histories found in textbooks, academic writing, and monographs subsume the border into the larger context of the frontier. In the process, those people living on the fringes—Gloria Anzaldúa's border dwellers and *atravesados* (troublemakers), Eric Gary Anderson's "aliens," and indeed entire cultures, or groups of Native Americans, Mexican Americans, and Mexicans—were not just pushed along the borders of the American frontier but were further relegated to the margins of American history.

In 1962, Jack D. Forbes, a Native American scholar of mixed Powhatan, Delaware, and Saponi heritage, worked to liberate many of the frontier's silenced voices by commenting on the ambiguity of the term "frontier" as it was understood and developed by Turner and his disciples. He writes:

> To the Turnerians, as well as many other writers, *the* frontier consisted solely in Anglo-Americans (or, occasionally, other Europeans). That which the

latter people were coming into contact with was not, to these authors, a part of the frontier; on the contrary, it was an obstacle to the frontier (63).

The border, then, in the Turnerian model did not exist because it could not exist. A close examination of the language Turner used to describe the movements and ideologies intertwined in the frontier does not factor into the metaphorical sweep, the grandeur of all that the frontier promised: freedom, liberty, and a resistance to the "domination of class." For Turner, in order for a border to exist, there must be no opposition to the continual westward expansion of Anglo and Euro Americans. This fact is explained in part by Forbes (1962) when he writes: "[T]he concepts of 'westward movement' (of Anglo Americans) and 'frontier' become virtually synonymous" to Turnerians who consider the frontier in terms of the one-way movement West of Euro Americans" (64). The vastness of the frontier was like democracy itself. Anglo and Euro American occupation in the Southwest wrestled the land not from Indians or Mexicans, but from wild nature itself. Further, frontier excess in the Turner paradigm metaphorically spoke to modernist inclinations surrounding the appropriation (or misappropriation) of "free" lands and the capitalization of a modern political and social economy—but only for whites, only for those who moved westward in search of a modern New World. Those who already occupied the West or Southwest, those who called the place home, were equated with the "uncivilized" landscape.

Kerwin Lee Klein's *Frontiers of Historical Imagination* (1997) broadly frames the narrative traditions by which historians, anthropologists, literary critics, and philosophers have explored and understood the European occupation of Native America in the American West. Beginning with Turner's frontier hypothesis and moving through breakthroughs in ideas about culture by anthropologists in the second decade of the twentieth century, Klein closes his multilinear history with works by Chican@s and American Indian scholars who reimagine and repopulate American frontiers with multiethnic characters and tropes. A particularly compelling aspect of Klein's postmodern critique of the writing of the history of the American West in the years following the broad-based acceptance of the Turner thesis is his re-formulation of the hero or heroine of frontier narratives as a subaltern subject.

Klein builds his view that history is the story of humanity's developing self-consciousness by foregrounding the idea that the "making of new frontier tales has traditionally begun by marking out a new hero" (271–72). For Klein, the hero of a frontier tale has always been an "outsider," a "subaltern hero" (272). Even Turner's middle-class males, whom Klein argues were yet subordinate to the "Great Men of Europe and the Atlantic seaboard," occupy this rank (272). So too do Walter Prescott Webb's arid "westerner"; William Christie MacLeod's "natives"; Américo Paredes's Gregorio Cortez; and Gloria Anzaldúa's *new mestiza*. To argue his point, Klein highlights Hegel's ideas of world history as a narrative of humanity's developing self-consciousness and subsequent liberation of certain peoples from a "voiceless past" (7) alongside a Kantian dialectic to overturn Turner's metaphor that history is the colonization of the West. Commenting specifically on G.W.F. Hegel's 1820 *Philosophy of History* and *Lectures on the Philosophy of World History*, Klein acknowledges the need to understand history as the sum of a trajectory that develops in space as well as time, because the "collision between people with and without history still structures public memory" (7). Because public and private memories factor in the interplay of history and the construction and configuration of human geographies in space, we must further account for the complex interplay of memory and the ways these embed structures of feeling into the historical record, subjects *Haunted* describes in detail.

In 1962, Edward Spicer published *Cycles of Conquest*. Like Bolton before him, and contemporaneously with Forbes, Spicer wrote about the Southwest as a space where Native Americans, Europeans, Euro Americans and Mexicans came together. These works and others opened up the American frontier from the constrictive bounds that most history textbooks had featured to date. The frontier signifies an imaginative, mythic space where forgetting and remembering, and creation and destruction, all take place; this is a core argument of *The Haunted Southwest*. Like Forbes, Spicer saw the Southwestern frontier in terms of contact—an interethnic situation. For Forbes (1962), ethnohistory *was* frontier history. Regardless of whether the "old" frontier histories focused on Euro American experiences, these experiences presupposed "any instance of more than momentary contact between two ethnic, cultural or national groups" (Forbes 65). With this in mind, Klein (1997) writes, "Forbes's idea of frontier as a space where two opposed cultures came together aligned with broader trends in contemporary thought" (207). Such thought, evidenced at least in part by the naming of Aztlán—the legendary ancestral home of the Nahua peoples—as the homeland of the Chican@ community in the late 1960s, focused upon borders, boundaries, ethnicity, and culture in such a way that "frontier and *frontera* became key words for multicultural textuality" (209).[6]

Thus, although historical narrative for a time seemingly failed to "emplot"—to use Hayden White's term as put into practice in *Metahistory: The Historical Imagination in Nineteenth-Century Europe* (2004)—the narratives of those "people without history" who call the Southwest home, a primary goal of *Haunted* is to show how the landscape itself retains and maintains as palimpsest stories and histories of others that subsume and counteract dominant frontier narratives. Recovery of narratives that yet embed the Southwest landscape is possible when we engage border theory, which I discuss throughout *Haunted* to conceptualize those continuous and interactive cultural zones that prioritize psychic, psychological, and metaphoric spaces and places of negotiation and belonging. A focus on relationships and attitudes toward the landscape coupled with how citizens view themselves as part of that landscape further embeds a discourse to accurately theorize the Bordered frontier as a mythic space predicated on the parallel necessity of incorporating place and place-making structures of inscription and belonging alongside aspects of space. A critique of frontier imperatives via the articulations of the Bordered frontier breaks open imagined and enacted spaces to show how the border and the frontier are complex, intertwined tropes that continue to configure identity on the Borderlands in the twenty-first century.

By the mid-twentieth century, then, scholars such as Forbes expressed a concern for the one-sided, ethnocentric view of the Turnerian concept of the frontier as virtually synonymous with the idea of "westward movement." In Klein's (1997) account, multiethnic inclusivity paves the way for new subaltern heroes—new voices—to emerge from the pages of Eurocentric narratives. Hegel's notion of history as the collision between people with and "without" history fulfills the promise of a new story centered in the concept of the Bordered frontier. Forbes's study of all sorts of frontiers—both in Europe and in the Americas—attended the works of scholars, including Chican@s, who would break open late nineteenth and early twentieth-century one-dimensional dialogues of the American Southwestern frontier. Importantly, Forbes's (1962) definition of the term "frontier" applies to "all cases of frontiers, whether occurring within the United States or elsewhere" (65). With this in mind, Forbes defines a frontier as

> an *inter-group contact situation*, that is, as any instance of more than momentary contact between two ethnic, cultural, or national groups[,] . . . an instance of dynamic interaction between human beings and involves such

processes as acculturation, assimilation, miscegenation, race prejudice, conquest, imperialism, and colonialism (65).

In his definition, boundaries are not clear-cut and do not exist in the abstract; rather, they correspond to political boundaries. As such, Euro Americans, Mexicans, Mexican Americans, and a multiplicity of Indian nations coincided within a dynamic landscape in the American Southwest. Fittingly, then, we must acknowledge, as does Forbes, that a "frontier complex, a multiplicity of frontiers in dynamic interaction" (69), has historically comprised the pattern of interaction in the American Southwest.

Turning again to Limerick (1987), she stipulates how a New Western history of the West further describes the ways that space, as a central component of the historical experience, bleeds into a process of infinite expansion predicated on a negation of the past. She writes: "Turner's frontier was a process, not a place. When 'civilization' had conquered 'savagery' at any one location, the process—and the historian's attention—moved on" (26). Larry McMurtry (1993) provides a literary description of this pattern of process in his novel, *The Streets of Laredo*. Crow Town, so named after the countless crows that still feed on the more than fifteen thousand rotted buffalo hides that had once been left to fester in the heaping Texas sandhills skirting the area, is an "evil" place that draws mostly bandits and outlaws. Years before the few rank huts and single dusty saloon of Crow Town were established, a large number of the great southern herd of buffalo had been pursued and killed by many hunters, including the Kiowa and Comanche. But the hide market collapsed, and the buffalo hides were left to rot in the sandhills about two hundred miles north of the Texas border. In time, to survive a stay in Crow Town became a "mark of pride to the young pistoleros along the border" (86). One outlaw, Tennessee Bob, became so maddened by the incessant cawing that he blew his brains out while playing a winning hand at cards. In a telling description:

> Like most of the temporary residents of Crow Town, he [Tennessee Bob] had gone there because he had more or less used up the West. His career had taken him from Memphis to Abilene, from Abilene to Dodge City, from Dodge City to Silver City, from Silver City to Denver, from Denver to Deadwood, from Deadwood to Cheyenne, from Cheyenne to Tombstone, and from Tombstone to Crow Town. Other renegades, whether Mexicans, Swedes, Indians, Irish, or American took the same route in different order. What they shared was a sense that there weren't too many places left where life was so cheap that the law wouldn't bother trying to preserve it (89–90).

McMurtry details the movements of renegades and outlaws to underscore the elasticity of the struggle over space in the West. His "list," meant to metaphorically evince a mythology of the West predicated on lawless activity, nonetheless rests on the production of space as a highly social process. Along these lines, and as regards Western literature, Jay Ellis (2006b) writes that a generic trope of the Western novel is one in which "lawless men (or lawful men in a lawless space) enact the violent subjugation of space until it becomes a place so constrained that it can no longer tolerate their inclusion" (87). Importantly, Limerick—and to some extent Weber and Forbes—invite us to examine and further break open the West as a place to be understood from within, from the point of view of those people who view the landscape as a center—a homeland—rather than an edge or periphery. Limerick's (1987) thesis asks that we strive to understand the West as a place of historic conquest, a meeting ground where "Indian America, Latin America, Anglo America, Afro-America, and Asia intersected" so as to better understand "the evolution of land from matter to property" (27). Regarding Turner's thesis, she writes: "Indians, Hispanics, French Canadians, and Asians were at best supporting actors and at worst invisible. Nearly as invisible were women, of all ethnicities" (21). According to Limerick, conquest of the West as place culminated in the drawing of lines on a map. The first stage of conquest involved the drawing of the lines; the second stage, which is still under way and contested, involves the giving of meaning and power to those lines (27). This echoes Saldívar's (1997) questions:

> How can a map tell us how the US–Mexico borderlands were once an ecological whole, with Mexico blending into the present-day southwestern American landscape? Can maps represent how, with independence in 1821, Mexico took over the Spanish borderlands only to have to fight off the United States in its quest to fulfill its manifest destiny? Can maps show how the Treaty of Guadalupe Hidalgo in 1848 added what Paredes calls "the final element to Rio Grande society, a border" thus inaugurating a new phase of the US–Mexico borderlands? (18).

At present, both academically speaking as well as in the colloquial imagination, it seems that we hear much more about borders than we do about frontiers. In the Southwestern United States, the Border Patrol, the Border Wall, and the increased policing of the border between the United States and Mexico have taken center stage, and although the frontier exists, the border seemingly subsumes it. Thus, whilst the focus has seemingly veered, it has shifted not just for political or ecological reasons; it has shifted, rather, as a result of the dialogic nature of borders and frontiers, the Bordered frontier.

IV. Hauntings and Haunted Landscapes: Towards an Ethics of Place

If the frontier in the United States is historically associated with growth and expansionist aims, then border studies and studies that focus on societies and cultures that people Borderland landscapes work not just to revise earlier narratives but to repopulate those narratives with missing players. In the twenty-first century, the frontier is and has become the border with inclusivity factored into it. But the American Southwestern frontier has always included Borderlands peoples, whether the historiography has incorporated such peoples or not. The relationship is not part to whole; it is whole to whole. One simply cannot exist without the other. Intrinsic to frontier stories—frontier histories—is movement. In this regard, the history of the American Southwestern frontier can be plotted from west to east. A north to south movement, however, was necessarily enacted not as a function of the frontier but as a movement in its own right, and with its own players.

The Treaty of Guadalupe Hidalgo that legislated the creation of the US–Mexico border at the Rio Grande continued a US policy of space-making when it annexed Mexicans into the US, effectively "re-graphing" the geography of a former Mexican region into the Southwest and further "bifurcat[ing] indigenous and mestizo identities" (Saldaña-Portillo 2006, 133). The border, however—this line of demarcation signifying a cartographically fixed and stable place—is an illusion, a way to imagine borders as fixed and stable. Indeed, as an ongoing and ever-shifting palimpsest of spatial negotiation between and among colonial, national, and Indigenous populations, the border, much like the ideology that frames the boundless manipulations of space that shape the core of the myth of the frontier, is *not* fixed and stable.

Frontier stories, by their very nature, are decidedly future-oriented. The classic western genre itself speaks to this in opening shots of countless films including *Stagecoach* (1939), *Red River* (1948), and *The Searchers* (1956). A staple of the genre, space in classic westerns is "waiting to be peopled," for here is an inherently American stage desirable as a "territory to master" (Tompkins 1992, 74). Even postmodern westerns like *Unforgiven* (1992) and *No Country for Old Men* (2007) begin with landscape shots wherein lies the promise of space in all its transcendent power and possibility. *Haunted* shows how narratives on the Bordered frontier tend not toward the future but coalesce within a timeless landscape predicated on a synthesis of past, present, and future recollections and imaginings; accordingly, narratives on the Bordered frontier disrupt a monologic frontier mythology.

By the 1960s, much of Western historical scholarship began to focus on the diverse and complex stories of minorities—Native Americans, Chican@s, Mexicans—many of whom had once comprised majorities during earlier periods as well as in the twenty-first century. These later histories fracture the chronological shape of Turner's model. In Limerick's (1987) assessment, the historical West was shaped by battles between people and access to the economic, political, and natural resources held by the terrain itself, rather than between groups of people themselves. The "unbroken past" of her title reflects the idea that the capitalist and expansionist aims of the Western frontier are alive and well up to the time of her book's publication. She argues that the "essential project of the American West was to exploit the available resources. Since nature would not provide it all, both speculation and the entrepreneurial uses of government were human devices to supplement nature's offerings" (86).

A historian by trade, however, Limerick's astute conclusions are circumscribed by historical fact and include few anecdotal and no literary critiques. Then again, Hayden White (1966) reminds us that "the historian can claim a voice in the contemporary cultural dialogue only in so far as he [*sic*] takes seriously the kind of questions that the art and the science *of his own time* [author's emphasis] demand that he ask of the materials he [*sic*] has chosen to study" (125). He urges a crossing of boundaries that ostensibly divides one discipline from another so as to open up "illuminating metaphors for organizing reality, whatever their origins in particular disciplines or world-views" (125). White recognizes "that there is no such thing as a *single* correct view of any object under study, but there are *many* correct views, each requiring its own style of representation," adding that "an explanation need not be assigned unilaterally to the category of the literally truthful on the one hand or the purely imaginary on the other but can be judged solely in terms of the richness of the metaphors which govern its sequence of articulation" (129–30). With this in mind, the Bordered frontier is a ruling metaphor of identity formation along and within the Borderlands. Furthermore, when we view the American Southwest frontier and the US–Mexico border through the lens of border theory, as it has been conceptualized both historiographically as well as literarily, we can more easily privilege a thematic critique based in ontologies of space and place in a particular region.

Haunted seeks to legitimize Borderland conceptions of community and justice in the public realm. But how do the unauthorized experiences and forms of knowledge of Borderlands peoples not just unsettle national realities of citizenship and belonging but push against those structures of meaning that have excluded them? More to the point, where do we locate these structures of meaning? In his study of the means by which undocumented workers are often criminalized based on national identity and cultural frames of reference that point beyond authorized truths, Pablo A. Ramirez (2010) probes the ways undocumented migrants expand the public sphere by disrupting political norms and legal definitions on the US–Mexico Borderlands. His study is framed by a discussion of the pro-immigration rallies of 2006–2007 surrounding the passing of H.R. 4437.[7]

Central to my discussion here, Ramirez indexes Michel de Certeau's (1986) ideas surrounding ethics, specifically the "ethical gap" that exists between what de Certeau describes as dogmatism and ethics to correlate the distance that marks the space between imposed laws and unsanctioned activity. For de Certeau—who pays particular attention to questions of the Other—ethico-political visions originate in the gap between "what is and what ought to be" (199). In other words, the antinomy between dogmatism and ethics marks a gap between "authorized" reality (which imposes laws) and the "effective operations" of "what ought to be," a distance that "designates a space where we have something to do" (199). For Ramirez, the 2006–2007 pro-immigration rallies "created an ethical force that disrupted political and legal models in order to propose new visions of democracy and incorporation" (2010, 51). As non-documented citizens, in both language and action, strived to move *beyond* authorized and sanctioned realities of the US nation, engaging in legal and ethical modes of narrating the nation that first imagined and then created "unauthorized definitions of family and community across national borders," they legitimized "borderlands conceptions of community and justice in the public realm" (51–52).

Ramirez delves into the fictional work of Helena María Viramontes and Daniel Chacon to suggest how the "unauthorized experiences and knowledges" of central characters illume the space between realism and borders, or "what is," and imagination and ethics—"what ought to be"—to show how these authors unsettle national realities of citizenship and belonging.[8] Although his focus is the positionality and often unjust criminalization of undocumented migrants/workers within the legal bounds of the US, his point is that, on the Borderlands, the Chican@ community is a necessary "disruptive foreign element" (2010, 52) that periodically embeds ethico-political projects not meant to sustain the dogmatism of the status quo but, rather, to interrogate and potentially restructure democracy on the Borderlands.

In the Borderlands, competing ideologies and peoples clashed violently or unremarkably. Eurocentric histories such as Turner's frontier thesis, with its roots in a Manifest Destiny that justified expansion and westward movement of Euro Americans, could not accommodate new structures or more inclusive systems of understanding. Moreover, although the overarching idea and support of a Manifest Destiny historically reads as the dominant ideological construct in the Southwest, it is clear that any consideration of a Bordered frontier within this geographical space must be accompanied by an understanding of the landscape and its influence on transforming individual realities and narratives. With this in mind, we must further engage the "interplay of history and geography, the 'vertical' and the 'horizontal' dimensions of being in the world" that Edward Soja (1999) writes about in "History: Geography: Modernity" (137). In so doing, we can "re-entwine the making of history" with the social production of space, as well as the "construction and configuration of human geographies" (137). Soja further turns to Foucault to conceptualize space as key to understanding how shifts in power result from space-making, a process I discuss in chapter 2 in terms of the power of naming practices as evidenced in my hometown of Laredo, Texas.

In *Borderlands/La Frontera*, Anzaldúa (2012) reminds readers of the ancient, continuous story that *mestizas/os* must recover on their way towards a new consciousness and a way of being in the world that moves beyond those "struggle[s] of flesh" and borders that result in *choques*—cultural collisions and incompatible frames of reference on the Borderlands (100). This recovery requires an understanding of how Indigenous and *mestiza/o* cultures on the Borderlands negotiate Euro American projects of modernity that tended to exclude "other" realities and histories. Laguna Pueblo author Leslie Marmon Silko (1996) echoes Anzaldúa's sentiment when she writes, "the ancient Pueblo people depended upon collective memory through successive generations to maintain and transmit an entire culture, a worldview complete with proven strategies for survival," further acknowledging that "the ancient Pueblo people could not conceive of themselves without a specific landscape" (268–69). A central tenet that links these two scholars' ways of knowing the world is epitomized in Paula Gunn Allen's (1986) characterization of a central tenet of Native American epistemology: "We are the land" (119). When discussing collective memory, I employ Paul Ricoeur's (2006) definition, which he expresses as "a collection of traces left by events that have affected the course of history of the groups concerned, and that is accorded the power to place on stage these common memories" (119).

The late New Mexican poet Sabine Ulibarrí encapsulates the significance of *la tierra*—the land—to Mexican Americans and *tejanas/os*. In the award-winning PBS documentary, *Chicano! Quest for a Homeland* (1996), he says: "The land was sacred because your parents and grandparents were buried there. Some of your children were buried there. And you would be buried there. The sweat, blood and tears of generations have filtered into the land; so it is holy, sacred . . . sacrosanct."[9] Ulibarrí speaks to an ethical connection to place, what Raymond Williams (1977) calls a "structure of feeling" that returns to past traditions and places of origin as a basis and orientation for continued belief. This echoes Devon G. Peña's (2005) view that "Mexican Americans tend to define nature as homeland, not natural resources or wilderness" (xxxii). Ulibarrí's sentiment further conjures a collective past, recognizing the claims others—our ancestors—have upon our bodies in the present. Michel de Certeau (1986) argues similarly. He writes: "While place is dogmatic . . . the coming back of time restores an ethic" (221). If we imagine that place and ethics are intimately connected, that, as Pierre Nora (1989) has so eloquently argued, in the modern world we have so many *lieux de mémoire*—sites of memory—because we no longer have *milieu de mémoire*, "real environments of memory" (7), then how do we capture the paradox of abusive systems of power that yet speak and make themselves known via memory and narrative? How do we account for McClintock's (2014) "administered forgettings" that leave spectral traces and temporal disturbances, forms of "ghosting" that can effectively repudiate official US doctrine and policies?

Not surprisingly, Pablo A. Ramirez (2010) turns to Anzaldúa to substantiate his claim that the Chican@ community necessarily adopts a "borderlands ethical stance" (51) when moving beyond sanctioned narratives of the nation in efforts to reclaim and encompass multiple cultural frames of reference that more equitably square with contradictions and difference. In this way, I am conversant with Ramirez, who concludes that, within de Certeau's ethical gap, the "unauthorized experiences and knowledges" of

xliv   *Introduction*

Chican@s that can neither be translated nor affixed to the dogma that is the legislative body become "ghosts" that "chip away at the structures of meaning that have excluded them" (53). In *Haunted*, these ghosts and specters reside not within the ethical gap between the legal realm that is and more equitable laws that should be, as claims Ramirez, but between the space between what delineates and indexes the frontier and the Borderlands.

The Haunted Southwest illustrates how, just as Ramirez argues that the US legal system cannot equitably account for or fully "translate" unofficial or unsanctioned experiences and systems of knowledge, neither can the system that is the American frontier fully interpret or express the system that is the Borderlands. Only a system such as the Bordered frontier, which *integrates* and synthesizes elements of both the border and frontier, can represent the ghostly matters and logics "contained" within and between these two competing realities. Significantly, *Haunted* moves beyond Ramirez's conception of a Borderlands ethical stance to incorporate aspects of place, which allows for the added elements of rootedness and orientation and is tied to the work of Tim Cresswell (2015), Mick Smith (2001), and others who interrogate forms of social and cultural geography alongside postmodernity, ecology, and forms of memory.

Modern theories of haunting and haunted landscapes are flashpoints by which to unpack the ways de Certeau, like Nora (1989) and McClintock (2014), understand modern forms of dispossession, exploitation, and repression. When effectively Othered narratives become trapped in the machinery of modernism and modernist practices, absences and spectral facets and configurations of those absences can be recovered by tracking through time and across those forces that make their mark by both being there and not. Moving across spaces of memory via practices of associative remembering legitimates relationships to the past that yet exist within the ethical gap between official dogma and "unofficial" activity. Reifying the legitimacy of cultural scripts that exist among the historical, the spiritual, and the affective—between the embodied and the silenced—can move individual agents to embrace new codes of ethics and ethical behaviors where contradictions of race, ethnicity, and culture play out. A goal of *Haunted* is to show how modernist frameworks that ostensibly dismantle deep-seated Indigenous social frames of reference that oblige individuals and communities to act on behalf of place are continually subverted by an ethics of place. Such a stance accords meaning to and shapes postmodern ways of being that account for rootedness and connection to embedded forms of knowledge that places a greater emphasis on memory and the non-human world.

The Haunted Southwest distills and links aforementioned aspects—all of which comprise the Bordered frontier—to remap the American Southwest on ethical grounds via an understanding of the political and social forces of haunting. I further proceed from Avery Gordon (2008), who provides us with a hermeneutics and a language by which to identify hauntings and acknowledge the material and social effects they produce, so as to establish "a reckoning" with their mechanisms (18). For Gordon, haunted landscapes and haunted bodies expose the cracks and riggings of distur- bances and disruptions that are not so easily silenced. Following Foucault, Gordon considers the politics of haunting as a path that can effectively reckon with the instruments and contrivances of haunting. Significantly, haunting, unlike trauma, seeks to produce an action, a future oriented "something-to-be-done" (xvi). This is reminiscent of Anzaldúa's (2015) need as a Chican@ to "bear witness to what haunts us" (10). Ultimately, it is Gordon's methodology in *Ghostly Matters* that gives us both the vernacu- lar and the tools to reckon with what modern history has rendered ghostly by tracing the insights of "structures of feeling" of those who *sense* broader social totalities still imbricated within violent systems of modernity (18, ital- ics in original). It is the individual's conscious horror of destruction and absence that foments those ethical relationships with what is dead but not buried, with what remains impalpable, transient, and ghostly.

V. Chapter Organization

The Haunted Southwest looks closely at characters both fictional and oth- erwise who are haunted and embody aspects of return and recovery— what scholars such as Stuart Cochran (1995) have termed "homing in" patterns—or who exist within haunted landscapes and therefore fear what *could* return. Uncovering and making visible the historical connec- tions between the border and the frontier in the Southwest allows us to explore the continuing coexisting and contested relationships between frontier and border ideologies that remain—however transformed— today. In order to fully understand how lives, and subsequent ideolo- gies, are mapped along the Borderlands, I re-situate the frontier within border narratives that are bound not by linear constructions of space but by a place-based poetics that posits a significant counter-discourse of return. This idea of return, I contend, is a missing element in the scholarship that informs the frontier paradigm; in *Haunted*, it signifies a key failure of the frontier vision.

In contrast, return and homing in are central to counternarratives of nation-making and identity in Mexican American and Indigenous conceptions of US–Mexico Borderland places. Just as for Native Americans and Indigenous cultures of the region, return is rooted not in static concepts of physical boundary lines arbitrarily visualized and plotted onto two-dimensional maps. On the contrary, an understanding of space and place as cyclical and non-linear attends aspects of memory, as it helps root geography and identity in such a way as to explode the mythologies and histories of the peoples of the Southwest. Cyclical time allows for a thematization of "the forward and backward movement of time" (Currie 2007, 37) that is associative, layered, and moves us beyond the logocentric linearity of a decidedly future vision espoused by the frontier myth. It allows us to interrogate the diverse temporal rhythms inherent in the Bordered frontier. *Haunted* shows how cyclical time within border narratives that are rooted in pre-Columbian notions of the interconnectedness of time and space remain an essential component of the historical experience that still challenges the hegemony of the frontier in the American imaginary. For example, David Harvey (2000) writes at length about the ways that capitalism "produces" geographical landscapes appropriate to a given "dynamic of accumulation at a particular moment" in history—landscapes that in turn may be re-built at a later date. The result, he argues, is that the "geographical landscape of capitalism" is made more and more sclerotic in time. Such fixedness and rigidity creates a major contradiction such that "loyalties to places (and their specific qualities) become a significant factor in political action" (59). As such, when we juxtapose conflicting ideologies of cyclical and linear time alongside Hayden White's (1996) musings about "historical time" (119), we unveil and ultimately disclose complexities of space and place as imperatives that undergird complex negotiations that play out within and between competing cultures, societies, and subjectivities.

Each chapter of *Haunted* moves across multiple spaces of memory and avenues of concomitant remembering to uncover cultural scripts that occur in those liminal spaces between the historical, the psychic, the spiritual, and the emotive and affective. Chapter 1 focuses on John Sayles's 1996 neo-western, *Lone Star*, to discuss the power of story as a historiographic device that coalesces identity on the Borderlands. The film engages aspects of literal and metaphoric borders to disclose a multiplicity of voices and show

how individual actors can effectively destabilize onerous public narratives with the goal of de-mythologizing and effectively "freeing" their own histories. Chapters 2 and 3 shift the focus to my hometown of Laredo, Texas, in the Borderlands to conceptualize how a century-old celebration couched in imperialist nostalgia and a rejection of place and memory continues to reify a unique class-based system in the Borderlands. The two main performances of the George Washington's Birthday Celebration Association of Laredo, Inc. (WBCA)[10] I discuss here foreground a modernist agenda couched in the capitalization of space and practices of mythogenesis that ultimately shape a nebulous civic identity based first in a denial of the Indian as Other and second, in avowal of an extant hierarchical class structure based in early colonialist formations. The performances of the WBCA hastened a shift in Laredo's identity from "a very considerable Mexican settlement" (Thompson 1974, 176) in the mid-nineteenth century to a modern American city that continues to reproduce what Cresswell (2015) refers to as "place memories" and "social memories" that effectively "contain" the experiences of the individuals who reside in Laredo (121). Paradoxically, place memories resulting from the main performances of the WBCA objectify Indigeneity and create specters of native inhabitants whose narratives continue to haunt the present in unexpected ways. Chapters 4 and 5 revisit western and Chican@ literary classics to show how a focus on landscape exposes a destructive linear vision of progress, an aspect associated with space and spatial poetics. Postmodern Chican@ texts such as Rudolfo Anaya's *Bless Me, Ultima* and Arturo Islas's *The Rain God* effectively shift the focus to the dictates of place-making, memory, and history, and in so doing fracture elements of the frontier mythology ostensibly privileged within frontier narratives by Cormac McCarthy and Larry McMurtry. The result is a recentering of race, ethnicity, and gender issues and an understanding of a place-based ethics that supersedes spatial imperatives which continue to both fracture identities on the Borderlands and silence Indigenous, more sustainable ways of being in the world. Chapter 6 coalesces elements from earlier chapters to frame Alex Rivera's speculative film *Sleep Dealer* (2008) as a challenge to controlling myths of progress that justify totalizing discourses of modernity that continue to choke the lifeblood of more sustainable patterns of being—that is, patterns related to Indigeneity and a land ethic that anchors place to the construction of both identity and community. The result—to use Walter Mignolo's (2007) term—is a "de-linking" with a rhetoric of modernity that continues to fracture and de-naturalize identities and communities via abstractions of the artificial, the unnatural, and the colonizing.

THE
HAUNTED
SOUTHWEST

CHAPTER 1

FORGETTING THE ALAMO ON THE BORDERED FRONTIER

"People liked the story we told better than anything the truth might have been."

—*LONE STAR*, BIG OTIS TO SAM DEEDS

John Sayles's 1996 neo-western mystery *Lone Star*—arguably one of the finest films about the interpretation of history on the US–Mexico Borderlands—is about dredging up truths that have been buried by official, subjective histories. In terms of the power of stories as historiographic devices that speak to individual and collective identity, the film beautifully captures how history lives in the present much more than it does in the past. Filmed in Del Rio, Eagle Pass, and Laredo, the film revolves around ideas about memory—both public and private—and how revelations about the past invariably reflect both the present and the future. This is made evident in the choices of several of the film's main characters who, when confronted with more accurate stories of their past, use that previously buried knowledge to redirect and restore their futures. *Lone Star* combines elements of the thriller and romance to stylistically and symbolically show how the people of the fictional town of Frontera on the US–Mexico border, where whites, Blacks, Chican@s, and Black Seminoles have historically co-existed, all remember the past in different ways.[1] It suggests that a certain fluidity has always characterized life in Frontera; the divisions between an imperialist, hierarchical history and emergent patterns that threaten old systems of living are in constant dialogue in *Lone Star*. In this way, the film explores the dynamic role of history through the development of literal and metaphoric borders. Further, the town of Frontera directly evinces the Spanish word *frontera*, which literally defines both the border and the frontier, making obvious the intrinsic relationship between the two.

The film revolves around the forty-year-old mystery of the death of former sheriff Charlie Wade, played by Kris Kristofferson, and the re-kindling of a romance between the present Sheriff Sam Deeds, played by Chris Cooper, and Pilar Cruz, played by Elizabeth Peña. Public discourse reveals that the townsfolk believe Buddy Deeds (Sam's father, now dead, played by Matthew McConaughey) killed the corrupt Charlie Wade, effectively mythologizing Deeds's actions as heroic. But throughout the story, the audience realizes that the film is more about people trying to live together in a liminal Borderlands space in dialogue with contested ideologies of race, ethnicity, and belonging. In the film, private and public histories set the scene for Sam to ghost back against a history that has been buried like Charlie Wade's bones, the finding of which catalyzes the film's action. Significantly, Sam Deeds is haunted by a suppressed history that has roots in the domestic space of the home, but which systematically empties out into the broader community to create a false narrative the entire town of Frontera has been led to believe.

Much has been written about *Lone Star*'s thematic edits, such as the many "elliptical dissolves" that erode "the frontiers of past and present" to foreground how the "consequences of time, memory, and history" work themselves out by our actions in the present (Campbell 2013, 203). It's in this way that Campbell concludes that it's a film "full of ghosts" (203). This strategy mirrors the circular logic of another Borderlands film that—on the surface—shows little affinity with *Lone Star*: Alex Rivera's 2008 sci-fi film, *Sleep Dealer*. Although superficially different in form and content, the editing styles of both films reveal parallels that invite audiences to make contact with the instrumentality of haunting and forms of historical accounting that compel a reckoning with modernity's violence. In both films, fluid camera techniques—pans, dissolves, and glides—thematically link style to subject matter. In this way both films transport audiences seamlessly from past to present as reminders of "the psychological power of history" and the "inability to break away" from narratives that affect main characters alongside an entire community (Ryan 2010, 229–30). I discuss *Sleep Dealer* at length in chapter 6. For now, however, it is useful to note further parallels: in both films, male protagonists are haunted by memories tied to dead fathers. In Sam's case, these memories are vulnerable to manipulation by the public narratives of the status quo. In *Sleep Dealer*, the protagonist, Memo Cruz, is both haunted and guided by the memory of his father's death, in which he inadvertently played a part. In terms of the father–son dynamic, both fathers in each film thrust their ideologies onto their sons, and both sons openly disdain such dogma. Both films are "grounded at the scale of a small place" (Arreola 2005, 39) to show how a modern infrastructure literally hegemonizes Indigeneity by shifting the power structure as it relates to a natural resource: water.

From Public to Private Discourse: The Alamo, Part I

Lone Star's narrative structure asks us to question the lessons of history from competing and conflicting points of view, as flashback scenes are seamless and reinforce the idea that the past bleeds into the present. For instance, during an early scene that at first seems to have little to do with the main storyline to discover Charlie Wade's killer, Pilar, a history teacher at the local high school, is embroiled in a heated discussion with a group of angry white parents who resent her inclusionary policies of teaching history—her teaching of the Alamo's history is the target here. When an angry "Karen"[2] admonishes Pilar for failing to teach what has "been set as the standard" in Texas textbooks, Pilar's rebuttal is: "I've only been trying to get across part of the complexity of our situation down here [, as in] . . . cultures coming together in both negative and positive ways." As the rhetoric between the Chican@s and Anglos in the room heats up, we begin to grasp that the *real* issue at stake here is the contentious nature between public, "standardized" history and the continued erasure of minorities' cultural and collective memory.[3] This scene makes obvious how the dominant Anglo society in Frontera *continues* to keep Mexican Americans, Chican@s, and African Americans vulnerable to manipulation by public narratives of the status quo. Pilar and the other Chican@s in the room admit and acknowledge the concept of counternarratives that can effectively embed wider collective memories of the Alamo's history. These can fracture ahistorical myths of individual success fixed securely to white "heroes" like Davy Crockett and James Bowie. Interestingly, it's a white woman, apparently another teacher, who clarifies Pilar's position. She says: "We're not changing anything. We're just trying to present a more complete picture." Karen's retort is a laughable "and that's what's got to stop." For minority citizens, the Alamo surrounds a public narrative that has been whitewashed for the benefit of Anglos.

Rodolfo F. Acuña (2017) describes how Hollywood films have used repetition as a "teaching tool" that continues to enforce stereotypes in popular films about the Alamo.[4] In the film, the forceful maintenance of the
Alamo's prominent and publicly recognized narrative parallels the public
narrative of Buddy Deeds.

The Anglo parents believe that history should be told *only* from the
perspective of the "winners," as stated plainly by a particularly angry male
parent whom Pilar suggests feels "threatened" by her practice of teaching a
more comprehensive history. For historian Tomás F. Sandoval (2001), this
deliberate revisionist strategy suggests alternate remembrances of things
past. More importantly, he submits that "the townsfolk are fighting over
Frontera's history not because of what it says about the past but because
of what it says about their present" (79). In this sense we come to understand how the town is searching for its "true" self via recovery of the past—a
through line that parallels Sam's quest. In this respect Sandoval follows
from Hayden White's (1966) directive that historians "establish the value of
the study of the past, not as 'an end in itself,' but as a way of providing perspectives on the present that contribute to the solution of problems peculiar
to our own time" (125). White reminds us that narrative is an essential component of the historical experience. As such, the audience slowly perceives
that the characters in *Lone Star* who are attempting to reconcile the past
with their present do so by way of efforts that lean towards justice.

Bones Not Recovered But Re-Covered: Perdido

Lone Star is a complex film that details how one's personal identity is defined
by familial and public histories. Through its reliance on revisionist methods of identity politics, the film demonstrates how colonialist impulses of
Western history have generally erased Chican@s and African Americans
from the landscape because they do not fit into the neat, white-centered
mythology of the west. As white sheriff Sam Deeds, Chicana history teacher
Pilar Cruz, and the African American army colonel Delmore Payne move
through the past and present social structure of Frontera, each comes to
terms with the ways that history is habitually "passed on in a deliberately
distorted fashion" (Sayles 1998, vii).[5] I focus herein on the decolonizing
moves Pilar and Sam make when Sam effectively de-mythologizes the public
narrative surrounding Buddy Deeds as Charlie Wade's killer—which marks
the lovers' departure from the public to the private sphere. Before delving
into Pilar and Sam's story, the parallel storyline of Perdido introduces us to

a significant "unjust foundation on which [the] town's social order appears to be constructed" (Whitehouse 2002, 302).

Sometime after the discovery of Charlie Wade's bones (figure 2), we learn that Buddy Deeds is being memorialized with an induction ceremony at the newly renamed Buddy Deeds Memorial Courthouse. Just before the public ceremony, we are made aware of "that crowd" of "troublemakers" led by Chicano reporter Danny Padilla from *The Sentinel*. Padilla has undertaken to dig up the truth surrounding the little town of Perdido, which was flooded in 1963 during Buddy Deeds' tenure as sheriff. In an earlier scene, Padilla reminds Mayor Hollis Pogue—Buddy's former chief deputy—and fellow Anglo businessman, Fenton, that Mexicans and Chican@s were forcibly evicted by Buddy Deeds when the dam was constructed. "1963.... They dam up the north branch to make Lake Pescadero and a whole little town disappears," bellows an angry Padilla. When Fenton replies how "that's ancient history," an infuriated Padilla counters with a retort about how Buddy and Hollis, as a result of the new dam infrastructure, "end up with lakefront property bought for a fraction of the market price." Although this subplot is never truly resolved, the building of the dam is key to understanding how the political machinery of Frontera functions. In fact, when we consider that the dam helped make Frontera a popular tourist destination, we see how control of a natural resource figures into the power dynamics of Frontera, a theme I revisit in depth in my reading of *Sleep Dealer*.

As a government official, Charlie Wade was obviously corrupt, as flashback scenes clearly demonstrate. Buddy Deeds was equally corrupt; however, his unscrupulousness was surreptitious. Charlie was a true villain who publicly extorted, threatened, and murdered in the light of day; Buddy profited from his position *privately*, secreting money, power, and favors subversively and factiously. The dominant political machine in Frontera initiated by Wade was preserved and reified under Buddy's tenure as sheriff—Buddy was just a lot more amiable and a lot less cruel. The induction ceremony illustrates how the public story of Buddy as hero must be protected not simply to maintain the status quo, but to honor, in perpetuity, his "deeds." Just as Buddy's story is fixed and stable in the public's mind, so too are the norms and political arrangements he meted out, for the courthouse now imprints onto the landscape a *lieu de mémoire*, a memorial site. Following Nora (1989), the courthouse marks the gap between memory and history such that it "ceaselessly reinvents [a] tradition" tethered to an "undifferentiated time of heroes, origins, and myth" further tied to an "eternal present" (8).

Figure 2: The discovery of Charlie Wade's bones catalyzes Sam Deeds' quest for the truth. From *Lone Star* (1996). File photo, https://www.imdb.com/title/tt0116905/?ref_=fn_al_tt_1

For the people of Frontera, Buddy signifies stability and equity—regardless of any "truth" Sam uncovers. Thus, when Sam eventually discovers that it was Hollis and not Buddy who killed Charlie Wade, and Hollis verifies that when the skeleton is revealed to be Wade's, citizens will presume that Buddy killed Wade so as to usurp his position as sheriff, Sam's reply is, "He can handle it." As Buddy is dead, this statement substantiates how Buddy's *legend* can handle it. Where human memory in *Lone Star* is continually shown to be dynamic and subject to manipulation and distortion, public memories must be forcefully maintained.

Whereas Charlie Wade wore his animus towards the Mexican and African American communities of Frontera openly, extorting money from members of these communities brazenly, the means by which Buddy Deeds amassed power and control in Frontera mirrors what Rodolfo F. Acuña (2017) has written about in terms of the ways that ruling elites keep dominant structures intact. The subtitle of his book, *Swimming with Sharks*, refers to contemporary forces of neoliberalism that plunder resources and public institutions with the goal of generating profit margins for the dominant society, which in turn "benefits from the control or erasure of minorities' collective historical memory" (x). Although *Lone Star*'s timeframe precedes the neoliberal landscape of the early twenty-first century that Acuña details, the film's emphasis on the political, economic, and social arrangements in Frontera is key to understanding the status quo's forceful maintenance of "public" history.[6]

As Sam makes his way to the courthouse for the naming ceremony, he is met by Jorge Guerra and Fenton. Guerra tells Sam that he has seen to it that Padilla's story has been "killed" by Eddie Richter at *The Sentinel*, a man we assume is the reporter's boss. Significantly, we later learn that Guerra will likely be elected as the new mayor of Frontera. When Sam indicates that Padilla has likely not backed off for good, both Fenton and Guerra redirect the conversation to "the new jail." Sam, clearly frustrated, responds: "We don't need a new jail. We're already renting cells to the feds for the overflow." Sam knows the construction of a new jail mainly serves the interests of the political machine and status quo, and he reminds both Fenton and Guerra that they have financial and political interests tied to the proposed project.

A few scenes later, Sam heads to Mexico to visit with Chucho Montoya, who he believes was witness to Charlie Wade's murder of Eladio Cruz, the man everyone, including Pilar, thinks is Pilar's biological father. Before Sam heads out, a Chicano deputy named Ray communicates to Sam that "the committee," whom he describes as "Jorge, Fenton, and all," wants him to "stand for sheriff in the next election." Sam indicates that he doesn't know if he even wants to continue in the position, and follows up with a question: "Do you think we need a new jail?" When Ray hedges and looks uncomfortably over his back towards what appears to be the present jail, he answers, "Well, Sam . . . it's a complicated issue." To this, Sam smiles glibly and responds, "Yeah . . . you'd be a hell of a sheriff."

From Public to Private Discourse: Structures of Feeling and the Decolonial Imaginary

As contrived histories are uncovered and freed, the unresolved violence of an imperialist past signified by the tenure of two corrupt sheriffs and the disappearance of the Indigenous town of Perdido pushes through. A turn to Raymond Williams's (1977) conception of structures of feeling, those dominant systems of belief that influence, explain, and factor into the social consciousness of individuals as they are "actively lived and felt" (132) guides our understanding of the ways changing forms attempt to meet emergent and newly emergent structures of feeling. Structures of feeling define a "particular quality of social experience and relationship, historically distinct from other particular qualities, which gives the sense of a generation or a period" (131). In *Lone Star*, the epoch of frontier expansion and colonization of the Southwest is signified by both Charlie Wade's and Buddy Deeds' acts during their respective tenures as sheriff in Frontera. Major conflicts arise as pre-emergent forms of Borderland articulations felt by the principal characters suggest formative processes that speak to new frameworks even as they contend with preexisting forms. Structures of feeling, then, that have been sedimented back into history may be silenced for a time, but they remain, even if they must be inferred. The film never lets the audience forget that entrenched myths and narratives can be destabilized when we collapse the time lag between past and present in such a way as to expose the stories that are still concealed in the interstices. In *Lone Star* the past and the present combine in long pan shots in two crucial flashback scenes that cement the idea that the truth often remains hidden in a character's memory. Panning shots in the film's two murder scenes—the first of Eladio Cruz and the second of Charlie Wade—erase any signal that a boundary in space and time has been crossed. Both scenes are narrated by characters that dig up a distant past in their memories to further emphasize the collapse between history and the present.

Emma Pérez (1999) ends *The Decolonial Imaginary* with a reminder that the history of the Alamo, which all Texans are charged to recall with pride and triumph, is a *story*, an Anglo narrative that "nags . . . for re-vision" (127). It is a self-reflective ending that speaks to her need as a Chicana to focus on those spaces, the gaps in the historical record, where colonialist mandates are exposed. Pérez proposes a "decolonial imaginary" where the oppressed and silenced—"colonial others"—not just flit between colonial and postcolonial spaces, but negotiate identity in ways that effectively uncover silenced histories (7). In order to free Otherness from the gaps of history, Pérez argues that we must look to "rupturing space[s]," which she describes as a time lag between the colonial and postcolonial. It is within this time lag, these gaps and interstitial spaces, that "differential politics and social dilemmas are negotiated" (6). By redefining Foucault's discursive archaeology as a method uniquely suited to discover the silences within the gaps that interrupt European and Euro American historical models of time, Pérez reconceptualizes individual histories with the intent of uncovering alternatives to "official" written, or otherwise sanctioned, history.

Although Foucault's archaeology—which explodes disciplines and categories—is important, what is crucial in the present reading of *Lone Star* is Pérez's use of Foucault's "genealogy" that "recognizes how history has been written upon the body" (xvi). Her challenge to official, public narratives is necessarily postmodern, as she reminds us that there is "no pure, authentic, original history. There are only stories—many stories" (xv). Traditional historiography produces fictive pasts that serve to negate "other" histories. To this end, Pérez employs the theories of Homi Bhabha, Michel Foucault, and Chela Sandoval, among others, to sharpen articulations and movements that take place within a third space of belonging, which necessitates that we rethink history with the goal of "freeing" it (127). Her book's title, *The Decolonial Imaginary*, refers to that which "teeter[s] in a third space [and] recognizes what is left out" of history (55). *Lone Star* illustrates how Pérez's concepts play out in contemporary treatments of historical pasts.

Bodily Activism and Coalitional Consciousness

In *Methodology of the Oppressed*, Chela Sandoval (2000) examines the junctures that connect the disoriented first-world citizen-subject who longs for a new sense of identity and redemption in a postmodern space to forms of oppositional consciousness that subordinated and colonized subjects engage in pushing through systems of power that do not speak to or for them (9). In *Lone Star* this juncture is represented by both Frontera itself and the complicated history that ostensibly separates Sam and Pilar. Sam Deeds labors throughout most of the film to expose the truth of history by working through past events via the uncovering of stories in all of their "present-ness" (White 1966, 132). Ultimately, his search for the truth turns the painful gaze of his own white colonialist history to the construction of his identity and his own body, a pattern reified in my reading of *Streets of Laredo* in chapter 4. Sam's search for knowledge ushers what Chela Sandoval (2000) calls "a coalitional consciousness" that marks the beginnings of a new "hermeneutics of love" with Pilar in a postmodern space (4). In this sense, Sam and Pilar symbolically represent a type of mirror image of the same decolonizing gaze: Sam, in his willingness to deconstruct and uncover the truth of his own history as evidenced by the colonialist, imperialist imperatives of his father, Buddy Deeds, and Pilar, in her position as a teacher who daily frames history in terms of revisions, counternarratives, and multiple voices.

Chican@s are making strides, politically and socially, in Frontera, as evidenced by the town's incoming Chicano mayor and the Chicano deputy who will presumably unseat Sam Deeds the following year as sheriff. In this sense, we can read Sam's body as a site of negotiation; once Sam learns the truth of his complicated history, both he and the audience acknowledge how his body represents a site of warring ideologies. As the son of a powerful white male presence in the Borderlands, his body is a marker of a colonialist historical past. However, this colonialist story offers him neither reprieve nor future. Soon after Sam and Pilar rekindle their romance, we are led to believe that Sam's life, at least since his return to Frontera, is as "empty" as the blank walls of the apartment he's been living in for the past two years. In fact, he's been waiting for Pilar to continue the story of his life. This underscores the idea that although Sam is obviously alive, his body signifies the ghostly shell of a being whose history has been ripped from him. Throughout the film, he is never entirely in the present; his longing signifies how he *feels* like a ghost. When Pilar asks him why he's hung no pictures on the walls, he answers, "There's nothing I want to look back on." They continue:

> Pilar: "Like your story's over."
> Sam: "I've felt that way. Yeah."
> Pilar: "It isn't. Uh-uh. Not by a long shot."

Cherríe Moraga (1983) writes: "Without an emotional, heartfelt grappling with the source of our own oppression, without naming the enemy within ourselves and outside of us, no authentic non-hierarchical connection among oppressed groups can take place" (44–45). This applies to both Sam and Pilar, who, like the audience, are yet ignorant of certain truths "in pointed contrast to Frontera's suppressed knowledge" (Magowan 2003, 23). Sam admits to Pilar that he returned to Frontera because "you were here." But it was the unearthing of Charlie Wade's bones, and Sam's subsequent "poking around" in the history of Frontera, that led him, finally, to Pilar.

For Moraga, fear and memory take place within the body, and it is the body that remembers and, more importantly, negotiates the historical, political, and social realms surrounding us all. Sam and Pilar take up the challenge, as Moraga says we must, not just to look at the nightmare of internalized racism within themselves, but to confront it and love it (49). Sam's willingness to traverse the juncture between past and present represents his emerging desire—conscious or otherwise—to connect with and ultimately carve an oppositional consciousness. This fact is epitomized in the re-kindling of his love for Pilar, which, in fact, has never died. Traversing this juncture necessitates union with the Other—Pilar. Bridging this gap, however, is key to unlocking a new-world citizenship that encourages a decolonizing global force as envisioned by Sandoval in *Methodology of the Oppressed*.

Negotiation and Compromise: Re-Forming Self and World

Rosa Linda Fregoso (1993), in her Oedipal reading of *Lone Star*, argues that the film does not truly represent a new social order because it does not decenter whiteness and masculinity. She writes: "[T]he white father–white son structure keeps the center intact and multiplicity at the margins of the story world" (56). For her, the masculine conflicts are "resolved" but the conflicts implicating the female characters—Pilar and her business-owner mother, Mercedes—are not. Although she rightly posits, when referring to the symbolic realm, that the film is first and foremost John Sayles's "reconstruction and vision" (60), and that the point of view of most of the film (in flashback or not) is masculine-centered, as it is Sam Deeds', she makes this point from the perspective of feminist film theory and cinematic mechanisms of spectatorship and identification. In this light, she writes that she refuses to participate in the "'white patriarchal gaze' and racial structures of vision that inform this film" (61). I would add, however, that we must consider that Sam and Pilar, during the first half of the film, negotiate the gaze equally, as they can only glimpse each other—first through bars, then through various "invisible lines" (Magowan 2003, 24) of glass. This is one way in which Sayles, who describes this film as "a story about borders . . . where I end and somebody else begins" (West and West 1996, 14), metaphorically evinces the ways in which all sorts of borders—race, class, sex, age—separate people.

Unlike Fregoso, I see Sam's *will* to uncover the bones of a buried local and familial history as, in effect, his challenge to the official story as evidence of what Chela Sandoval (2000) calls a "decolonizing stance" (4). Sam is the product of an Anglo-American father who was instrumental in perpetuating a colonialist regime in Frontera, but Sam's quest for knowledge and truth turns the gaze of his own colonialist history to the construction of his own identity, his own body. As previously noted, his search for knowledge ushers what Chela Sandoval calls "a coalitional consciousness" that marks the beginnings of a new "hermeneutics of love" with Pilar in a postmodern space (4). In essence, Sam and Pilar symbolically represent the need to not just question the dominant narratives of public and institutionalized history, as does Pilar, but personal and familial histories, as does Sam.

José E. Limón (1997) argues that *Lone Star* revises much of the traditional iconography surrounding Anglos and Mexicans in a Borderlands space. In his study of enduring American cultural iconography of Anglo-American and Mexican relations in Texas, he revisits traditional representations of the American cowboy, the Mexican female figure of illicit sexuality, and the "prim and proper" Anglo female figure to flesh out a theory of ambivalence that plays out in partial and unconscious challenges to the ruling cultural order (604). Although Limón links Pilar to traditional images of the "racial-sexual Other," he concludes that her character actively "revises the image of the Mexican woman at the sexual and social margins of society" (612). Through her position as an educated woman with activist inclinations, Pilar assumes what Limón describes as the conventions of "the Anglo schoolmarm" (612). In this way, her body, which signifies the body of the colonized, becomes "a site for witnessing a fissure or decentering within the colonizer" (610). Moreover, he argues that Pilar's social status as a public-school teacher sets her on equal footing with "whatever cultural capital still accrues to [Sam] as an Anglo in the 1990s" (612). Importantly, Limón privileges the space—a café owned by Pilar's mother, Mercedes—where Sam and Pilar finally unite physically to conclude, following from David Montejano, that "the politics of negotiation and compromise have replaced the politics of conflict and control" (quoted in Limón 613). I push Limón's conclusions further to argue that the lovers' union signals the beginnings of a "rhetoric of resistance" in which their bodies, in the language of Chela Sandoval, transform into a methodology of emancipation based in a differential consciousness. For Alan P. Barr (2003), it is love that provides the means for Sam and Pilar to "cross divides," transcend barriers" of race, and, as we learn in the last moments of the film, incest, to venture toward "new frontiers" (372). Crucially, their union signals the means by which love becomes "reinvented as a political technology, as a body of knowledges, arts, practices, and procedures for re-forming the self and the world" (Sandoval 2000, 4).

Dissolving Borders and Destabilizing History: The Alamo, Part II

The historiographic function of *Lone Star* rests in the fluidity and re-negotiation of a politics inscribed on the body that culminates in the revisionist impulses of the historical truth by the main characters. By the film's end the borders between the past and present, and black, white and Mexican have dissolved. So too have the borders between truth and lies. All the same, whether or not an authentic, lasting alliance between Sam and Pilar will be forged remains to be seen. At the film's end, it appears that Sam has come to terms with the primary source of his oppressive disquiet, those ghostly structures of feeling so carefully manufactured by his father and others in the public sphere that have haunted him his entire adult life. This is continually signaled by his will and readiness to uncover the truth of his father's "deeds."

While investigating the death of his father, Sam increasingly becomes more willing to destroy his father's image, thus metaphorically subverting the patriarchal, imperialist hegemonic rule symbolized by the mythic Buddy Deeds' tenure as sheriff. Throughout the film, Sam has worked to uncover the primary source of a private haunting expressed by a false public story that has silenced the fact of the genealogy he shares with Pilar; they are in fact half-siblings. The fact that Pilar and Sam *choose* to remain together despite the knowledge that they share the same father symbolically speaks to the idea that the two have resolved to engage in a type of "bodily" activism. Moraga (1983) insists that no authentic, nonhierarchical connection among oppressed groups can take place without an emotional, heartfelt grappling with the source of one's own oppression—we must know and name the enemy both within and outside of ourselves (45). Emma Pérez, too, reminds us that historically, disenfranchised groups have often created their own postcolonial imaginary when they can otherwise not succeed in breaking from earlier colonial formations. With this in mind, Sam and Pilar use their bodies as sites to map a rhetoric of resistance.

The final scene in the film concludes with a long shot of Sam and Pilar facing a torn, blank drive-in movie screen (figure 3). They have agreed to suspend the "rule." When Pilar says, "I can't get pregnant anymore if that's what the rule is about," it is not merely the biological rule against incest that they have suspended but a rule inscribed in the narrative that dominates the burden of history. At the film's end, the hope that the lovers envision is shared by the audience; we can imagine that Sam and Pilar, who have successfully destabilized the historical narratives they at one time believed they had been born into, have made strides in freeing and de-mythologizing history so as to, in Pérez's (1999) words, "consciously remake the narrative" (127). In this regard, the film makes a distinction between entrenched public history and counter-hegemonic interpretations of that history in ways that seek redress. Truth comes at a price, and both Sam and Pilar realize that the truth is contingent upon one's stance on a tenuous border that was historically created and sustained by the politics of identity. We can take the narratives of history as they are, or we can make a final distinction about

Figure 3: Sam Deeds and Pilar Cruz face the decision to remain together despite the knowledge that they are related. From *Lone Star* (1996). File photo, https://www.imdb.com/title/tt0116905/?ref_=fn_al_tt_1

history as it has been written and intervene to create more accurate histories of our own.

This is evident when, in the final lines of the film, Pilar says to Sam: "We'll start from scratch. All that other stuff. All that history. To hell with it, right? Forget the Alamo." As a place of *cultural memory* for both Anglos and Mexicans, the Alamo as legendary functions similarly to Buddy Deeds as legend; both should be able to "handle the truth." In fact, as a site of cultural memory, the Alamo *must* be capable of accommodating the competing claims of disparate groups rather than the one distorted version that Glenn Whitehouse (2002) argues remains tied to the United States' "civil religion"—the paramount "value placed on individualism almost to the exclusion of any sense of debt to society or past" (296). For Whitehouse, the lovers' decision to "forget the Alamo" signals their need to escape from an unacceptable *"ethical* situation" tethered to the Alamo as a symbol of partisan politics, contradiction, and hypocrisy (297, italics in original). When Sam and Pilar refuse what Whitehouse considers the tragic consequences of the past, the result is that they are no longer bound to the divisions created by the actions of their parents and the previous generation. For Whitehouse, offloading historical baggage such as that tied to the Alamo's contradictory significance for entire groups of people such as Mexicans and Chican@s marks the lovers' departure from the public sphere to the private sphere. As such, their decision speaks to their shared commitment to "discount the importance of public life and history . . . in order to seek a purely private happiness" (301). In their rejection of the whitewashed "winner's" narrative of the Alamo, Sam and Pilar underscore "the *demand* that memory

places on us to evaluate our personal and social history in terms of justice"
(Whitehouse 303, italics in original). Forgetting the Alamo, then, speaks
directly to what modern history has rendered ghostly. We can, however,
undo the tangled machinations of those spectral presences that haunt our
bodies and the landscapes we call home when we commit ourselves to extri-
cating and unburying the entwined stories of the Bordered frontier.

Lone Star illustrates how a reexamination of ideas about storytelling, time,
and personal identity foment the exploding of official public histories based in
the subjugation of both fact and personal memory. In the American Southwest,
relationships between the physical environment and the ideologically driven
constructions of borders create a complicated convergence point of fluidity
and tension. Sam's quest for the truth of history begins with the unearthing
of Charlie Wade's body—now bones—and ends with his transcending barriers
of race, ethnicity, and even incest. His union with Pilar at the film's end signals
the means by which love becomes "reinvented as a political technology" and a
process for "re-forming the self and the world" (Sandoval 2000, 4). Because the
American Southwest evinces borders, boundaries, and tensions of space and
place, an understanding of the metaphoric and imaginative power of these complex constructs that moves beyond lines plotted on physical maps helps us to
both theorize and understand the complex negotiations silenced voices navigate
in efforts to uncover alternatives to public written histories.

In *Lone Star*, the Bordered frontier can be seen in Sam and Pilar's obverse
movements, as illustrated by Sam's uncovering of the truth and Pilar's daily
framing of history for her students. In the end, both Sam and Pilar ghost
back against the story an earlier generation ingrained in their respective
memories, a story so powerful that it left its bitter mark on their bodies, for
an audience *senses* how throughout their adult lives they have remained, like
ghosts, partly with each other but mostly without. However, as the burden
of history is lifted in the film and those ghostly aspects of their adolescent
romance—a passionate devotion literally snatched from their lives by Buddy
and Mercedes—move Sam and Pilar beyond feeling towards action, we see
how, in shaping a new story, they can begin to fill the shape of that absence.
Indeed, all the narratives that comprise the film reflect a personal discourse
of loss attenuated by entrenched public histories. In chapters 5 and 6, I discuss critical regionalism and ecology in the Southwest to illustrate how a
broader conception that accounts for the connections and contradictions
between and within borders and frontiers at the regional level can speak to
wider national and global concerns.

CHAPTER 2

GEORGE WASHINGTON
ON THE BORDER

I n *Lone Star*, we see how history can be covered over, hidden, and concealed like Charlie Wade's bones. History, too, can be disappeared, as was the aptly named town of Perdido, which literally translates as "lost." Conversant with the historical writing of Américo Paredes and Arnoldo De León, Anna Adams (2007) explores how personal histories in the film are metaphorically aligned with Frontera's political history to remind us how, for the most part, Anglos and Euro Americans have, at least throughout the nineteenth and early-twentieth centuries, written and overwritten the history of Mexican Americans, Mexicans, and Native Americans on the Borderlands.[1] This is made manifest as Sam and Pilar fill in the gaps of personal, familial histories that, in time, reveal an incongruity with narratives made public by an earlier generation, namely Buddy Deeds and Mercedes Cruz. In the film, the audience is made to acknowledge how the borders between truth and lies are complex and onerous to maintain. Further, the *public* preservation of a fabricated past is preserved and sustained by erecting markers—monuments—that continue to fill the shape and essence of the immediate landscape, or a landscape's present, as evidenced by slapping the name of Buddy Deeds on an existing courthouse.

Adams asserts how, in the film, citizens who "have been excluded from the official history texts" are granted "equal time" (346). Further, we also deduce that the story of Perdido can remain suppressed only for so long, as

Sam himself indicates to both Hollis and Fenton, that the Chicano reporter Danny Padilla has likely not backed away from the story for good; the town may have vanished from sight but not from mind and memory. Perdido's story demonstrates how the production of space is deployed as a means to render silent the rich heterogeneity of Indigenous people in an existing Borderlands community. Similarly, the courthouse is more than a physical marker; a turn to Lefebvre reminds us how the production of space further binds re-presentations of space symbolically to the landscape. The naming of the courthouse after Buddy Deeds is a perpetual marker and reminder of how the law functions in Frontera. Finally, the repercussions of silenced personal histories may preclude the shape of one's future happiness and self, as is the case with Sam, who, before the discovery of Charlie Wade's bones, found it necessary to forget how Buddy and Mercedes forcibly separated him from Pilar as adolescents. Similarly, Mercedes chooses to maintain the falsehood that she is of "Spanish" heritage, rather than acknowledge her true Mexican history. In yet another seamless transition to the past, Mercedes flashes back to the evening when, as a young girl, she illegally crossed into the US by swimming across the Rio Grande. Throughout the film, however, Mercedes blatantly and fiercely disidentifies with her Indigenous heritage, a pattern I turn to now, and which we also find evidenced by an earlier generation in Arturo Islas's *The Rain God* (1984), which I discuss in chapter 5.

Part I: Jorge Wachinton, aka *George Washington Gómez*

Américo Paredes's complex novel, *George Washington Gómez* (1990), is rooted in the bodily negotiations that the main character, Guálinto, must undergo. Written between 1936 and 1940, a heightened period of national assimilation for Mexican Americans and Chican@s, the novel is an early example of canonical Chican@ literature in which the main character disavows his Mexican racial and cultural identity in order to embrace a fully "American consciousness," a model of behavior similarly espoused by Mercedes in *Lone Star*. The novel's ironic title reflects the protagonist's bifurcated development under the strain of cultural and political clashes and pressures in early twentieth-century Jonesville on the Grande, a fictional city that corresponds to the city of Brownsville, Texas. Broadly, the novel details Guálinto's development as he negotiates aspects of his Anglo-Texan environment, often alongside episodes of abuses by the Texas Rangers, Euro American land grabs, and external racism in educational and societal systems.

For George Washington Gómez—called Guálinto by his family and friends—the South Texas Borderland experience creates such a conflict of identity that incompatible ideas result in behavior that appears contrary to his character, as his identity is entwined in an actual, as well an imagined, history. As a child, Guálinto fantasizes about being a border hero. A precocious, intelligent child, he has the luxury of a stable household and loving and caring guardians. These facts, however, do nothing to quell his resentment and animosity toward the *angloamericanos* in the novel. Throughout the novel Guálinto struggles with assimilating into American culture while denouncing what he imagines as a shameful Mexican heritage aligned with what Saldaña-Portillo (2016) describes as the *indio bárbaro*, a generic deployment of "Indianness" necessitated for the acquisition of space in the Borderlands. Ramón Saldívar (1993) discusses Guálinto's "checkerboard consciousness" to comment on the centrality of an ongoing dialogue between contending discourses that cannot be "resolved into one voice" (159). In fact, a Borderlands dialectic nominally and literally marks Guálinto's body such that he exists within a spectrum of possible identities "as a subjected representation of the imaginary relations to the real conditions of existence in the early twentieth-century borderlands of south Texas" (158). I believe that the contradictory systems of knowledge that Saldívar posits as a "dialectics of difference" (159) that shape Guálinto's identity can be found in the fissure between border and frontier paradigms—the Bordered frontier. Saldaña-Portillo, too, focuses on the "psychic consequences" that result from Guálinto's "disavowal of indigeneity" in terms of what she identifies as a Southwestern racial geography that effectively splinters the protagonist's psyche to such a degree that "a psychosis is triggered" (142). I focus here on the final section of the novel during which Guálinto returns to Jonesville as an educated married man with a successful career before him. The section titled "Leader of his People" ironically grounds a set of choices that establishes and roots his worldview. His return shows how Guálinto's seemingly impossible task of developing into a heroic figure lies in a failure not of historic determinism rooted in a clash of Mexican and American cultures, but his failure to integrate the past into his future—a failure of what Mario J. Valdés calls the "historical imagination" (quoted in Márquez 1994, 84).

Some years after leaving Jonesville, Guálinto returns to South Texas as a lawyer. But unlike his childhood companions, Elodia and El Colorado, he is not an "organic intellectual . . . in the making" (Pérez 1998, 45), for he *chooses* not to be. Earlier in the novel, before Guálinto kills Lupe García (aka Arnulfo Miranda)—the seditionist who is later revealed to be his uncle—his boyhood friend, El Colorado, admonishes him to use his anger and his past knowledge to "get people to listen" (250). But Guálinto resents the fact that he has, since his birth, been asked to be a "leader of his people," as evidenced by the "great man's name" (16). His resentment is manifested in the shame he feels towards his dead father. At one point, he yells at his uncle Feliciano: "My father was just an ignorant Mexican! He got it into his head I was going to be a great man. A great man! And he saddled me with this silly, stupid name!" (193). By the novel's end, Guálinto has married Ellen Dell, a blond with "a long Anglo-Saxon face" (283). The negation of all that his name promised his mother and father is complete upon meeting Ellen's father, an ex-Texas Ranger who may have had a hand in killing Guálinto's father, Gumersindo, during the last days of the seditionist uprising that comprise the backdrop of chapter 1. Ellen's father says to Guálinto, "You look white, but you're a goddamn Meskin" (284). With this pronouncement, Guálinto decides to "legally change his name to George G. Gómez" (284). Further, he emphatically proclaims that neither his wife nor his children will learn Spanish—his native tongue—because "[t]here's no reason for them to do so." What's more, he insists that his children "will grow up far away from here" (301). It is interesting to note, however, that although the narrator declares he keeps the "G" in his changed name to honor his mother, Saldaña-Portillo (2016) observes that the G "is the resistant Indian character of his youth who haunts the adult George" (150). Not surprisingly, the eradication of his birth name secures and is testament to his decisive disidentification with his culture, his people, and the place he once called home.

A key scene in the novel surrounds the killing of Lupe García (later revealed to be Guálinto's uncle and brother to his mother). When Guálinto kills Lupe, Saldaña-Portillo maintains, he metaphorically kills a Mexican heritage he never really comprehended (149). She further describes García as an "*indio bárbaro*" who "haunts the narrative as a ghostly apparition," sporadically appearing and disappearing across the Southwest landscape tactically and at will (144). Indeed, just before this murder—for which Guálinto is labeled a hero by American law—he stumbles upon a dance filled with "his people. The real people he belonged with . . . not the 'Spaniards' like the Osunas" (247). Here, he meets the pretty, dark-skinned Mercedes, a girl very different from the girl he has desired throughout the novel, the rich "white-skinned beauty," María Elena Osuna (243). Although he vows to return to Mercedes and her welcoming home, he does not. Instead, he begins to carry a knife, and his animosity towards his Uncle Feliciano, his name, and the future his family has always wished for him foment indifference, hate, and guilt. Be "a great man and help my people," he scolds a deeply saddened Feliciano. "I'm not going to be a great man. I'll just be another Mexican with the seat of his pants torn and patched up. And I don't want to help my people. What for? Let them help themselves, the whole lot of ragged dirty *pelados*" (265). By this point in the novel, he believes his Uncle Feliciano to be a coward, and he seethes with a hatred of all Anglos: "They were the cause of all evil, he thought. They came, they took away everything we had, they made us foreigners in our own land. An Anglo had taken away his girl, the same Anglo had ruined his sister. Because of the Anglos he would never find decent work" (273). These are the musings of a desperate and downtrodden boy, and as readers we fully understand Guálinto's despair. We are, however, not prepared for his ultimate transformation.

During a final conversation with Feliciano, we realize the extent to which Guálinto has negated his own past, disidentified with it, separated from transpersonal time and space so absolutely that he is "an individual alone," a man "without context" (Bevis 1987, 590). Where the killing of his Uncle Lupe metaphorically speaks to the slaying of a Mexican ancestry he never embraced—whether through shame or misunderstanding—the legal erasure of his name is the final nail in the coffin of alienation that he ultimately chooses for himself. After attending a political rally held by some of his old friends, the "members of the executive committee of Latins for Osuna" (292), Guálinto disdainfully refers to them as a "bunch of clowns playing at politics" (300). Feliciano, who has just learned that his nephew's job entails spying on his old comrades on behalf of the US Army, ruefully retorts: "Then you see no future for us." Guálinto replies,

> I'm afraid not. Mexicans will always be Mexicans. A few of them, like some of those would-be politicos, could make something of themselves if they would just do like I did. Get out of this filthy Delta, as far away as they can, and get rid of their Mexican Greaser attitudes" (300).

In the end, then, Guálinto is nothing more than a pawn of the US government, ironically the very faction that once stole his homeland from under his feet.

Guálinto refuses to embrace the specter of his ancestors, instead crushing them under the burden of his own history and ultimately embracing a frontier ideology of limitless growth oriented only towards the future.

Feliciano, however, successfully destabilizes the frontier ideologies that have
labored to fissure his Mexican identity. In so doing, Feliciano orients himself toward a new more inclusive consciousness. Through Feliciano, who
assumed responsibility for his nephew Guálinto after Guálinto's father was
murdered at the hands of the Texas Rangers in chapter 1, "we get to see
the political machine at work in Jonesville, where he and the Gómez family relocate" (Pérez 1998, 35). Feliciano, once himself a *sedicioso*, neither
represses his history nor wholly assimilates into an American system that
seeks to erase the Mexican; instead, he subverts the frontier ideology in ways
that empower Mexicans while undermining the new American system of
government. He joins his old comrade, "El Negro," now the chief of customs who goes by the name Santos de la Vega, in a "little venture" to import
goods into Mexico duty free. Both Feliciano and de la Vega understand that
gold and land are "the only things that stay with you, the only real wealth
in the world" (81). Both men acknowledge that the old ways of keeping all
of the gold that one can out of the "Gringo banks" is important as well.
During the Depression years, when the market crashes and the Gringo laws
take over the banks, Feliciano, who "never trusted banks," will use part of
his money "to buy land from the old Gringo who rents to me now" (192).
Importantly, he explains to Guálinto that the "backward *ranchero* way"
(192) has allowed them to come out ahead in the end. In this light, I agree
with Saldívar (2006) that the "novel pulls from the residual elements of traditional culture the patterns that conceive the subject and then interrogates
those patterns in the light of its dominant, modern formation to suggest
other, untried designs for imagining a new ethnic consciousness" (149).

　　The memory of a homeland deeply flavors one's aims for the future. In
George Washington Gómez, Mexicans like Feliciano who embrace the past
do so in an effort to mediate between an emergent American way of life and
the residual knowledge of a very recent Mexican history. The forces at play
in the construction of a border consciousness are entwined not just in an
ideological battle at the subjective level, but conflicting narratives of space
and place. In this sense, Guálinto remains an emblem not of place but of
the vast, blank expanse of Southwestern space, and, as such, he is utterly
lost. By the novel's close, he is "not comfortable with the way things ended."
Indeed, he remains haunted by nightmares that leave him "with a feeling
of emptiness, of futility . . . fighting battles that were won and lost a long
time ago" (282). Neither a border hero nor a leader of his people, he is only
George, a man born in South Texas who will make money at the expense of

"his people" and his *tierra natal*. This fact not merely makes him no better than the Anglo Americans he once despised, it paints a far worse picture of him, for he has become the colonial agent he once spurned.

Critical Regionalism and Heritage Sites: Shaping a Modern Narrative in Laredo

As Renato Rosaldo (1989) and other scholars have observed, individuals like Guálinto, and indeed entire communities, often exhibit nostalgia for past events, events that exist in the imagined ideals of subjects who now occupy different spaces and who yearn for an idealized vision of a historical past. Such "imperialist nostalgia" can foment an oppressive ideology; citizen subjects who re-create the imagined ideal and labor under such conditions celebrate an oppressive condition. The emotion of nostalgia invokes the attempt to establish both a "more genuinely innocent" time and an "earlier epoch" (108). Seemingly relatively benign, such nostalgia facilitates the colonial agent's shift from a complicit reference point to innocent bystander. It is this pose of "innocent yearning" that attenuates the unsettled aspects of conquest that speak to a broader pattern of westward expansion on the Borderlands.

In this chapter, I detail a story early elite Laredoans created as a prime example of a colorful campaign that places the achievements of an affluent few at the center of history while pushing Indigenous actors to the margins. In creating the heritage industry known as the annual George Washington's Birthday Celebration (WBCA), Laredoans with privilege and power packaged and sanitized place and history on the US–Mexico Borderlands. As I describe herein, this incredible event exemplifies how an understanding of haunting can advance scholarly critique in terms of justice. Before moving toward issues of ethics and justice, which I detail more fully in chapters 5 and 6, it is useful to situate early efforts that inaugurated and shaped the celebration. A critical regionalist perspective, as put forward by José E. Limón (2008), opens a dialogue that is transnational and global while attentive to local complexities. Critical regionalism moves beyond oppositions of space and place in ways that allow us to conceptualize how people relate to land and region in their sociocultural fullness while considering relationships—often adversarial—that exist globally. Although the concept of "globalization" in many of its current iterations is beyond the scope of this study, it nonetheless provides an entry point to acknowledging shifting systems of consciousness as these exist in a multinational space like Laredo at a time when an incoming power structure sought to instill a consciousness that was both localized and yet securely tethered to a broader national identity. Further, a critical regionalist approach enables our apprehension of how colonialist and national imperatives of space overwrote a landscape of Manifest Destiny in Laredo that effectively subverted existing property arrangements.

Within the dynamics of globalization lies a basic paradox entwined by the dualities of tradition (the past) and progress (the future), a contradiction that further plays out spatially, along a geographical axis, and temporally, or in terms of historical processes. Because modernity generally suggests a continuum, what Roland Robertson (1996) describes as a "general homogenization of basic experiences in a temporal, historical mode" (27) that developed in the US alongside the decimation of Indigenous peoples, he redirects the more generalizing notion of globalization to Anthony Giddens' term, "globality," which speaks to globalization as a consequence of modernity (27). Where globalization, broadly, "compresses" the world (35), and as such the complexities of space and time that redound adversarial relationships between the local and the global, globality more accurately speaks to conditions that have facilitated the diffusion of modernist principles that interpenetrate geographically distinct civilizations. Thus, although Limón cautions against "the impulse to set global and local into immediate opposition" (177), we can look to terms like "glocal," introduced by Richard T. Rodriguez (2008) in response to Limón, as a further way to acknowledge how the global and the local intertwine to obtain "a politics of both collaboration and conflict" such that we can better understand the coexistence of "two groups in a common public sphere" like Laredo (184).

As I recount here, when the Great Sachem of the Improved Order of Red Men (IORM), Yaqui Tribe # 59, A. C. Hamilton, first declared Laredo as "truly a Red Man's city," he particularized a national story in a localized context in a very particular transnational and regional setting.[2] Peña (2020), too, concludes how a "specific goal" of the IORM fraternity brothers was "to unequivocally claim Laredo, Texas for America" (33). Such a claim appropriated rituals that served as a "differentiation strategy" of patriotic ideals intended to "authenticate their Americanness and to claim political legitimacy" (33). These rituals effectively caused a disruption of Laredo's identity as a once-Mexican settlement and seeded their reactionary project as an aspect of globality. In glocal terms, then, the IORM instilled a language, a setting, and a host of actors bound by a new story of globality, one that could effectively "contain" the space of the nation, the thrust of American exceptionalism, and a modernist story of conquest.

Like creation myths, elaborate traditions are often invented to bolster certain stories. Just as nations and nation-states invest in monuments, museums, and industries that secure a sense of power and pride, and speak to a sense of national awareness, so too do localities look to place-making to provide distinctiveness and visibility. Cresswell (2015) turns to David Harvey to illume how groups create sites of "heritage, where a sense of rootedness in the past and in place is provided for the consumption of locals and tourists" (95). Heritage industries package place and history in sanitized ways to attract tourists and capital. What happens then when a heritage industry is not oriented towards actual, truthful traditions, legacies, and histories of the place? For Harvey, it is those powerful institutional forces in society that often devalue or destroy existing geographical configurations in the move to develop new infrastructures. Moving from the abstract to the specific, Harvey's work speaks to the ways that the politics of place can be both "reactionary and exclusionary" (90). This is a pattern found in the annals of Laredo's history.

Part II: George Washington's Birthday Celebration as Origin Story

Since its inception in February 1898, Laredoans on the Texas–Mexico border in South Texas have carried out an elaborate month-long celebration in honor of George Washington's birthday. Begun by the fraternal organization IORM as a patriotic celebration to unite Laredo—a predominantly Spanish and Mexican Borderlands space—to the greater US, the celebration re-creates events following an imagined script that includes two garish performances: an "Indigenous" pageant presided over by Princess Pocahontas, and a Colonial Presentation and Ball. This chapter details how the WBCA encompasses a *lieu de mémoire*, an institutionalized public memory in which Laredoans continue to treat Indigenous cultures as abject. The result underscores the ironic compromises of a border performance that precipitates the representation of space as a symptom of colonial and national imaginaries in the United States. In Laredo, the spatial enterprise that is the WBCA illustrates what Saldaña-Portillo (2016) describes as a "graphing of the geo" that designates the ongoing, multilayered processes of space-making that have shaped the Borderlands by subverting existing property relations or creating new spatial relations between and among Indigenous peoples and incoming

Spaniards or Euro American colonialists (19). Further delving into issues of race, class, and gender alongside the historical imperatives that ushered the widespread adoption of an idealized and outright false narrative—which continues today—further guides our understanding of the ways individual agents engender a collective memory at the expense of a truly multicultural national narrative.

Because I grew up steeped in the traditions of the WBCA and have participated in various capacities in the celebration, I take an ethnographic approach to a place-based analysis of the celebration as well as draw from the Latin@ narrative form of *testimonio*. Chandra Talpade Mohanty (2003) and others have described *testimonio* as a genre of writing steeped in both memory and history that skirts and mediates issues of resistance, truth, and authenticity in the circulation of stories of subaltern or socially marginalized citizens. This crucial mode of rewriting historical memory, which I discuss further in my study of *Sleep Dealer* in chapter 6, is key to remembering and recording the experiences and struggles of Indigenous peoples. This chapter highlights how authorized scripts that shape public history, like those of the WBCA, can effectively subvert what Nora (1989) contends are "real environments of memory" (7). Real and actual environments of memory often remain hidden beneath the façade of modern topographies. In the twenty-first century, much of Laredo's complex social history remains buried under a heritage industry steeped in an imperialist nostalgic imagination promulgated by an elite, powerful few. The WBCA is an integral part of Laredo's collective memory. Nonetheless, those not familiar with Laredo culture, politics, and social life often question the seemingly contradictory impulses behind this time-honored, often outlandish celebration—with good reason. Why does a city that boasts a population that remains over 95.6 percent Hispanic so vehemently and garishly celebrate a slew of American icons who have little or no association with the US–Mexico border or the American Southwest?

In Laredo, the Other exists within a fragile space where insider and outsider have survived symbiotically, and in the interests of an elite few. The Other in this paradigm is a historical Indigenous presence whose erasure was necessitated in order to first redeem and then continually reinforce modernist, colonialist priorities in the Borderlands. What is remarkable in this particular border place is the fact that alliances were neither historically nor primarily based on ethnicity, but on class. These alliances, contend Yoder and LaPerrière de Gutiérrez (2004), remain: "In contrast to conditions found in major Hispanic places throughout the United States, the stark social disparities that exist in Laredo are not racial or ethnic in nature" (75).

This chapter focuses historiographically on race, gender, and, to some extent, class in a Borderlands space to demonstrate the accommodation of a Eurocentric, linear narrative in which Indigeneity is not just negated but made virtually invisible by the widespread adoption of a particular legitimating story. An examination of the historical imperatives ushering the widespread adoption and dissemination of the narrative surrounding George Washington on the border helps uncover how individuals with power and status engender a collective memory at the expense of an inclusive, and truly multicultural, narrative. The historical accommodation of Anglos and Mexicans in Laredo, on the far edge of the American frontier, reveals how a very particular national identity was carved within a fluid, highly permeable geographic space. Those with money, land, and means wrote, perpetuated, and participated in the story; all others in the space became, and are yet, subject to it. In the following chapter, we see how a group of women—the Princess Pocahontas Council—ghost back against this story to bring forward the past in a way that allows it to undermine the false memories that fracture the nostalgic vision of the WBCA—although not without its own perplexing import.

Cultural geographer Daniel Arreola (2002) reminds us that cultures are produced and subsequently reproduced through forms and practices ensconced in spaces. Although cultural geography is one way to assess culture, and in Arreola's study an apt model to apprehend the evolution of the cultural features of the distinct ethnic region that is South Texas, such a model occasions us to explore the spatial abstractions of region, place, and landscape in terms of individuals who shape, and are consequently shaped by, that region. Arreola's regional study of South Texas points towards an understanding of "the ancestral geographic roots of the residents, how the region came to be formed politically and demographically, how identity is vested through cultural representations, and how the region is emblematic of a particular identity, and, therefore, different from other cultural regions" (4). Because, Arreola argues, different cultures "make place" in quite particular ways, diachronic studies of "human-place bonds" (4) yield insight into signifying frameworks particular to the social situation of individuals in a given landscape. People are not just bonded to the places in which they live and dwell, but landscapes can act as "signifying frameworks" through which social systems are communicated, experienced and even reproduced (5).

Laredo has shaped its identity through its cultural expressions. The city rests on the US–Mexico border and so has always been highly permeable, as demonstrated by a vernacular that exemplifies and nurtures the use of a distinctive Laredo dialect enmeshed in a mixture of Spanish and English—Spanglish. Although linguistic registers are beyond the scope of this study, shifts in naming practices reveal imperialist objectives and reinforce a colonialist push to forge a modern, nationalist identity. A few key examples of name changes in Laredo show how public spaces are identifiers of broader hegemonic practices that had taken root by the end of the nineteenth century. These practices transformed Laredo into what it is today: a burgeoning binational, bicultural city that identifies itself as "The Great International Gateway of the Two Republics" (152), and "the primary trade route connecting Canada, the United States and Mexico" (LDF online).

What's in a Name?

In 1755, Laredo was officially designated Villa de San Agustín de Laredo, "said to be so named after the town of Laredo on the Bay of Biscay in Santander, Spain" (Wilcox 1938, 86). By 1848, the name of the province had changed. After 1848, with the signing of the Treaty of Guadalupe Hidalgo, Laredo became a decidedly "American" town; Laredoans who desired to become part of Mexico founded the adjacent city of Nuevo Laredo on the Mexican side of the Rio Grande. Early competing hegemonic forces wrought changes and laid the groundwork for the emerging identities of Los Dos Laredos, as the region is commonly called in the twenty-first century. This coincided with an emerging nationalism and an industrialized worldview that sought to define, and often redefine, itself at the local level. Dion Dennis (1997) observes how South Texas "maintained much of the population, culture, language and sensibility" of its adjacent nation of Mexico, further arguing that "the definitional distinction between an American and Mexican identity was (and often still is) extremely precarious and vulnerable" (par. 5). As such, we can look to specific instances of national patriotism and citizenship among Laredo's early elite who shaped an identity and ideology that remains today. When we push conventional methodologies of geography and social science to look beyond traditional disciplinary lines of inquiry, we uncover the power relations at work in the construction of individual and collective spacialities as well as the consequences of those constructions. As Soja and Hooper (1993) have concluded, "[s]pace cannot simply be metaphorical; it is connected to material geographical realities and it is constructed out of unequal social relations of power" (185). In Laredo, we can read these relations of power as they have become "tied to relations of production rather than to national origin" (Sánchez 1983, 19).

Public records indicate that the original families who settled in Laredo in 1755 came from Spain; along with them came Mexican Indians from the interior of Mexico, probably Tlaxcaltecas. The end of the US–Mexico war of 1848 created a boundary of the Rio Grande and divided the landholdings of Laredo families. Early naming practices show that initial settlers in Laredo borrowed their neighborhood names from churches they later established, as in San Francisco Javier. Laredo historian Stan Green (1993) describes how "immigrants from Mexico did not bring with them the same traditions as did the immigrants from Europe. . . . [C]ivic impulses found their scope not in the general body politic, but in that nearer realm of the neighborhood" (1). Names that designate landmarks, such as Chacon (so named after Chacon Creek), El Tropezon (The Big Stumble), Cantaranas (croaking or singing frogs), and Siete Luces (seven lights, named after a local *cantina*) are additional early neighborhood names that indicate a strong network of family and neighborhood allegiances rather than "civic activism" (1). Anglo newcomers who began arriving after the 1880s, however, appropriated and conquered in many ways, not just militarily—a pattern begun with the founding of Fort McIntosh in 1849, and by which "for the next 100 years, with two brief exceptions, the United States Army and its influence would be present in Laredo" (Thompson 1974, 165).

El Azteca, chronologically the second neighborhood to appear in Laredo, remains the oldest surviving neighborhood in the area. Located east of the historical central business district, at least a portion of this barrio was named El Ranchero for a store that would grind corn and sell the *masa* (cornmeal) to local residents (Yoder and LaPerrière de Gutiérrez 2004, 63). This southernmost barrio was home to an early laboring class of mostly Mexicans. The first Laredo neighborhood, San Agustín, was composed mostly of leading ranchers who built their town residences as close as possible to the San Agustín church and plaza. Historically, the third of Laredo's neighborhoods was St. Peters, "which became home to the Anglo Americans and Europeans who poured into Laredo after the railroads came in 1881" (Green 1993, 5).

Newcomers to the region routinely named and renamed towns, places, and sacred spaces. In 1755, as noted earlier, Laredo as a city was officially designated Villa de San Agustín de Laredo (Juarez 2001). At this time, there was only one church, San Agustín Church. The area around the church, San Agustín Plaza, in keeping with the Spanish colonial practice of designating plazas as sites for "public meetings, corrals for wild cattle during Spanish round-ups, and places for relaxation," was designed to serve as the center of civic life and the pivotal space from which the entire town's plan evolved (Nixon-Mendez 1995, par. 1). In 1902, Mayor Albert Martin (1889–1972) officially changed the name of the plaza to "Martin Plaza." Albert Martin was the son of Raymond Martin, who emigrated to America from France in 1849 and who by 1860 "was the wealthiest man in Webb County" (Thompson 1986, 114). The name was made official in the city records. It is unclear when the name was officially changed back to San Agustín Plaza; the name had been changed by May 2001 when the Webb County Historical Commission officially "adopted" the plaza (Juarez 2001). Originally, the street names surrounding San Agustín Plaza were Calle Real, Calle San Francisco, Calle San Jorge, and Calle del García. Other streets in the colonial settlement were named for the institutions they led to—for instance, Calle Convento (Convent Street) and La Calle del Agua (Water Street).

Another instance of the naming of a crucial, identity-making public space that shows the thrust of US nationalism on a previously native Mexican identity is seen in the changed name of another plaza. The plaza known today as "Bruni Plaza" has undergone various name changes throughout its history. The 1885 Sanborn Map shows the block as a "public square." In 1900, the name "plaza" is used to indicate the site. In 1891, the Hijos de Juarez (Sons of Juarez), a mutualist society that provided relocation assistance, burial insurance, and fraternal networks for Mexican immigrants, occupied the large building on the west side of the plaza. Due to its proximity to this building, the plaza came to be known as Juarez Plaza. By September 1, 1931, the plaza had been re-named in honor of Antonio Mateo Bruni, an Italian immigrant who came to be one of Laredo's most prominent citizens (Nixon-Mendez 1995, par. 4). In a memo from the historic preservation officer, Nina Nixon-Mendez to Alfredo Castillo, director of parks and recreation, dated November 30, 1994, Nixon-Mendez writes: "Bruni Plaza . . . is a reminder of two important developments in Laredo's history. It embodies the spirit of the Spanish founders who carved a town out of the brush country. Secondly, it is a testimonial to the progressive minded citizens who emigrated to Laredo in the latter part of the 19th century" (par. 1). The naming of the plaza appears to be one way to show the population, which was mostly

Mexican and who remained politically tied to the mother country from which it had been severed in 1848, who was, or who was trying to be, boss. In the twenty-first century, the evidence, embossed on a memorial on the grounds of Bruni Plaza, remains in the words of A. M. Bruni: "God has given us political power to be used for the welfare of the people."

In 1767, Juan Fernando de Palacios, the governor of Nuevo Santander, New Spain, "officially designated Laredo as a villa, a central plaza laid out, and issued *porciones* or land grants" (Nixon-Méndez and Thompson, 1). After the Civil War, Mayor Samuel Jarvis expanded the traditional Spanish plaza town plan. Edmund J. Davis appointed Jarvis mayor of Laredo on July 15, 1868, through an order from Major General D. C. Buchanan, then commander of the 5th Military District. On August 17, 1868, Mayor Jarvis's first signature appears in the city minute books. The entry, by an unnamed alderman, pertains, in some measure, to the width of the city streets. The entry is in Spanish. The second entry, that of January 2, 1869, acknowledges that a "new map," which appears to have been devised by Mayor Jarvis himself, was instituted in place of the old. This entry, too, is in Spanish: *Se resolvío: que el mapa nuevo de la ciudad hecho por el mayor sera conocido [unintelligible word] de esta ciudad en lugar de el Viejo.*[3] According to archivist Joe Moreno of the Laredo Public Library, no copy of the original city map before 1869 is available. By the time Jarvis's term as mayor had ended in 1872, the city minutes had shifted to the English language.

With his new map, Jarvis named Laredo downtown streets alternately for American and Mexican heroes. In true confluence of nation, religion, and a spirit of bi-nationality, Jarvis and the city fathers named out the streets coming from the river as alternating generals and military heroes from Mexico and the US: Zaragoza, Lincoln, Hidalgo, Farragut, Matamoros, Washington, Victoria, and Scott. The intersecting avenues were given religious names: San Eduardo, San Jorge, San Enrique, and San Francisco.[4] Jarvis also took the occasion to name some streets after his children: Santa Cleotilde, Santa María, and Santa Zarita. Important to the present discussion is the implication of power Jarvis held in designating what Laredo streets were to be called as well as changing those names he deemed appropriate. Jarvis, a native New Yorker from a wealthy socialite family, ultimately expresses the role of colonial power to rename.

In regard to naming practices of public streets and plazas in Laredo, a Euro American, colonialist influence to push and further instill US nationalism on a population of residents who had, at one time, been Spanish, then

Mexican, and who called themselves *tejanos*, attempted to erase, or at least cover up, an earlier identity. The naming of streets in public spaces in the border town of Laredo is one way of showing that the established order corresponds to those who assume responsibility for the naming (Cantú 1995). In nineteenth-century Laredo, several forces intent on making the national identity of the community correspond with the geopolitical identity of the new elite, however at odds this may have been with an earlier geocultural identity, coalesced to rename these public spaces in the heart of this old city. This short discussion on naming and re-naming initiatives is an apt introduction to the Washington's Birthday Celebration held every year in Laredo since 1898, for it underscores how Euro Americans redefined public spaces in their efforts to chisel the landscape to fit their nationalistic ends. Euro Americans further appropriated a story—that of the Sons of Liberty/Red Men—tied to a cultural hero and bound to an existing "American" discourse so as to construct and ultimately perpetuate a specific ideology based in a mythology of the Indian as Other.

Revising Laredo's Story: Red Men Enact Place

Just as a privileged class of Laredoans with power and means changed the names of public spaces, so too are the beginnings of the WBCA tied to "peculiar representations of nationalisms and identities in the interzone between languages, cultures, classes, genders, and histories" that "differentially express the historical, material, and semiotic motifs that mirror the logics of power in this interzone on the Rio Grande (Dennis 1997, par. 3, 4). For Saldaña-Portillo (2016), generic conceptions of Indianness, portrayed as civilized Indians or barbarous *indios,* were deployed alongside Spanish and Euro American colonial practices as a means to coalesce and render silent the heterogenous cultures of Indigenous people in the United States. Further, an American ambivalence in which American Indians serve as "oppositional figures against whom one might imagine a civilized national Self" (Deloria 1998, 3) continues to shape how successive generations of Laredoans—myself included—have, and continue to be, socialized.

Since its inception in February 1898, and unabated by the Mexican Revolution, two world wars, a national depression, and the 1970s oil crisis, Laredoans have carried out an elaborate celebration in honor of George Washington's birthday.[5] Participants of the celebration's formative and most influential performances have always been members of the oldest, wealthiest, and most powerful families in Laredo; recurring family names are steadfast reminders of the elite class structure represented by the event. In 1848, Laredo came under US rule, and Americans began arriving. After 1881, the year the Texas–Mexican Railroad first came to town, Euro Americans with capital, business connections, and political influence began to make their mark on Laredo. At this time, Laredo's population was comprised "of about eighty percent of Mexican extraction and twenty percent of American ancestry" (Wilcox 1942, par. 5). Elliott Young (1988) cites the coming of the railroad in Laredo as coincidental with the city's full integration into the international capitalist system and, more importantly, American society. For Young, the coming of the railroad symbolically marks the divide between a Mexican past, with its "jacal and adobe shanties" and an Anglo present and future with "capitalists, artisans, and two-story brick buildings" (52). Similarly, the celebration underscores a marked attempt to break with the Mexican past. An early *Laredo Times* article by noted Laredo historian Seb S. Wilcox chronicles the inception of the WBCA by the IORM, a secret fraternal order of all-male membership linked to the early Sons of Saint Tammany societies formed in 1783 by former officers of the Continental Army (Davis 1990, 59). This lays the foundation for understanding the impulse behind the Bordertown extravaganza.

In 1897, veteran San Antonio newspaperman Charles M. Barnes traveled to Laredo with the purpose of organizing a lodge around the patriotic IORM, of which he was district deputy and great sachem.[6] The Laredo charter, whose motto is "freedom, friendship, and charity," was issued on May 29, 1897, and designated the local chapter Yaqui Tribe No. 59. "The local lodge grew . . . and soon numbered among its members the most prominent men of Laredo of both American and Mexican ancestry, all loyal citizens" (Wilcox 1942, par. 4). According to Robert E. Davis (1990), great chief of records, Great Council of the United States, early Tammany Societies such as those established as early as 1789 in New York and Philadelphia, and later in Rhode Island, Kentucky, and Ohio (Deloria 1998, 47), have "direct links to the Society of Red Men [not to be confused with the IORM] formed at Fort Mifflin in 1813. . . . Each May 12th the Society held a 'grand celebration' in honor of Chief Tammany, with Indian dances being performed at some public place" (70). According to Davis, with each successive year the celebrations became more raucous. With the War of 1812, Secretary of War General Henry Dearborn ordered "all military persons to cease from taking part in the excesses of the Tammany Society" (71). After 1812, the celebrations ceased entirely, and the society slid toward extinction. Tammany "ideals," however, were passed along to a new order called the Society of Red Men. Regarding the name change, Davis (1990) writes:

> They wanted a *new* organization. One not tainted with politics. . . . What could be more natural than to turn to that rare breed of men who loved freedom more than life and fought to the death to protect their liberty, a simple people who lived with nature, but were fierce and proud, the American Indian (85).

According to Wilcox (1942), before 1898 and prior to Barnes's arrival in Laredo, Laredoans in this border space had only celebrated Mexican holidays such as Cinco de Mayo and Día 16 de Septiembre. Charles Barnes and the new IORM, that "patriotic body of Yaqui Tribe No. 59 conceived the idea of fittingly celebrating a purely American holiday . . . to kindle the fires of patriotism in the hearts of a border city" (par. 5). Historically, and continuing into the twenty-first century, the WBCA is a distinctive extravaganza that "blurs all sorts of traditional boundaries while producing new ones" (Treviño 2005, 46). It is a social drama charged with political import and valuation based in a revisionist historical narrative that dates back to the "oldest fraternal order of American national origin" in which upwardly-mobile married white men "summoned up an imagined mythic past in which risk-taking and male hierarchies were celebrated through secret macho rituals of racial transformations, first from a 'paleface' to a 'red man' and then up the hierarchy from a brave to a 'sachem' or 'a keeper of the wampum'" (Dennis 1997, par. 6). The reinscribing of specious "Indianness" as an icon of uniquely white male privilege instilled an important, and lasting, sociopolitical objective. From as early as 1905, full-time politicians made their way to Laredo to join the festivities, where politicos and Laredo's privileged citizens learned early on that it was "the best occasion of the year to make a political point" (Green 1999, 248). Furthermore, argues Green, the Washington's Birthday Celebration gave birth to the phrase that "every February the State Capitol was transferred to Laredo" (242).

Identity Making, Accommodation, and Awakening Patriotism

Border scholar David Montejano (1987), like Arreola (2002), argues that "being Mexican" in Laredo derived its meaning within the social and political context provided by local class structures. Whereas class signifies an economic identity construction, in terms of the WBCA, class is tethered to a partisan bureaucracy that effectively politicizes affluence and nationalism, a pattern that continues to oppress and exploit participants in the two performances I detail here. The legacy of colonial rule in Laredo is grounded in ways that Mexicans and Anglos have historically worked together to represent and propagate a social order that partially derived from a localized structure and system of class rather than race. In this sense, the memory of the Laredo chapter of the Fraternal Order of the Red Men, Yaqui Tribe #59, remains a signifier of social and cultural relations in Laredo today.

Historically, most nineteenth-century Laredoans—rough-hewn ranchers and their families—spoke mainly Spanish, even after Laredo "was given American political structure for city and county" under Captain Mirabeau B. Lamar during the Mexican War of 1846–1848 (Green 1999, 3). In later decades, European and American newcomers married into local families, resulting in an ongoing process of Americanization and Mexicanization. Montejano's "relaxed class analysis" of race relations in Texas guides our understanding of class, ethnicity, and, ultimately, identity in the area. He delineates four "race situations": Incorporation 1836–1900, Reconstruction 1900–1920, Segregation 1920–1940, and Integration 1940–1986, to examine the complex, ultimately accommodationist relations between Anglo Americans and Texas Mexicans—*tejanos*—in Texas from 1836 to the present. This notion of cooperation is key to understanding the Birthday Celebration as a major force that embodies central social struggles of Laredo's population and ultimately shapes the public memory.

The 1898 *Laredo Times* article that professed the annual commemoration of Washington's birthday as an effort to "awaken patriotism on the border and make us realize that we live in the United States" is integral to understanding what is at stake in the hearts and minds of elite citizens who fashioned a tenuous identity for Laredo throughout its history (Young 1988, 55). Gilbert Hinojosa (1987), like Montejano (1987), agrees that early Mexican families provided an entry for whites in Laredo's elite circles and helped to mitigate racial tensions in the area. In this regard, Laredo's demographic and political structure historically compelled inclusionary practices among *tejanos* and whites. Additionally, in Laredo, "Mexicans could be invited to join the U.S. nation as equal partners because a significant portion of them held political and economic power" (55). This economic and class structure, in which the seeds of the WBCA were sown, remains today.

The 1898 celebration, the first of its kind, was a civic success that culminated in 1923 with Laredo's receiving a state charter. The festivities are

described by Young (1988) as a "ritual of inversion" in which elite men—
mostly Anglos but at least one Texas Mexican—"played Indian" in a mock
attack against city hall. Lower socioeconomic classes and visitors watched
the performance from the sidelines. This spectacle "pitted Laredo's forces of
order, including its primary political institutions, against the forces of disor-
der"—American Indians and Indigenous citizens (58). Tejanos, who consid-
ered themselves "white" Mexicans, in reenacting a scenario from the annals
of manifest destiny reinforced a sense of common destiny among Laredo's
Mexican and Anglo population. In this way, whites and *tejanos* exoticized
Indigenous populations as "Other" and set in motion a system that continues through the present in the language of class and culture, in which *tejanos*
occupied a "transitional position in the racial hierarchy" (71). Montejano
(1987) argues that whites and Mexicans, during the period of "segregation,"
enjoyed friendly and relaxed associations where Mexicans owned land and
had political power. Being "Mexican," he argues, drew its meaning within
the social and political context of local class structures (252). His analysis
of the 1930 census speaks to the rationale by which *tejanos* identified themselves as white. Jerry Thompson (1974) writes that in the mid-nineteenth
century,

> Laredo thus developed a somewhat different socio-political pattern than
> that which characterized other areas of the state. True, Laredo came to
> experience discrimination, but discrimination of a different nature, mean-
> ing that the discrimination was socioeconomic rather than racial. The
> upper-class, both Anglo-American and Mexican-American, tended to dis-
> criminate against the lower class of the town with a force perhaps worse
> than that in any other area of the state (161).

Even during the early twentieth century, when racial violence had spread
throughout South Texas, Laredo never experienced the brutal mass killings
and lynchings that occurred elsewhere throughout Texas. Jovita González
argues that on the border, "descendants of the old grantees" demanded and
retained certain privileges (quoted in Montejano 1987, 114). This mirrors
Hinojosa's (1987) assertion regarding the security that was claimed by both
Laredo Mexicans and whites via stable family relations. He concludes that
"the complex relationship that developed between Euro Americans and
Mexican Americans was often mutually beneficial and never outwardly
hostile. The coalitions that evolved were not principally ethnic; instead,
they pitted the privileged, whether Anglo, European, or Mexican, against
the poor" (68). In Laredo, elite members of Mexican and Euro American

families "intermarried so long ago that no one in their right minds would attempt to make ethnic distinctions" (Swartz 2006, par. 16).

The WBCA is a testament to the complex negotiations of power between affluent Mexicans and Euro Americans that continues to demark class structures in a given geopolitical space. Mary Pat Brady's (2002) study of what she calls the "manipulation of space" (52) in her hometown of Douglas, Arizona guides our understanding of the colonialist imperatives that have historically defined the space and parameters of the celebration and its basis in a fraudulent, nostalgic reality. Brady's analysis, which begins by positioning the construction in 1912 of the Southwestern Railroad Depot in Douglas as a signal of the triumph of Anglo hegemony over the region and the beginning of the capitalization of the border, helps us conceptualize how the Borderlands town of Laredo negotiated a conflictive coexistence of dialectically opposed temporalities: one Mexican, agrarian, and premodern, and the other a US cosmopolitan modernity. Similarly, analyses of communal, identity-making performances through the years must focus on the role of narrative as well as the transformations of the production of space in which that narrative is performed. To this end, the work of Raúl Homero Villa (2000), alongside Soja's, further explains the manipulation of space as a social process. Villa's work, which shows how memory is central to understanding the spatial practices that produce form and meaning in the *barrios* of Los Angeles, helps us understand how citizens from distinctly different social and cultural backgrounds vie for communal physical space.[7] Although in Laredo, the radicalized social activism of protest and dissent which forged the Chican@ activism of Los Angeles was seemingly "worlds away from most of us on the border" (Treviño 2005, 39), studies such as Brady's help unbury the memories of alternative spatial narratives hidden beneath the façade of an imperialist nostalgic imagination promulgated by a privileged class.

CHAPTER 3

PRINCESS POCAHONTAS
GHOSTS BACK

February 1984, Laredo, Texas

I am "Princess Happy Butterfly," and I represent the great Cherokee Tribe of Tennessee in the annual Princess Pocahontas Pageant. The event, which the organizers call "mystical and magical," is both a performance and a variation of its sister presentation, the Society of Martha Washington Colonial Ball.

As Princess Happy Butterfly, I am *not* happy. Instead, I am hot and nervous in my fringed cerulean blue suede outfit, and the genuine owl feathers in my hair itch. This is all my mother's fault . . . her idea. My costume is ornate and elegant. Adorned with thousands of glittering and clinking beads, it took ten protracted months to design and weighs forty pounds. A tenth-generation *tejana*, I did not have a *quinceañera*; instead, I, along with fourteen other high school girls, am "presented" via the Washington's Birthday Celebration of Laredo as a member of the Princess Pocahontas Court of 1984. My escort Henry does not want to be here either. I have never been to Tennessee.

•

As a member of the 1984 Princess Pocahontas Court, I portrayed a mythic figure from an imagined past—Princess Happy Butterfly—the name given to me by the all-female members of the Princess Pocahontas Council (figure 4). For one year prior to our "presentation" in the pageant, we fifteen young women endured countless tea parties and luncheons, learned professional horsemanship skills, and were formally instructed on how to publicly present ourselves in a graceful, confident, and genteel manner; we were, after all, debutantes.[1] Furthermore, although my escort Henry and I represented the Cherokee Tribe of Tennessee, neither of us, nor any of the other members of the Court, were ever instructed in any way regarding specifics of the tribal nations or peoples we were portraying; we were merely "representatives" who were chosen by a cadre of professional and working-class women to participate in *their* conception of history. In this sense, we were mimics, role playing in a very specific re-presentation of history. So, too, did my friends who served as debutantes in the older, more traditionally established Colonial Ball play the roles of "Marthas" by portraying ladies and contemporaries of the founding fathers. Both festivals, which involve "masked" performances and processions and serve as a type of "coming-out" ritual for each young woman presented, encompass what Homi Bhabha (2006) has described as a "desire to emerge as 'authentic' through mimicry" (126). In Bhabha's conception, the play actors of the WBCA represent an "*ironic* compromise" and a "desire for a reformed, recognizable Other, *as a subject of difference that is almost the same, but not quite*" (122, italics in original).

The falsely nostalgic visions that entwine both performances remain a testament to the maintenance of racial, gender, and patriarchal hierarchies that have historically oriented both Euro American and Mexican subjectivities in the border community of Laredo. The elite cadre of established Laredo families represented by the Society of Martha Washington who, year after year, fashion a "royal" ensemble in order to propagate a vision of power and wealth do little to undermine the efforts of the Princess Pocahontas Council. In fact, the Princess Pocahontas Council is equally complicit in creating, sustaining, and, finally, participating in a forced political theorization of power based in the subjugation of history. This chapter, like the previous one, puts forward a troubling element of haunting that speaks to a particular animated state of colonial hegemony coded within the yearly performances of the WBCA. The initial goals of the IORM and later the Society of Martha Washington—steeped in a mythic ethics of space—continue to factor (and fracture) the social consciousness of individuals as they are lived and relived in perpetuity. The two celebrations I detail here show how "the past is made metaphorically equivalent to the present;

Figure 4: "Princess Happy Butterfly" and escort, 1984. Courtesy of the author.

and the present appears simply as a repetition of persistently recurring structures identified with the past" (White 1991, 616). Returning to Gordon
(2008) reminds us how hauntings manifest abusive systems of power such
that their impacts are felt in everyday life, particularly "when they are sup-
posedly over and done with . . . or when their oppressive nature is denied"
(xvi). Gordon references forms of slavery here, but repetitive colonial enterprises that first generate and then immortalize blind spots where "home
becomes unfamiliar, when your bearings on the world lose direction, when

the over-and-done-with comes alive" (xvi) are themselves specters, as they alter the experience of being in time, for every year Laredoans return to a time where the "trouble" of colonial space-making enterprises are restored, have presence, and demand attention.

Cristina Ibarra deftly illustrates, in her acclaimed 2014 documentary, *Las Marthas*, how the Colonial Ball/Presentation is more than an assimilation ritual, as it speaks to a way of life that celebrates individual members' and, accordingly, certain Laredo families' "place in society as the elite" (Anchondo 2014, 40). The film follows two young women, both Martha Washington Society debutantes, during the grueling year prior to their presentation in the February pageant.[2] Most of the young women who will serve as debutantes in the Colonial Pageant know from childhood that they will be presented at the ball; these include daughters, granddaughters, and nieces of original members, the parents of whom presume this presentation from their child's birth. Others, however—generally no more than one per year—may be invited to participate. Such invitations do not come easy for these non-legacy daughters, as tradition breeds a sense of demarcation and class consciousness that quite obviously sets "legacy daughters" apart from "guests." The same, however, cannot be said of the young women who will portray Native American figures in the Princess Pocahontas Pageant, as there is no "birthright" attached to this event. In this chapter, I discuss how the ghostly presences of American forefathers, foremothers, and Native Americans—real or imagined—have laid claim to Laredoans' social consciousness. As Norma Cantú asserts in *Las Marthas*, the celebration upholds early, landed elites' collusion with Anglo newcomers to the area to "affirm their existence and their right to govern, their right to the land, their right to be the *patrón*." These specters have veritable presence and demand our attention, as they mark the perennial reinvocation of an early battle in Laredo: the battle for place.

•

¡Ay, mi'jita, I just love it! All that *history*!

My mother beams when I ask her about her membership in the Princess Pocahontas Council of Laredo since its beginnings in 1980. It is an integral part of her elite identity and position in Laredo social circles. She is not a "Martha," a member of the most privileged social club in Laredo. But she has a voice in choosing who will portray Pocahontas and receive the key to Laredo in the annual WBC; this constitutes a certain level of social clout.

Yet it is her response to my question of *why* she spends so much time on an event that lasts one evening that is especially telling. The space that she negotiates with her reply is huge and brilliant—just like one of the Marthas' $25,000 debutante gowns. The Spanish prefix, *"Ay, mi'jita,"* that rests so comfortably within her English sentence, solidifies my roots as a Laredoan. But it is the tight, little square my mother's mouth makes as she so exuberantly delivers the word "history" that speaks volumes. She is passionate and resolute. As secretary of the council, she helped write several pageant scripts. She knows they are full of history. What I can't figure out is what she means by "history." Pocahontas was never in Laredo . . . and neither were George or Martha Washington. In fact, the key performances of the yearly celebration are couched not in historical fact, but a manufactured, mythical interpretation of history that reveals a lot more about the city's present identity than its historical reality.[3]

The Society of Martha Washington and the Princess Pocahontas Council

In Laredo, the Birthday Celebration is a defining factor of individual and collective identity. An examination of the popular celebration held here every year since 1898 guides our awareness of the need for an elite few to recurrently reaffirm white and largely class-based dominance at the expense of a wider, native population. This fact mirrors Philip J. Deloria's (1998) conclusions surrounding "playing Indian" and the role and meaning of race in US history. Because "Indianness lay at the heart of American uniqueness," Deloria concludes that there was "no way to conceive an American identity without Indians. At the same time, there was no way to make a complete identity while they remained" (37). Historically, this is a crucial fact of life in Laredo, where, in the words of Dion Dennis, "George Washington was recoded as a South Texas foundational and legitimating signifier for the [earlier] patronist system" (1997, par. 12).

The two events that, arguably, comprise the heart of the GWBC—the Colonial Presentation and Ball and the Princess Pocahontas Celebration and Pageant—are performances that represent fields of negotiation entwined in the politics of identity and exclusionary rituals that separate Laredo's newer and older elite. In 1939, the celebration held its first colonial pageant featuring thirteen young debutantes who represented the thirteen original colonies; the number of "debs" now featured is generally twenty or so. Because the present study focuses on manipulations of space and mythologizing patterns borne from such stratagems, I do not focus on other, later elements of the yearly celebration. These include a Mr. South Texas luncheon, a jalapeño festival, a *noche mexicana* sponsored by the local League of United Latin American Citizens (LULAC) council, a barbecue, a parade, a golf tournament, and countless other attractions and events during the month of February. The combined events of the annual celebration—the largest of its kind in the US—bring in up to $20 million of revenue during the month of February. Finally, an important feature of the celebration is the international "Bridge Ceremony," which serves as a kind of "welcoming ceremony" between officials and dignitaries from Mexico and the United States who exchange *abrazos* (hugs) to symbolize amicable relations between the two nations.[4]

By 1923, the celebration events had grown to such a magnitude that a corporation was formed. On February 2, 1923, the Washington's Birthday Celebration Association of Laredo, Inc. received its charter from the State of Texas. During the 1924 celebration, "social and civic minded ladies of Laredo conceived the idea of a gorgeous night pageant depicting Martha and George Washington and the original 13 colonies" (Wilcox 1942, par. 32). This production proved so popular that in 1939 Monsignor Dan Laning founded the Society of Martha Washington. The grandiose Colonial Pageant and Ball have remained under the auspices of the Society of Martha Washington to this date. Pocahontas figures centrally in the earliest WBCA celebrations. She is not the focus of her own organization and pageant, however, until 1980.

In 1904, Pocahontas, in her first WBCA incarnation as "bearer of peace," appeared on the scene when the Yaqui defeated the settlers during a performance—described by Margaret Nething (1999) as "a classic cowboy-and-Indian spectacle of several chapters" (211)—at Laredo City Hall. She appears after the cowboy-and-Indian skirmish in which the Yaqui ransacked city hall, and the Cavalry came to rescue of the local cowboys.

> A bugle was heard playing. Attention now focused on the East end of the plaza where the beautiful Queen of the Yaqui Tribe appeared with her entourage. After Pocahontas arrived at City Hall, six braves lent assistance as she gracefully dismounted.... [T]he captives were brought downstairs so she could meet them (212).

Pocahontas was then given the key to the city of Laredo—a practice that continues today—in a symbol of peace and goodwill. Beginning with the first Pocahontas performance by Naty Matherne in 1898, all subsequent performers have received the key to Laredo in the WBC; this practice signals the start of the month-long celebration as well as the Grand International Parade. Perhaps most telling is the title that the Princess Pocahontas Council (PPC) gave the 1998 celebration: "A Celebration of Peace—Our Dawn of Democracy." The printed 1998 pageant overview provides crucial insight into the relationship between the WBCA and Pocahontas:

> As delegates of the newly independent American colonies, Mr. Benjamin Franklin and Mr. Thomas Jefferson met to discuss certain communications received from President George Washington. . . . As the two gentlemen leave, they reflect upon the tranquility that has existed among these [tribal] nations since the early 1600s when Chief Powhatan, of the Powerful Powhatan Confederacy, had provided the basis for that peaceful co-existence. They also reflected upon the role that his daughter, the beautiful Indian maiden Pocahontas, with her friendship and genteel manner, had added to that peacefulness and to the successful colonization of Jamestown. At that time, Chief Powhatan had hosted a great celebration to commemorate this peace which still prevailed in their homeland. Let us return to the early 1600s and share in that celebration (6).

Since 1940, the Society of Martha Washington has retained sponsorship of the increasingly extravagant Colonial Presentation and Ball. It is arguably the most exclusive social club in Laredo. Furthermore, although my mother and the other members of the Princess Pocahontas Council—all women— have a voice in choosing who will portray Pocahontas and receive the key to Laredo in the yearly Washington's Birthday Celebration, the Princess Pocahontas Pageant has been called the "poor cousin" to the Colonial Ball and presentation by at least one scholar (Young 1988, 83). As a Laredoan steeped in these traditions, I find this designation to be fitting. The members of the Princess Pocahontas Court often cannot afford to be "Marthas"—the colloquial moniker ascribed to the Society of Martha Washington debutantes—and they generally do not fall into the strata of working-class young women in Laredo who are socialized by means of a *quinceañera*. They are, rather, middle- and upper-middle-class young women who dress up like Indians to "help Laredo project an image of racial and national harmony" (85).

Although the figure of Pocahontas has been represented since the earliest celebration in 1898, it was not until the fall of 1980 that a group of Laredo women conceived the idea of "creating an organization to enhance the role of Princess Pocahontas during the annual festivities of Washington's Birthday Celebration and keep alive the customs and legends of a vanishing race" (Barrera 1999, 215–16). According to Dennis (1997), the Princess Pocahontas Pageant and Celebration represent "an alternative American Indianist ritual" meant to "reflect the legitimacy logics of the emerging professional class" (par. 13). In this way, the women of the Princess Pocahontas Council—upwardly mobile *tejanas*—"display each year a romanticized, 'Orientalized' (in Edward Said's sense of the term) version of the 'American Indian' that is absolutely benign, compassionate and benevolent" (par. 15). Elaine Peña (2020) chronicles how she attended a Princess Pocahontas pageant, which she describes as "an elite event" in 1996 and being "secretly confused by the voice-overs and choreography that narrated Native American tribal histories" (3). She recounts how what she knew of the history and culture of North American Indigenous tribes "did not match up with the spectacle" she was watching (3). It is this reconfiguration of "Indianness" that allows the members of the Council to effectively distance themselves from Mexicanist identifications, and instead absorb a reimagined ancestral history (and a highly improbable one, as it is tied to an Algonquin figure, rather than a Yaqui, Toltec, or Aztec figurehead).

These patterns of disidentification ostensibly relegate the goals of the Princess Pocahontas Council alongside the older, more firmly entrenched performances of the Society of Martha Washington. The resultant disidentification with the actual and Indigenous is reminiscent of the generational disidentification exhibited by Mercedes in *Lone Star* and Guálinto in Paredes's *George Washington Gómez*; we also find this pattern in Arturo Islas's *The Rain God*, which I discuss in chapter 5. Here, then, is a group of multiethnic, disenfranchised subjects who have identified an absence within a deeply entrenched celebration couched in imperialist nostalgia. Ostensibly, the women of the PPC Council have labored to reinscribe a genealogy of the silenced. The paradox, however, lies in the sheer absence of veracity in their narrative. The story the Princess Pocahontas Council yearly tells certainly ghosts back against the obvious social erasure of Indigeneity perpetrated for a century by first the Improved Order of Red Men and then the WBCA, but it's just another imagined script that has institutionalized a pernicious false memory at the expense of accurate historiography.

Initially, the Princess Pocahontas Council was formed as a result of Laredoan Velia Uribe's interest in the annual role Pocahontas played in the broader Washington's Birthday Celebration. According to the 1998 *Princess Pocahontas Council Periodical*, the group's interest was threefold:

1. To support and enhance the role of Pocahontas and her court in the celebration.
2. To provide greater opportunity for the community to participate more fully in the celebration by sponsoring youth-oriented activities.
3. To revise and promote interest in the customs and legends of the American Indian culture (2).

Although the PPC retains this spirit, in past years it has become increasingly evident that the Princess Pocahontas Pageant is making strides to approach the ostentation level of Society of Martha Washington members—who clearly reflect position, wealth, and class in Laredo. When I was "Happy Butterfly" in 1984, my beaded gown cost about $1,200 to make. During this same year, the gowns of many of my friends who were "Marthas" cost $5,000 to $6,000. In 1992, when my brother René was Ysela Tijerina's PPC escort, his costume cost roughly $5,000 to make; Ysela's costume cost roughly $7,000. Today, each Colonial gown generally costs upwards of $20,000, and each PPC outfit may cost upwards of $12,000 to $14,000. Indeed, it is ironic "that families would spend so much money on a daughter's debutante gown in a city with some of the poorest people in the country" (Young 1988, 84).

The Shape of the Other and the Return of the Abject

The majority of people in Laredo can only afford to *view* these balls and pageants as part of the Grand International Parade that always closes the events for the year rather than participate in the masked events. Additionally, these celebrations are tangible products as well as performative expressions of Otherness that fortify the familial and individual status of future generations of Laredoans. These overt displays of power and status continue to shape class-based divisions such that a colonial imagination has seemingly been absorbed into the very fabric of the community (figure 5). For example, in *Las Marthas*, legacy daughter Laura Garza Hovel, in discussing her final performance during the Grand International Parade the morning following the Colonial Ball, remarks how the parade is "not just for the upper class," a clear pronouncement of internalized classism. So too do viewers discern non-legacy daughter Rosario Guadalupe Reyes's precarious positionality as differentiated from the others: she labels herself an "oddball" and comments on how her parents "tried so hard to keep me there." In *Las Marthas*, we further discern how parade spectators—enthralled by first

Figure 5: Society of Martha Washington debutantes and escorts on stage at the Laredo Civic Center. File photo, LatinoUSA.org. https://www.latinousa.org/2014/05/02/laredo-celebrates-george-washington-photos/

sight of the extravagant and elaborately costumed debutantes rolling by on flatbed trucks—will likely forever remain sequestered from participation in these excessive displays of wealth and status. Just as *Las Marthas* depicts Laura and Rosario as clearly demarcated in terms of binary categorizations of legacy versus non-legacy members, so too are Laredoans demarcated as those with social capital and those without, as the unquestioning allegiance to these romanticized colonial icons continues to shape space in the city.

Mikhail Bakhtin called metamorphosis "a mythological sheath for the idea of development—but one that unfolds not so much in a straight line as spasmodically, a line with 'knots' in it. This chronotope structures time around moments of biographical crisis which show how an individual becomes other than what he was" (quoted in Morris 1994, 181). This is an important concept relative to the young members of both the Princess Pocahontas Court and the Colonial Ball and Presentation—theirs is a rite of passage construed around a particular national identity as well as class structure. The members of both parties effectively signify costumed manifestations of what Rosaldo (1989) refers to when he describes imperialist nostalgia as a lament against that which one has destroyed. These annual masquerades perpetuate an invented image of racial and national harmony, what the postcolonial theorist Homi Bhabha (2006) describes as an "authorized" rendering of Otherness (126). In this sense, select Laredoans—themselves colonial agents—bemoan the history they are complicit in transforming. Again, what is significant is how such nostalgia belies the innocence of colonial actors. These parties flatter and perpetuate what they wish to acknowledge as their own "civilized" identities. Yet they can only accomplish this by referencing an imagined past in which their complicity in destroying Indigeneity and a Native American populace is conveniently erased. Moreover, although this border landscape has changed greatly in recent decades due to global factors of migration, urbanization, industrialization, and increased border militarization, Mario Barrera's (1979) model of internal colonialism, which he posits as "a structured relationship of domination and subordination, where the dominant and subordinate groups are defined along ethnic and/or racial lines, and where the relationship is established and maintained to serve the interests of all or part of the dominant group" (193) is particularly useful in understanding the historical dynamics that helped manipulate the expansionist and exclusionary policies of a select few who have wielded economic and political power since the late nineteenth century. By further foregrounding the ideals of nation formation in Laredo within a theoretics that underscores time, space, and the ironic compromises of imitation, we are better poised to understand how these particular actions that embed a nostalgic and false historical memory figure in the production and concretization of identity in Laredo.

Julia Kristeva's (1982) ideas surrounding the abject shed further light on the complex rituals of inversion that the Princess Pocahontas Pageant continues to generate. Importantly, the ceremony both denies and glorifies Native Americans in a complex mimetic ritual. Regarding abjection, Kristeva asserts how it "is above all ambiguity" because "it does not radically cut off the subject from what threatens it" (9). More importantly, one experiences abjection only if an Other has settled in the place and stead of one's Self. The Self must not simply identify with and incorporate this Other; rather, the Other "precedes and possesses" the Self, and such possession causes the Self to be (10). Furthermore, spatial ontologies as they relate to Victor Turner's view of the "communitas" of performance that involve a liminal, transitory experience from one symbolic domain to another further illuminate the underlying stakes negotiated in the "playing out" of the dramas entwined in the two WBCA performances I have been discussing. Participants, like spectators, are taught to validate these oppressive, ahistorical power structures.

The Princess Pocahontas Pageant, like the Colonial Ball, "reaffirms the cohesion of a social group to its communitarian structure through participation in a time of revitalization" (Mesnil 1987, 191). In her analysis of the social and historical reality in which carnival operates, Marianne Mesnil, following the work of Mircea Eliade, Michel Freitag, and Bakhtin, demonstrates how the "dynamic nature of the carnivalesque festival is thus a function of the relation between the reference group and the global society in power" (190). Carnival as Christian feast does not apply here. However, I do believe that the performances of the Princess Pocahontas Court are at least partially aligned with carnival from an anthropological standpoint, in that a goal of the performance is to shift the standing of the mostly middle-class young women in the eyes of the broader populace. In Bakhtin's societal model, the carnivalesque festival is rebellious and oppositional to the hegemonic society. In this sense, the performances of the Princess Pocahontas Court become expressly charged with political import, especially when we recall how the women of the PPC strove to incorporate their voices alongside the inveterate Society of Martha Washington. The performances of the Princess Pocahontas Court ghost back against the entrenched story of the Society and speak to structures of feeling that echo a desire to re-vision what has been deceptively sedimented into history. The performance, however, is also a space of negotiation within which the politics of identity for those presented are reconfigured alongside the political force of haunting. The paradox is the story that is being ghosted back, or against the entrenched narrative of the Society—that what originated in the suppression of Indigeneity and history—is itself a suppression of factual history. Thus, both performances impart Richard White's (1991) conviction how, "in myth, time brings no essential change" (616).

Performing Indianness

Performances are generic ways to embed traditions. Their repetitions situate actors in time and space, structuring individual and group identities in such a way as to produce "an intricate counterpoint to the unconscious practices of everyday life" in terms of stylistic and marked "expressions of otherness" (Kapchan 1995, 479). As ritualized modes of cultural expression, performances carry a high degree of reflexivity and agency for the individuals involved. In her historical analysis of performance, Deborah A. Kapchan turns to Victor Turner's symbolic view of performance to stress how large-scale cultural-display events must be examined as "semiotic modes of cultural expression" (480). In Turner's view, socially dramatic performances like carnival not only fabricate meanings in highly condensed symbols, but also comment, critique, and subvert those symbols in such ways so as to transform the social, psychological, and emotional being of individuals while continually "enfolding" citizens into the larger community (quoted in Kapchan, 480). The communal action, while highly self-reflexive at the individual level, carves a space for a shared reality. For Turner, this shared, communal reality, which he called "communitas," is most often experienced in liminal states—in the "transition from one symbolic domain to another" (480–81). This is significant, as both of the events discussed here serve as coming-of-age rituals for the young women involved.

As Philip Deloria (1998) argues, although the import of Indian Others depended on the "changing social and political struggles of white Americans, they also relied upon the shifting circumstances of real Indians" (43). Just as by the mid-1820s the American government began to systematically remove American Indians west of the Mississippi, so too did this movement usher the removal of American Indians from American life and into American history.[5] As regards the symbolizing aspects of Pocahontas in US popular culture, Joanne Barker (2002), in seeking to uncover how the broader narrative of Pocahontas functions, appraises the countless versions of the story of Pocahontas in US popular culture. In her search for the "real" historical Pocahontas, Barker turns to the writing of Cherokee scholar Rayna Green to conclude that the "transfiguring" of Pocahontas by a multitude of incarnations within "U.S. nationalism's mythic structures" has worked to generally serve the goals of men and US colonizing systems (316–17). For both Green and Barker, the appropriation of Pocahontas's story more often than not erases "a multitude of historical and cultural sins from the pages of U.S. history" (318–19). The story of Princess Pocahontas in Laredo evinces a broader pattern surrounding the systematic removal of Indian nations from their lands, nations, communities, beliefs, languages, and stories. Like so many narratives that embed the historical figure of Pocahontas, the story Laredoans have appropriated for Pocahontas strips her of any vestige that veritably speaks to her own culture, or even political or social agenda, for that matter. Rather, it transforms her into a modern agent of US nation-building.

Similarly, Paula Gunn Allen (2003), in what she calls her "biomythography" of Pocahontas, cautions that readers must negotiate the narrative of Pocahontas on various levels in order to fully understand her world.

Pocahontas cannot be known as "fact"; more importantly, neither can she nor her people be known outside of the spirit-centered world of the Indian. Facts alone, often privileged in Western narratives or biographies, cannot account for that "which moves through a people . . . its heart, its *manito*" (10). Pocahontas's world, and thus her *actual* story, exists as continuity within a Native "life system" that encompasses a "community of living things, geography, climate, spirit people, and supernaturals" (4). Gunn Allen, then, locates Pocahontas within that space that Brewster E. Fitz (2004) posits "points both forward and backward," an echo of circular notions of time (239–40).

In her examination of modern American Indian literature, Gunn Allen (1987) writes that such narratives must reflect "the deepest meanings of a community" by "carrying forward archetypes through the agency of familiar symbols arranged within a meaningful structure" (565). The nature of continuity, she argues, is "to bring those structures and symbols which retain their essential meaning forward into a changed context in such a way that the metaphysical point remains true, in spite of apparently changed circumstances" (573). This trajectory is manifest in Islas's *The Rain God*, a subject taken up in chapter 5, in which I show how the novel's protagonist locates a subjective equilibrium within a continuous interplay of the forces in his ethnic and cultural universe. Just as colonial patriots—forebears of the Improved Order of Red Men—dressed as Indians not to disguise themselves, but to signify rebellion and separateness from the British, so too do Laredoans continue to "play Indian" to separate themselves from a nebulous identity based first in a denial of Indian as Other, and second in avowal of an extant hierarchical class structure based in early colonialist formations.

Early colonialist imperatives remain firmly entrenched in Laredo social and civic structures, as is evidenced by the Princess Pocahontas Pageant and Presentation. The appropriation of Native American culture and identity—what Shari M. Huhndorf (2001) calls "going native," has for years remained encoded as part of the racial dynamics of conquest in Laredo. Although it is important, then, to frame the WBCA, and specifically the Princess Pocahontas Presentation and Pageant, in Laredo within a theoretics of space, it is also imperative to comprehend Laredo's unique history in terms of the demographic and geographic significance of Mexico and Mexicans who, from the outset, were incorporated into the politics of nation building and identity formation. Because, in Laredo, the demarcation of Other exists along a tenuous continuum where insider and outsider have survived symbiotically, and in the interests of an elite few, a historically based, post-colonial analysis of the physical details of the landscape as it is inextricably linked to Laredoans who actively shape that landscape into a space of lim-inality and negotiation yields crucial insight into the continuing pattern of classism that has historically split not different races or ethnicities in Laredo, but different classes.

Lieux de Mémoire and De-Linking Narratives of Coloniality

Laredoans have created a *lieu de mémoire*—a site of memory that presup-poses the will to remember while simultaneously "block[ing] the work of forgetting" (Nora 1989, 19) that modern history so often calls for. Pierre Nora's contributions to the study of *lieux de mémoire* are extensive and not unproblematic. His three-volume study of places that embody French national memory is indebted to a commitment to understanding France's national past in terms of history and memory.[6] As such, it is a springboard for an understanding of the ways that history is "never an innocent oper-ation" (9–10). And although the strict binary Nora creates of history and memory is both problematic and polarizing, his insistence on the ways the modern historical age has seemingly abandoned what he calls "real" and "true" memory while simultaneously erecting sites that have "no referent in reality" (23) is one way to conceptualize the artificial reconstructions of nation signified by the two main performances of the WBCA. Real memo-ries, argues Nora, are "social and unviolated, exemplified in but also retained as the secret of so-called primitive or archaic societies" (8). He grants a wide swath to his study and classification of sites of memory, discussing archi-tectural sites, memorials, places of refuge, and even "living" sites such as pilgrimages. For my purposes here, I borrow from his discussion to focus on topographical sites, "[w]hich owe everything to the specificity of their location and to being rooted in the ground" (22). For Nora, although there exists a historical continuity to such sites, they nonetheless signify a dis-connect between the way modern history seemingly "collapses" truthful, unaffected memory in favor of "dictatorial memory," which he argues is "all-powerful . . . a memory without a past that ceaselessly reinvents tra-dition, linking the history of its ancestors to the undifferentiated time of heroes, origins, and myth" (8).

In denying Laredoans access to the true history of the Spanish Mexican culture that originally shaped the region, in shifting the focus of origins from Laredo's descendancy from New Spain to America's "founding fathers" and New England, ruling classes in the area effectively silenced the collective values of generations of native Coahuiltecans, Jumanos, Caddos, Karankawas, Yaqui, and even Aztecs that "were part of a great exchange network of trade routes that evolved over centuries" throughout the region (Moreno 2006, 157). When the *actual* cultural heritage of Laredo's landscape was effaced wholesale by a colonialist narrative tied to an eternal present in which the colonial annually triumphs as the supreme emblem of modernity, those social and intimate storehouses of memory associated with ancestral traces and repetitions became fragmented and splintered. Nora reminds us: "*[L]ieux de mémoire* occurs at the same time that an immense and intimate fund of memory disappears, surviving only as a reconstituted object beneath the gaze of critical history" (11–12). There is hope, then, in reconstitution and in shifting the focus to what yet lies beneath the narratives of the WBCA, of what remains as trace. We cannot predict or know what *should be* remembered, but we must also acknowledge that the "cult of continuity" (Nora 1989, 16) in the form of the WBCA is only an aspect of the highly visible remembered past. The past the WBCA celebrates is solid and steady. It is material, symbolic, and functional, and so embodies the three aspects central to *lieux* that Nora conceptualizes (19). Thus, although the "fundamental purpose" of *lieux de mémoire* is "to stop time, to block the work of forgetting, to establish the state of things, to immortalize death, to materialize the immaterial" (19), it must also be clear that *lieux de mémoire* revise aspects of memory as regards place and place-making. Because "memory attaches itself to sites" (22), recovery becomes central to understanding dominant and dominated aspects of both place and memory that entwine *lieux de mémoire*.

The WBCA as Heritage Industry: The Capitalization of Space

Following the footsteps of French Marxist theorists such as Henri Lefebvre, who by the mid-twentieth century began to incorporate spaciality in postmodern geographical analyses, Edward Soja (2011) privileges space alongside time and human geographical patterns to show how space is not structured by its own autonomous laws, as earlier twentieth-century Marxist analysts proposed, but, rather, is "a dialectically defined component of the general relations of production, relations which are simultaneously social and spatial" (78). Because, he argues, human patterns of being in the world exist simultaneously and dialectically in time and space, an emphasis on relations of production helps us conceptualize how the construction of a specious narrative, replicated and regenerated in and over time, reproduces a semiotic motif that mirrors the uneven logic of power in a historically contested space. Hearkening back to the discussion of *Lone Star*, Sam Deeds' quest for the truth of his history is buried under a fraudulent public memory that has his father, Buddy Deeds, murdering the corrupt Charlie Wade in an act of justice. This very public narrative, which has mythologized Buddy Deeds as heroic, turns out to be false; Buddy didn't kill Wade, another deputy did. Regardless of the fact that Sam and Pilar know the truth behind the story, the town of Frontera never will, for capital, power, and public memory are at stake. So too is Laredo's true history buried under a sanitized façade meant to be easily and readily consumed by the public as well as to fortify a tourist economy.

There is a tension, then, that spatial mobility and capital bring to the permanence of place. Tim Cresswell (2015) reads David Harvey's discussion of the Baltimore community he lived in at one time—a community that, in light of a gruesome murder, found it necessary to "gate" itself off from the wider black community at large—as an example of a radical reconfiguration of a place that is differentiated, exclusionary, distinctive, and that provides a "sense of pride and belonging" as well as attachment (95). Perhaps most significant to the present discussion is how the residents of Guilford Baltimore consciously and deliberately created a place—a gated community—that could effectively contain a sanitized experience of living for residents who could afford to live there as well as the retention of capital investment. In 2001, the Guilford residential community was first listed in the National Register of Historic Places, effectively marking the neighborhood as a "heritage" site, or one in which "a sense of rootedness in the past and in place is provided for the consumption of locals and tourists" (95). There is a certain simplicity, if not quite dangerousness, to a logic that suggests groups of people can define themselves *against* outside forces (read: threatening others) who are excluded from a particular vision when enacting place. Just as the gated community of Guilford exemplifies place-making processes that serve to secure the power and authority of a particular group, it problematizes, if not alters and reshapes, individual and collective memories. Regardless of the process in which the collective memory of one group of individuals is often made concrete through the formation of a particular place, "this production of memory in place is no more than an element in the

perpetuation of a particular social order that seeks to inscribe some memories at the expense of others" (97). In Laredo, the facts of modern life force
us to reckon with the ways capital investment in place-making is often done
at the expense of defining one group to the detriment of another group who
is not and cannot be included in the "particular vision" of the place being
enacted (97). This pattern plays out in the film *Sleep Dealer*, which I discuss
at length in chapter 6.

Ultimately, the performances of the WBCA must be viewed as negotiations of power that involve crossing from one spatial-temporal continuum to another. History, and more importantly the *memory* of a particular
accommodationist history, figures greatly in the production of identity and
power in Laredo. As such, Mary Pat Brady's (2002) analysis of the transformation of space in Douglas, Arizona—a model that delineates the processes
that shape how places "are understood, envisioned, defined, and variously
experienced" (7)—further elucidates the idea that subject formation relates
to spatiality and the ongoing, often contradictory production of place at
the local level. In her study of how perceptions of space have altered due to
a changing, increasingly globalized economy on the border, she describes
how the production of place is entwined in ontologies of time and space.
More important, however, is her idea surrounding how the establishment
of the US–Mexico border necessarily demands an understanding of how
subjectivities are simultaneously produced within a contested geographical
space. She uses the term "subjectivity-in-process" to argue that a *mestiza*
consciousness emerges in relationship to spaciality and the ongoing production of border spaces. Place-making, then, is integral to identity-making
in the Borderlands. She writes that the border "is produced through a nostalgia that imagines its (former) tranquility and that necessarily belies the
three centuries of conflict that have engulfed it. In other words, these border narratives depend on an understanding of space, of place, as immobile
and fixed not as process" (51). According to Brady, identity-making activities create place. This mirrors Limerick's (1987) assertion surrounding the
myopic Turnerian vision of the frontier. She writes, "Turner's frontier was
a process, not a place. When 'civilization' had conquered 'savagery' at any
one location, the process—and the historian's attention—moved on" (26). I
turn to ideas surrounding place and process in the following chapter, in my
discussion of haunted cowboys and ruling ideologies of space in Western
narratives.

Historically, the WBCA was instituted as a patriotic celebration to unite

Laredo with the greater United States. Nonetheless, "the historic, geographic, and demographic significance of Mexico and Mexicans on the border had to be incorporated into the very concept of America . . . . Indians, however, who held little or no political and economic power on the border, were portrayed as foreign enemies" (Young 1988, 50). This idea of a native elite cooperating on a social, political, and cultural scale in a complex mimetic performance entwined in a falsely nostalgic mythos of a "Native" history is at the heart of identity formation and politics in Laredo. The Washington's Birthday Celebration encompasses an institutionalized public memory in which Laredoans have historically treated Indigenous subjects as abject. Ironically, however, what is abjected remains as palimpsest or, as Limerick describes, as "something in the soil."[7] Although the key performances of the Washington's Birthday Celebration serve as both reminder and metaphor for the social transformations necessitated by white and Mexican elites in order to cling to a tenuous economic and political stronghold, so too does the abject continue to return, albeit in equally disturbing ways.

CHAPTER 4

HAUNTED COWBOYS

I n the preceding chapter, I discussed how one story has shaped and perpetuated a dubious public memory in Laredo. The heritage industry
that is the WBCA reveals how a broader narrative of westward expansion
morphed into the manipulation of a colorful and romanticized story that
capitalizes on the formation of a falsely situated creation myth for an entire
city. This idea mirrors Limerick's (1987) assertion regarding how the "origin myth" of Anglo America both explained American exceptionalism and
romanticized the brutal reality of Euro American conquest as the American
West took shape. In Laredo, we see how elaborate traditions were invented
to bolster and commercialize an origin myth for a young city. Where
Thompson (1974) draws attention to the American Civil War as setting in
motion Laredo's path towards a capitalist modernity when it became an out-
let for contraband Southern cotton, Adams (2008) details how Laredo continued to build upon its identity as a commercial trading center throughout
the nineteenth century. Limón adds that this progression "reaches a kind
of cultural climax with the city's 1898 celebration of George Washington's
birthday" (7).[1] With this in mind, we can trace how the narrative first created and then sustained clear boundaries that further served to distinguish
a premodern society from a distinctive and visible modern place that could
instill a sense of pride and belonging for individuals who saw the need to
devalue and destroy the city's earlier identity.

  In this chapter, I turn to postmodern literary fiction by two influential authors of the American West—Cormac McCarthy and Larry

McMurtry—to illustrate how, as in Laredo, the dream of an imagined, mythic West is little more than a lamentation of a West that in fact has never existed. Where the IORM awakened a spirit and iconography tied to benevolent colonizers as social insurance guaranteeing the maintenance of economic and class divisions in Laredo—a structure of feeling subsequently embraced by the Society of Martha Washington—the Princess Pocahontas Council summoned an equally specious narrative of idealized Indianness even as it ghosted against these earlier efforts. Further, the Society concretizes and re-presents spatial practices as a symptom of colonial and national imaginaries that *maintain* the shape of frontier apparitions, effectively silencing the factual historical memories of this once-Mexican community. In this chapter, I move backwards in time to illustrate how fragile the line is between myth and truth in the American Southwest. The novels I consider here complicate borders as extensive eulogies for a variant of American optimism that has faded by the nineteenth century and that will not survive into the twentieth century. Further, where we are asked to "forget the Alamo" in *Lone Star*, the novels addressed here characterize contemporary "frontier" literature that laments the forgetting of the Alamo.

I focus on McCarthy's border trilogy and McMurtry's *Streets of Laredo* due to these works' points of convergence surrounding the power of stories and the way stories both organize and impose order on our worlds; these works are deeply invested in the myths that shape our lives as they offer up extended critiques of space and spatial practices in the American Southwest. A close reading of these novels invites a further consideration of shifting patterns of memory as a movement from myth to truth. It is this movement, shaped by the playing out of an imagined frontier ideology in nascent dialogue with an actual Southwest Borderland, that shapes the ethical gap between past and present, or what is and what ought to be. Whereas in Laredo, past and present are made metaphorically equivalent in myth through the repetitions of the WBCA, in the novels under discussion here, present articulations of place shatter the unsustainable, ahistorical myth of the past but also contain the still-longed-for imagined frontier.

The crumbling foundations of a frontier ideology in these novels make themselves known in the landscape and the bodies of major players. As the bedrock of frontier pursuits totters, moral frameworks that act as guides for corrective measures manifest as structures of feeling. In these novels, the myth is a vestige by which characters construct a matrix of meaning that ultimately misrepresents worlds and ways of life either vanished or vanishing. Where the worlds of the protagonists, built upon specious beliefs and patterns, reveal themselves as either waning, defunct, or outright impossible, so too do the hearts and minds of characters disclose themselves incapable of continuing to internalize archaic, destructive, and deceptive narratives. A focus on history, memory, and a linear vision of future progress associated with a frontier mythology further exposes these ostensibly frontier narratives as Borderlands stories in disguise. When we deconstruct patterns associated with space and a spatial poetics of unlimited expanse, increase, and movement, we see how the myth of American progress and rugged individualism becomes hemmed and curbed by environments of memory and the authenticity of rooted cultures and the legitimate experiences of place. Further, when we recenter issues of race, ethnicity, and gender in narratives that shape the Bordered frontier, we see how a place-based ethics must supersede historical and contemporary imperatives of space that continue to fracture identity.

Finally, the protagonists of these novels illustrate how individuals can either make contact with what haunts us, as does Captain Woodrow Call in *Streets of Laredo*, or disavow the phantoms of modernity's violence, as does John Grady Cole in McCarthy's border trilogy. To make contact with hauntings requires making visible and known the joint mechanisms of the Bordered frontier; to remain haunted by an anachronistic frontier mythology is to continue to misunderstand the empirical evidence ensconced in the landscape itself, for it is here that history and subjectivity shape social life. Finally, and recalling Gordon (2008), this chapter illustrates how we *must* be haunted by history in order to move forward, for ghosts always demand their due, as they effectively pull us into nascent structures of feeling that we come to "experience as a recognition" (63). Accepting these specters as symptoms of loss or felt absences, as does Captain Call, "simultaneously represents a future possibility, a hope," as such reckonings are attempts born *"out of a concern for justice"* (64, italics in original). Recognizing past oppressions from the vantage point of the ghost, then, reinscribes an ethical center to the Bordered frontier that moves beyond sanctioned narratives of the nation to encompass multiple cultural frames of reference that more equitably square with contradictions and difference.

Lost in Space: *All the Pretty Horses* and *Cities of the Plain*

Cormac McCarthy's border trilogy is a unified body of work comprised of *All the Pretty Horses* (1992), *The Crossing* (1994), and *Cities of the Plain* (1998).

The bookend novels are devoted to the protagonist John Grady Cole, and the hinge novel tells the story of Billy Parham. In the trilogy, John Grady and Billy assume conventional mythic roles found in historical Western narratives that are situated between two key frontier paradigms: the myth of progress and the primitive-pastoral myth. *Horses* builds upon the myth of American progress and individual promise, a "rose-colored and stereotyped cliché of the national symbolic," in which the "sacred cowboy" image is glorified and romanticized (Spurgeon 2005, 89, 86). This venerable image is shattered in the final novel of the trilogy, *Cities of the Plain*. In *The Crossing*, Billy Parham is tempted by the heroic possibilities of a primitive-pastoral dream that begins with returning a pregnant she-wolf to her home in Mexico. His dream ends in desolation and loss even as it hints at the promise of regeneration—a theme picked up in the closing pages of *Cities*. The boys' adventurous quests, typical of the *Bildungsroman*, enable their move from innocence to experience as they push forth into unknown territories of the American Southwest and northern Mexico. Situated along the US–Mexico Borderlands, the novels embed a spattering of Spanish to remind readers of an accounting of stories and histories from both sides of the border. Parallel realities continually push against the frontier myths both John Grady and Billy embody to instill a reckoning that evokes de Certeau's (1986) notion regarding how the recuperation of time can effectively reestablish an ethic tied to place and place-making practices.

John Grady Cole's actions are grounded in the ideals of a frontier mythology predicated on a future vision that does not easily accommodate memory or alternative historical narratives. This absence of history and memory leaves him adrift in time and space by the end of *All the Pretty Horses*. In the first chapter, John Grady leaves the ranch he grew up on in San Angelo, Texas after the death of his grandfather. The year is 1949, and we are given to believe the ranch will be sold. Having lost financial and legal ties to the place, he has no moral obligation to stay. As a result, John Grady and his friend Lacey Rawlins travel southward in an attempt to move backwards in time to a place where they imagine the codes of the Old West still hold some value. Although John Grady's lineage is embedded in the Texas landscape, a longer history that echoes of displaced nations and buried places will haunt him throughout both *Horses* and *Cities*. As the two ride towards Mexico, they encounter a "dream of the past" that speaks of an earlier time. McCarthy's lyrical prose conjures riders of "lost nations" who have come down out of the north, all of them pledged in blood and redeemable in blood only. When the wind was in the north you could hear them . . . nation and ghost of nation passing in a soft chorale across that mineral waste to darkness bearing lost to all history and all remembrance like a grail the sum of their secular and transitory and violent lives (5).

John Grady's survey of the landscape embeds his sense of alienation and longing and parallels his rootlessness, for he is "like a man come to the end of something" (5). A stark foreshadowing of things to come, John Grady and readers alike feel the weight of the lingering spirits of ancient Indigenous nations. In mythologizing these nations and Indigenous warriors, McCarthy suggests that violent, colonizing histories do not simply remain as memories but as constants that suffuse a structure of feeling linked to history and protracted reminders of place. This rootedness bubbles up from the landscape: "[B]ut the warriors would ride on in that darkness they'd become, rattling past with their stone-age tools of war in default of all substance and singing softly in blood and longing south across the plains to Mexico" (6). Significantly, John Grady's being and body sense the weight of memory, but these are not his memories, they're ghosts, spirits entombed in the cultural past, scars of more ancient histories, more deeply entrenched narratives.

John Grady Cole signifies an "American Adam"; self-reliant and confident, he is the "inventor of his own character" (Owens 2000, 111). When John Grady and Lacey leave Texas, they enact the myth of American progress, free of memory and external constraint, shaping their illimitable selves by whim and choice (Pilkington 1973, 175). They do not consider, however, that when they travel into Mexico they will encounter codes, histories, and truths of a culture beyond the scope of American laws, values, and ideals. For example, before their arrival in Mexico, Rawlins studies a map he's picked up in a café and notes that "[t]here were roads and rivers and towns on the American side of the map as far south as the Rio Grande and beyond that all was white" (34). Rawlins muses that the vast area to the south "ain't never been mapped" (34), but John Grady explains that the area has indeed been mapped; however, this particular map does not indicate the mapped territory. The map fits their purpose: when they cross into Mexico, they face blank space. This underscores John Grady's spatial dream of frontier promise as an empty slate. Rawlins is a comrade whose frontier vision never equals Cole's. In fact, Rawlins becomes increasingly aware that his friend's dream will lead to trouble, reminding readers that the "Manichean Mexican landscape" that Cole moves through is "a projection of the tension between

his steadfast romantic ideals, and the cruel, capricious world around him"
(Cooper-Alarcón 2014, 144).

As the two venture south in search of a promised land filled with ranches,
horses, and opportunity, they meet the young gunsel, Jimmy Blevins. When
the three cross the physical border of Mexico they strip naked, suggesting
what Harold Bloom (2004) calls a "baptismal scene" (24) that symbolizes
rebirth. This scene anchors a broader theme of crossing both physical and
metaphoric borders. It insists on an understanding that the trappings of one
world—the frontier—be peeled away or divested upon entry into Mexico,
further instilling in readers a distinction between the US and Mexico, civilization and wilderness, past and present, and myth and truth. The crossing
of metaphoric borders holds equal weight. For instance, when the boys reach
the Hacienda de Nuestra Señora de la Purísima Concepción in Coahuila,
they believe they will be free to live out their fantasy of cattle ranching in
an Old West paradise. Moreover, John Grady immediately has eyes for more
than the ranch; he falls in love with the beautiful Alejandra, the *hacendado*'s
daughter. Although John Grady proves his worth as a skilled horseman with
the *hacendado*, Don Héctor, earning a private room and the boss's good
favor, he soon learns that Mexico is not paradise and he is not Adam. The
crossing into Mexico marks the movement from myth to truth in the novel:
John Grady will not "own" horses, land, or Alejandra because, as a *norteam-
ericano*, he has no right to them. There are other borders, too. The borders
of race and class are manifest in the eventual failed relationship between
John Grady and Alejandra.

In *Horses*, Mexico is a region of memory, and these memories continually haunt Cole's maturation. Mark Busby (2002) writes about Mexico as a
land of history and the Southwest as one that deemphasizes history: "If the
American frontier hero pushes west into a historyless land, then when that
figure turns south and crosses the border, he encounters a land with a strong
and troubling past, for Mexico represents a country with a lengthy and dis-
tressing history" (144–45). Throughout the trilogy both John Grady and
Billy necessarily withdraw from familial memories as they pursue American
ideals; in Mexico, however, the boys are continually confronted with lessons, often in the form of long sermons, that speak to entrenched histories
and stories that threaten their paradisiacal visions.

The crossings John Grady undergoes are not bound by history or memory, and so the frontier vision that spurs him onward is continually subsumed by contrasting memories and stories of other peoples and other

nations. In Mexico, John Grady's "code" is as ephemeral as the clothes he and his companions shed when they cross the border; his code means nothing in Mexico. While in Mexico, the boys are not bound by the time period in which the novel's action takes place, 1949–1951; instead, they cross into the past. Cooper-Alarcón (2014) writes, the "farther into Mexico the Americans ride, the farther back in time they ride as well, culminating with their arrival at the hacienda" (148). When John Grady begins his doomed affair with Alejandra, he attracts the attention of the Dueña Alfonsa, Alejandra's great-aunt who speaks at length with John Grady. Her complex stories are meant to instill a lesson about differentiating between dreams and realities, and they foreground a main conflict in the trilogy: the tension between our idealized visions and the not-so-ideal realities they often engender. The Dueña tells him: "In the end we all come to be cured of our sentiments. . . . The world is quite ruthless in selecting between the dream and the reality, even where we will not. Between the wish and thing the world lies waiting" (238). This foreshadows another painful history lesson—the one provided by Eduardo the pimp in *Cities*. To help "cure" John Grady of his sentiments, the Dueña sees to it that Alejandra will never see John Grady again. When John Grady and Lacey are arrested and taken to a Saltillo prison they manage to escape, unlike Jimmy Blevins, who is also being held but is killed. We later learn that the Dueña has bought John Grady out of prison in return for Alejandra's promise that she will not see him again. Pilkington (1973) reminds us that Alejandra ends the affair because she acknowledges "the obduracy of centuries-old conventions and customs" (320). What Alejandra appears to understand, and John Grady does not, is that there are limitations to their affair, and these are based in family, class, and nationality. In the trilogy, love alone is insufficient when crossing such borders.

Upon his return to the US in the final pages of *Horses*, John Grady is confronted with a vision similar to the one he encounters after his grandfather's death. This time, he confronts an Indigenous tribe camped just outside of Iraan, Texas, "a scattered group of their wickiups propped upon that scoured and trembling waste" (301). These Indians have "no curiosity about him at all. As if they knew all that they needed to know. They stood and watched him pass and watched him vanish upon that landscape solely because he was passing. Solely because he would vanish" (301). Unlike McCarthy's earlier description of warriors who "would ride on in that darkness they'd become," John Grady, at the novel's end, is described as only one man, not a "nation" or "ghost of nation," but one man, one shadow—albeit one shadow composed of horse and rider. This final image of John Grady who rides and passes "like the shadow of a single being. Passed and paled into the darkening land, the world to come" (302) provides a thematic close to the novel. John Grady's vision is peopled not by *his* ancestors, but by American Indians who once roamed the land freely, nations whose domestic ties are directly linked to the ground under their feet, and, as such, remain.

In both *Horses* and *Cities*, John Grady Cole makes remarkably unreasonable choices in the two romantic quests that structure each novel. Alejandra proves to be a fantastic overreach of his cowboy code, as does Magdalena, the prostitute in *Cities*. Just as the *hacendado* reminded Cole in *Horses* that "one country is not another country" (145), so too do the Dueña Alfonsa's words regarding the "odd durability for something not quite real" return to haunt John Grady in *Cities of the Plain*. *Cities* opens in 1952, at which time John Grady's plans for reclaiming his grandfather's ranch that first set him in Alejandra's direction have faded; his plans now are to fix up an old domestic space on the New Mexico ranch he works with Billy Parham. Although John Grady's hopes are quite reasonable—a home of his own with a woman he loves—his actions remain haunted by the constraining space of a frontier mythology that cannot contain his imaginings. Eduardo the pimp, who "owns" the doomed Mexican prostitute, imparts this lesson, but it comes too late.

The central action of *Cities* surrounds a team of cowboys who face an uncertain future in a dying industry. In the novel, Billy Parham, who we meet as a boy in *The Crossing*, is a world-weary twenty-eight years old and John Grady Cole is nineteen. The men make regular forays into Ciudad Juárez, and it is here where John Grady meets and falls in love with Magdalena. Once again, however, his romanticized expectations and lack of knowledge of Mexican history and culture force the conclusion that "the chivalric roles promised by cowboy mythology are ultimately impossible to fill" (Ellis 2006a, 221). When Billy visits Juárez to ask Eduardo the pimp if he can "buy" Magdalena so that she and John Grady may marry in the US, Eduardo tells Billy that his friend "has in his head a certain story. Of how things will be" (134). He cautions Billy that the thing that "is wrong with this story is that it is not a true story. Men have in their minds a picture of how the world will be. How they will be in that world. The world may be many different ways for them but there is one world that will never be and that is the world they dream of" (134). The frontier is the bedrock of John Grady's identity, but the tension between his desires and Mexico as a place with a geography, culture, and heritage of its own is more powerful, and ultimately more deterministic, than lofty ideals. In *Cities*, John Grady must suffer the unintended consequences bound by this truth.

At the end of the novel, during his fight to the death with Eduardo, John Grady is reproved by the latter one last time for underestimating the reality of the truth in favor of imagined dreams rooted in a frontier ideology of limitless pursuit and increase. Eduardo says: "Your kind cannot bear that the world be ordinary. That it contains nothing save what stands before one" (253). He continues, juxtaposing the vast spaces of the frontier with Mexico as a place with a solid makeup: "But the Mexican world is a world of adornment only and underneath it is very plain indeed. While your world—your world totters upon an unspoken labyrinth of questions. And we will devour you my friend. You and all your pale empire" (253). Indeed, Eduardo "sees" what John Grady and Magdalena cannot, or will not see—that their love is based on false promises that cannot be reconciled given the violent subjugation of space that has become constrained by the imperatives of a historically contained Mexican place.

The border and the frontier are alternate ways to experience and know the world. Memories are like scars, reminders of a past that will always remain, however changed. The Mexican police officer, the captain whom Billy visits after he identifies the body of Magdalena, reminds us that the past must bleed into the present in order that events in the past are given their true weight. The captain tells Billy: "Every male in my family for three generations has been killed in defense of this republic. Grandfather, father, uncles, brothers. Eleven men in all. Any beliefs they may have had now reside in me. Any hopes. . . . They are my Mexico and I pray to them and I answer to them and to them alone" (243). Here, familial memories ground the Mexican captain, and we are again reminded how the past is hemmed and circumscribed by an ethics of place that these boys are not entitled to, and so their yearnings and visions give way only to the dream. This is important when we consider Jay Ellis's (2006a) observation that "[d]reams in McCarthy point more to delusions, beliefs, and provisional truths, more than to larger truths" (5).

The Misapprehension of Place: *The Crossing*

In *Horses* and *Cities*, John Grady leaves Texas and encounters and comes to terms with Mexicans—cultural and ethnic Others—who crush his dreams, which are revealed to be no more than artifacts of a frontier myth that has lost its valence. In *The Crossing*, which takes place before and during World War II, Billy Parham encounters the Other in nature, a she-wolf that he traps and intends to return to her Mexican homeland. The novel is composed of four sections, each consisting of an instance of crossing the border from Parham's home in New Mexico into northern Mexico, around the state of Chihuahua. Billy first travels into Mexico to return the trapped wolf; the second time, he enters Mexico with his brother Boyd to search for his family's stolen horses after his parents have been murdered; the third and fourth crossings revolve around the search for Boyd and Billy's subsequent return to the US to bury his brother's bones. Entwined in these sections are various stories told by different travelers. Time and again, in the form of stories from so many people, it seems that we are heading toward some inescapable conclusion of McCarthy's. "Bits of wreckage. Some bones. The words of the dead. How make a world of this? How live in that world once made?" says the *gitano* to Billy (411). *The Crossing* is perhaps the most haunted, and haunting, novel of the trilogy—a complex novel of return, recovery, and loss. In this chapter I focus not on the many crossings that frame the novel but on the first section in which Billy captures the she-wolf in an attempt to apprehend the paradox of place.

In the bookend novels, Texas and New Mexico are home to a myth that has lost its potency. In contrast, Mexico is described as "a mythic and exotic other that is increasingly shown to be as much a product of American fantasies as of indigenous reality" (Cant 2008, 206). Mexico, for Susan Kollin (2001), "becomes a region where the hero from the north of the border loses his bearings and his sense of identity" (580). In *The Crossing*, Mexico parallels the she-wolf in that it is "wild . . . inscrutable . . . unknown" (580). Billy is the primitive-pastoral hero who leaves his home to battle against a mythology and dreams that internalize the material and social effects of hauntings to illustrate how such are both transmitted and received. Billy's quest ends in failure and both he and readers remain haunted by the pastoral vision represented by the she-wolf, who signifies loss, and lack of recovery and salvation. Barcley Owens (2000) argues that the she-wolf with a belly full of pups symbolizes the "sins of mankind" (79). The she-wolf signifies the obliteration of wildlife and wild spaces ushered by the unfettered encroachment of the cattle and ranching industry in the Southwest; in Mexico, the wolf is little more than a commodity to be exploited by the whims of men.

Out of Time and Place: The Wolf as a Relic of Place

Billy obsessively seeks to capture the wolf, which he eventually does, illustrating his initial grasp of the inscrutable wild and unknown. Curiously, he commits to return her to Mexico without so much as a goodbye to his family. Turning freely and quickly from the domestic, it seems a distant, mythical past is a force great enough to catalyze his actions. This reveals that Billy both acknowledges the mythic past and feels he has a claim to it based on his skill at capturing, stringing out, and muzzling what to him is a sacred emblem of that past. Billy himself is a paradox: his home and any obligation he has to his family appear to matter little to him, yet he feels morally obligated to return the she-wolf to her rightful place. Perhaps this is because wolves manifest early in the novel as an aspect of Billy's nightly dreams to suggest a mythical, primal connection that either naturally, or as premonition, bubbles up from Billy's unconscious.

What "noisy silences and seething absences" (Gordon 2008, 200) does the wolf represent for Billy? I suggest the wolf signifies the superposition of worlds in the novel; it is from a different (past) world and a different (past) time. The wolf signifies how the past is both force and moral compass that continues in the present. Whether surfacing from the primal depths of the Mexican mountains to the south or within Billy's own subconscious, the wolf abides in a parallel reality and all but vanished time and place that Billy seeks to know and is compelled to bridge, but in a most cruel and uncompromising fashion, he will not. Billy seeks to abide in the wolf's world, the world he recalls from his dreams, but the wolf's world signifies not a parallel reality, not simply a deep dive into primitivism or the inscrutable wild, but an obliterated way of life and a vanished world, covered over by the built environment that likely compelled its initial journey into New Mexico.

Throughout the novel, Billy hears tales and stories in many guises and from diverse travelers, but he heeds little of the narrative messages he "witnesses." As such, Cant (2008) surmises that he remains outside of the "cultural matrix" that both he and Dianne C. Luce (1999) explore in McCarthy's oeuvre. The capability for narrative, says Luce of *The Crossing*, is the means by which human beings formulate the stories that contain our past and give meaning to our present (208). In this regard, *The Crossing* "is the story of a boy who discovers too early and too crushingly what cannot be held and whose spirit suffers a grievous wound" (211). Although his parents are brutally murdered in the novel and his brother Boyd is subsequently killed in Mexico, the unhealable wound, the scar that forever marks Billy, surrounds his failed quest to return the wolf to what he imagines is her proper place. In Mexico, corrupt authorities confiscate the wolf and Billy loses his grasp on her for a time. When he locates her, she is a sideshow entertainment fighting for her life in a wolf-baiting ring. Billy shoots her out of mercy and trades his gun for her carcass. When he buries her, the sound of her pups, a soft smothered chorale emanating from the soil that echoes Billy's smothered desires, the cultural script that he was born into is once more manifest. Billy's youthful longing to know and integrate the Other is mercilessly dashed. Regardless that all manner of travelers pontificate, sermonize, and orate at length about all manner of responsibility and experience, Billy will never reconcile the trauma signified by the murder of the she-wolf and her unborn pups. Such traumas, buried like so many bones, will mark his hands and scar his heart.

Time and again, the travelers Billy meets on the road in Mexico allude to a space between, a thing he can never know. Some time before Boyd's death, a Mexican *ganadero* "hold[s] his hands forward one above the other, a space between. As if he held something unseen shut within an unseen box." With this gesture, he tells Billy: "You do not know what things you set in motion. No man can know. No prophet foresee" (202). We know that Billy has dreamed of wolves as a boy in New Mexico and by this point he has been forced to kill the wolf out of mercy. In the novel, Billy dreams of wolves, and he tries "to see the world the wolf saw" (51). His attempts to restore order to the wolf's world by seeking to deposit her safely home in Mexico mirror his own attempts to find a place in the world, a home of his own. Although Billy forms a bond with the wolf, his quest to restore the wolf to her place in the world will cost him any sense of home, of security and attachment, that he once had—however tenuous. His alignment with the wolf is one of responsibility, and he knows he is "a man entrusted with the keeping of something which he hardly knew the use of" (79). As such, just as "the wolf knew nothing of boundaries" (119), neither does Billy. But he will learn, and this lesson will cost him any sense of place he ever, no matter how fleetingly, embodied.

Billy's capacity for taking part in his own narrative or the world's "matrix" is not restored in either *The Crossing* or *Cities*, where, as an old man of seventy-eight, he is still homeless—a *huerfano*. In both novels, Billy "picks up the road metaphor with its connotations of wandering, avoidance and entrapment within the illusion of linear time-boundness" (Luce 1999, 212). This being said, it is Billy's dejection and anguish at the end of *The Crossing* that empties the Southwest most poignantly of any romantic illusions it once held—whether real or in dreams. It is the final image in the last pages of the book of Billy holding his face in his hands and weeping for an old dog—"[r]epository of ten thousand indignities and the harbinger of God knew what" (424)—that illuminates the vast frontier space before him as one fully defiled and profaned. The irony that the "false" dawn—ostensibly the nuclear explosion at the Trinity site that occurred on July 16, 1945—is what prompts Billy to call the dog back from the growing darkness is not lost on readers. The atomic detonation in the final pages of *The Crossing* further sets in stone that which can never be made whole again. Billy recognizes that his fate is tied to that of the old dog's—both are part and parcel of the world's matrix, and it seems neither will ever have a place, a home to call their own.

As readers, we must acknowledge that, with the wolf's death, Billy comes to know "what cannot be held," and perhaps it is for this reason that he continues to pursue a nomadic existence. As Billy's dreams increasingly become nightmares, and as he loses everything he once had, we are forced to reckon with the limits of our human power over the wild as well as the narratives that form our deepest longings. By the novel's end, we realize that Billy has paid an insurmountable cost for the price of his primitive-pastoral dream. Just as the crippled old dog he sees at the end of the novel has written across its body, "ten thousand indignities," so too is Billy's body thus writ, and therefore haunted by stories he once held as truths, but which experience reveal to be otherwise. Billy cannot return the she-wolf to her rightful home because her home no longer exists. Towards the end of *Cities*, we are privy to Billy's hands as an old man, full of "ropy veins that bound them to his heart. There was map enough for men to read. There God's plenty of signs and wonders to make a landscape. To make a world" (291). Perhaps the homeless dog, like the she-wolf, is more attuned to the heart of things, and Billy's driving away the dog remains, as Luce points out, "a cowardly disavowal of his connectedness to the matrix of the world that includes horror and loss and grief" (212). This appears to be evidence of McCarthy's own ambivalence regarding the fatal nature of the Southwestern mythology that informs the actions of old cowboys like Billy. We find this ambivalence in McMurtry as well, as the following discussion of *Streets of Laredo* attests. Even so, Billy's ultimate failure rests in the fateful undertaking that is his initial quest. Perhaps this is because his abstract ideals have no rootedness in place, or perhaps it is because his mind and heart so easily retreat into a romantic sense of place that they cannot be effectively contained within a frontier vision. It seems Billy will never be let loose of frontier constraints; it is this which gives power and resonance to the final image of Billy as he weeps, alone, on a road that will, once again, take him to no place, but, rather, to more empty spaces.

McCarthy's border trilogy is replete with universal meanings about human nature and significant lessons of Western and national history. The West is full of stories grounded in a pastoral-primitive nostalgia where the hero's idyllic dreams come to fruition in a wilderness setting. Both Billy's quest and John Grady's dream are doomed to failure. Billy represents the primitive-pastoral hero who, tested and almost spiritually broken by the wilderness experience, remains a wanderer, *un huerfano* at the conclusion of *Cities of the Plain*. Like John Grady, Billy must learn that there exists an essential continuity between our present concerns and the concerns of history. The boys' dreams, which encompass so much of the spatial imagery of the Southwest, and the figurative imagery of borders and frontiers are singular, and, as such, little match against the social and cultural backdrop of a Mexican landscape, a place steeped in history and memory. In the trilogy, the boys' willful dreams are continually overshadowed by Mexican and Indigenous realities told to them in the form of stories or embedded in the landscape; these concrete remembrances disrupt their idyllic pursuits. In this sense, the boys remain haunted by unsettled, unresolved histories of collective violence and cultural and social issues signified by their crossings into Mexico.

Chopping Away at the Myth: *Streets of Laredo*

Streets of Laredo is the final and darkest installment of Larry McMurtry's saga of the American West that began with the publication of the Pulitzer-Prize–winning *Lonesome Dove*. A postmodern novel of fragmentation and loss in which McMurtry deconstructs the Western mythology of rugged individualism and cowboy gods, *Streets* employs inversions, reversals, and symbolic "cuts" to parallel the broader ideological shifts of major characters' mindsets and preconceptions. The novel's emphasis on a plurality of voices exposes liminal spaces and convergence points where subjects can effectively disrupt outmoded ideologies and forge new connections. *Streets* is framed by tropes central to Borderlands texts: physical, psychic, and emotional transformation and accommodation serve to overturn a traditional frontier mythogenesis and point towards a more inclusive Borderlands consciousness.

Elsewhere, I have written about *Streets* as a novel where major players transgress existing borders to denote a third space, a meeting point where they may effectively disrupt outmoded ideologies and forge new connections.[2] In this chapter, I focus on Woodrow Call's body as a dying emblem of the frontier myth. In the novel, McMurtry literally and figuratively chops away at the frontier myth, as evidenced by the loss of body parts and structures of feeling associated with the frontier myth. Both Call's body and the landscape itself suggest the means by which the power and rootedness of place, in time, can render spatial signifiers ghostly. In the novel, Call is compelled to confront the presence of such signifiers as he battles between his violent history and his increasing invisibility in the present—a battle that plays out and is marked on his body. Although he remains haunted by echoes of his former self throughout much of the novel, McMurtry grants Call entry into the security of place by the novel's end, a fate not shared by Billy in *The Crossing*.

When Euro Americans moved westward into the already-occupied spaces of the American Southwest, the geography did not categorically shift from an agrarian, premodern society to a more cosmopolitan one. On the contrary, this "manipulation of space," as Mary Pat Brady (2002) calls it, yielded a palimpsest of sorts (52). In *Streets of Laredo*, this geographical palimpsest may be read on or of the body, as McMurtry's use of the loss of body parts is a metaphor for human loss and an increasingly obsolete frontier mythology. Bodily mutilations that occur throughout the novel are initially associated with Mexicans, possibly reflecting the fragmentation of a culture and a people disenfranchised by the effects of westward movement. In time, however, maimings, cuts, defects, and missing body parts equally assault whites, indicating McMurtry's commitment to cleave away at the frontier myth and its accompanying cowboy hero.

The novel opens in the last decade of the nineteenth century. The frontier has been pushed to its southern and western limits, and the Comanche have for the most part been relocated. Mexicans have long accepted the Rio Grande as the US–Mexico border, and rangering and cowboying as a way of life have lost their foothold and given way to farming, ranching, and a more fixed urban structure. These changes are evidenced by the railroad, which is central to the novel's action. Part I, titled "A Salaried Man," underscores the shift in the relations of space and power on the frontier. Captain Woodrow Call, "the most famous ranger of all time" (132), has been hired by the Eastern robber baron and railroad president, Colonel Terry, to hunt the notorious Joey Garza. Call is nearing seventy, but he still takes on occasional assignments to bring in petty criminals to make his living. However, the nineteen-year-old Joey Garza—who learned his vicious ways from the Apache—is no petty criminal. A postmodern villain who smiles as he kills, Joey has a "cold nature" that there "is no accounting for" (404).

Keeping the rail lines running and money in the pockets of the "gringos" Joey steals from catalyzes the novel's plot. To track down his quarry, Call must first travel by train before he proceeds into Mexico on horseback. Before he embarks on his journey, he laments the transforming landscape, as he has not yet shed the trappings of an earlier horse culture and the limitless sense of space it intimates. He tells Charles Goodnight, his sometime friend and owner of the small line cabin in Quitaque Call sometimes occupies, that "traveling by train weakens the memory. . . . A man that travels horseback needs to remember where the water holes are, but a man that rides in a train can forget about water holes, because trains don't drink" (17). Call's lament hints at the new ethos he will be forced to confront: the necessity of a new character needed to function in the modern world.[3] If he is to survive, he will need to embrace place. Later, Call admits that what he and men like Goodnight "were doing was only the shadow of rangering, anyway" (38). From the onset, then, Call is a decentered subject. Long a symbol of the ranger and adventuring cowboy on horseback who protects pioneers and settlers, Call is now a salaried man, not hunting the Comanche or Kiowa but protecting the interests of corporate empires.

Ends and Beginnings: Identities in Process

As a boy, McMurtry and his brothers caught sight of the last of the great cattle drives from their barn-top vantage on Idiot Ridge on the fringe of the plains in Archer County, Texas. His earliest recollections form the stuff of his creative concerns, and they are suffused with memories and impressions of the borders between frontier and civilization, myth and reality, past and present. Born "of a people who had lived for years on the fringes of civilization, who could see both into the vastness of the plains and into the culture of the East," McMurtry straddles the boundary between divergent worlds (Lich 1988, 13). A son and grandson of frontier cattlemen, McMurtry speaks the native language of his frontier soil and generates characters as functions of their setting. Scholars Mark Busby, Tom Pilkington, and Lera Patrick Tyler Lich concur that McMurtry combines elements of anti-myth alongside mythic elements of a cowboy god whose home was the frontier and who celebrates the ideals of freedom and adventure appropriate to the boundless spaces of the frontier. This is especially true in *Streets*, which reflects the author's deep ambivalence towards a shifting landscape quickly moving from an agrarian, rural way of life to a more urban one.

McMurtry maintains that all of his novels begin with a "culminating scene" that illustrates a closure of sorts: "I don't know what's ended and the writing of a novel is a process in which I discover how these people get themselves to this scene" (Bennett 1980, 13). This idea, when combined with McMurtry's ambivalence towards his home state of Texas and the myth of the west he grew up both idolizing and disdaining, compels a postmodern reading of *Streets* that foregrounds the nature and necessity of change. Just as the landscape shifts and gives way to place, so too are the old ranger's movements continually upstaged by characters who embody place: women, Mexicans, and American Indians. Call is not the novel's hero, and his many failures parallel the ways McMurtry uses the "metaphor of physical fragmentation to allegorize the unreasonable paradigm that result[s] from the beloved myth" (Nickell 1999, 12). Throughout the novel McMurtry's self-reflexivity combines with historical references and locations during a time of profound transformation to illustrate how Call's cognitive disorientation mirrors the societal trauma the myth of the West has wrought for Indigenous, female, and Mexican bodies silenced by the same myth. Call, however, is a subjectivity-in-process, and so, when the trappings of space reveal themselves for what they are—vestments of a confining, outdated ideology—Call embraces a different story bound by the ethical and moral requisites of place.

The expansive Southwestern landscape is a repository of memories in *Streets*. First, Call and Goodnight muse about it. "Often the two men would sit, largely in silence, looking down into the canyon until dusk and then darkness filled it. In the dusk and shadows they saw their history; in the fading afterlight they saw the fallen: the Rangers, the Indians, the cowboys" (16). Yet, always, McMurtry's ambivalence remains. The "old ones" of the West, as Call calls them, are vanishing, their diminishing attire evidence of loss. Goodnight thinks about his cowboys, who "wore the[ir] guns from wistfulness. . . . [T]hey wanted to feel that they were living in a West that was still wild" (362). For Call, however, it is not diminished attire, but a diminished self that he grapples with throughout the novel. Furthermore, although the vast Southwestern landscape inherently counteracts the idea of borders, its location on the edge of Southern and Western culture along the Rio Grande and the border of Mexico necessitates an awareness of place and borders. McMurtry (1979) writes:

> I grew up in a post-frontier mentality in Archer County in the 30s and 40s and yet my grandparents were among the very first white people in my county: and I knew, as I was growing up, numerous people who had been really, literally, in the first generation of white people in West Texas and who settled the land, and, who, in settling the land, had acted upon and developed a set of values, a set of beliefs, a set of traditions and customs that really went with the frontier way of life and that were designed to insure certain things, namely . . . survival of the settlement (27–28).

When we consider these ideas alongside Pilkington's (1973) claim that McMurtry's "ambiguous love affair with his homeland" stems from ideas surrounding "birth and death that he is most concerned with" (174), we can read how the death of all that signifies space in the novel gives way and ultimately yields to place, and the safety, security, and community that place signifies.

Streets complicates the oppositions of space and place intrinsic to the frontier mythology. As illustrated in McCarthy's border trilogy, such conflicts are based in the historical prioritizing of vast, open spaces that tied men like John Grady Cole, Billy Parham, and Captain Woodrow Call to a life of journeying and the search for fixity, or rootedness. Unlike the border trilogy, which offers no solace for Billy or John Grady, McMurtry concludes *Streets* with a merging of the dualities inherent in the Bordered frontier to produce a synthesis rooted in the domestic imperatives of place. In so doing, he prioritizes the feminine alongside new approaches to a cultural politics of difference. In *Streets*, two women—Lorena Parker and Maria Garza—upstage Call's actions. A Borderlands text at heart, the novel subverts frontier priorities by repopulating an ostensibly frontier narrative with "missing" players.

Transformation is a key element in *Streets* that obliges characters to "remake and reclaim" narratives of hope and belonging contrary to those they have previously embodied (Pérez 1999, 127). Ideological transformations in the novel are written on the body, and they take place alongside shifts in power relations that arise from the questioning of male-dominant cultural practices. Lorena, as well as Maria and Call, all renegotiate the politics inscribed on their bodies in such a way that conflict and control yield to negotiation and compromise. Lorena, the ranger Pea Eye's wife—whom, like Pea Eye, we first meet in *Lonesome Dove*—has transformed herself from prostitute to wife to schoolmarm and, finally, savior. Lorena does not just physically accompany Call on his quest—her earlier transformation fore-shadows Call's path to consciousness.

When Lorena first speaks with Charles Goodnight about Joey Garza and, more specifically, Mox Mox, the "manburner," and second killer/villain introduced in Part II of the novel, she reiterates that Goodnight is needed in Quitaque. She says, "This whole part of the country needs you. You're the man who built the school. . . . You brought the doctor here. You paid for the courthouse." In contrast, she says, "Nobody needs Captain Call" (242). By the novel's end, however, Call *is* needed. Teresa, Maria's blind daughter, needs him. When Call first rides into Ojinaga during his hunt for Joey, he finds the old scout Billy Williams caring for Teresa and Rafael, Maria's two children. Although the young Teresa cannot see Call, she "thought the man might be a king, from the way he made the air different when he looked at her." She is soothed by Call's voice, and she hopes that he will stay with them for a while. Call, too, is drawn to Teresa, as he discerns "something in her quick expression that was unusual" (289). He muses about the child, wishing he "had a bauble to give her, a ribbon, or a locket, or some such trinket" (290). This scene foreshadows a reconciliation of forces, of ideological struggles on the Borderlands. In time, Call will move from "ruling" the frontier to reigning in a young girl's heart.

Saved by The Other: Women and Renewal

In the opening pages of *Streets of Laredo*, Pea Eye, who has rangered with Captain Call for over thirty years, initially refuses Call's order to accompany him in the search for Joey. As Pea Eye has always proved loyal before, Call determines that, "The woman had won. In the end, it seemed they always did" (38). Indeed, Pea Eye is deeply conflicted at the prospect of leaving his family's farm in Quanah. After weighing his loyalties to Call, on the one hand, and to Lorena and his growing family on the other, he decides to stay in Quanah. Later, when Charles Goodnight admonishes Pea Eye for not accompanying Call, Pea Eye decides his choice was made in error. Lorena acknowledges that Pea Eye's history is the culprit: "She could change her husband's habits, and she had, but she couldn't change his history, and it was in his history that the problem lay" (162). She recognizes that Pea Eye's history is mired in a hierarchical binary that bisects an outmoded ideology and the ongoing production of the border as place:

> That was what it was, too: woman against man. Her body, her spirit, her
> affection and passion, the children she and Pea shared, the *life* they shared
> on the farm that had cost them all her money and years of their energy. It
> was that against the old man with the gun, and the way of life that ought to
> have ended (160–61).

Lorena's remark presages loss, but it is a loss marked by renewal, most notably for Call. The novel begins with a decentered Call, but this turn does not
mean his death. Rather, it suggests his inevitable metamorphosis alongside a
changing landscape and the reshaping of a way of life in the Southwest. This
illustrates the dialogic nature of the Bordered frontier, a site of inherent,
often embedded discourses that account for memory, history, and subjectivities in process. This is the discourse at work in *Streets of Laredo*. The material marker of the border in the Southwest—the Rio Grande—furnishes the
geographical fragmentation in the novel; the many crossings illuminate the
Southwest as a fragmented space; border theory dialogues with the third
space in ways that break open subjectivities in process.

Call suffers from a diminished sense of self throughout the novel.
Along his quest to find and kill Joey, he acknowledges that "[n]ever before
had he followed his instincts and come up totally empty" (371). His arthri-
tis at one point becomes so bad that several "days passed without his even
unsaddling his horse. He was afraid he might not be able to pull the saddle
straps tight again, with his sore hands" (372). Additionally, he begins to
second-guess his decisions. Lorena entreats Call to let her ride with him to
search for Pea Eye, who leaves Lorena and their family after being admon-
ished by Goodnight for allowing Call to hunt Joey on his own. Call tells
her, "I don't know that I can protect you. . . . I let the Garza boy slip right
by me and kill Roy Bean. Then I let Mox Mox get away. That's two poor
performances in a row" (391). Call has never failed before, for he is well
aware of the "way of the frontier. If you failed in vigilance, you usually
died. Rarely would the frontier permit a lapse as serious as the one he had
just made" (422–23). Call's lapses and failures are not tests; he has proved
himself many times throughout his long career. Rather, they are "cuts" to
his psyche. Call's loss of body parts announces his further break with the
frontier myth.

Late in the novel Call is seriously wounded by Joey Garza. He suffers a
bullet lodged close to his heart, has one leg amputated by Lorena, and is facing the loss of his left arm. Yet he still lives, and Lorena does not understand
what will become of him:

Even if she wrestled him onto his horse and got him to Presidio and they found a doctor, what could the doctor do? And what would there be left for him if he did live? He couldn't hunt men anymore. He wasn't a rancher. He didn't farm. He had lived all his life by the gun, and now no one would ever want him for his fighting abilities again. Better that he had died—he wouldn't have this suffering, and he wouldn't have to live as an old cripple (454).

Maria Garza is Joey's mother and midwife to the town of Ojinaga, a Mexico border town opposite to Presidio, Texas. Joey hates his mother and considers her a whore simply by virtue of her sex. When Lorena rides into the village of Ojinaga with a wounded Call in tow and tied to his horse, Maria, having endured an earlier transformation of her own flesh in Crow Town, demonstrates a radical shift in consciousness. Call killed both Maria's father and brother during his early days as a ranger:

> The name sent a chill through her. She had loved her father and her brother. They had done no more than take back horses that the Texans had taken from them. No living man had caused her as much grief as Woodrow Call: not the four husbands, three of whom beat her; not the gringos, who insulted her, assuming that because she was a brown woman, she was a whore (61).

Although she holds a newly sharpened knife in her hand, Maria "didn't raise the knife and she didn't strike" (458). Call's wounds, his torn flesh, now marked by both Lorena's cutting off of his left leg and Joey's bullets, signal to Maria an alternative ethical and political authority against the dogmatism of power once held by Call. Although he is still Other, their encounter signals a moment of an alternative perspective:

> Though he bore the name of the man who had killed her father and her brother, Maria knew he was no longer that man, the one she had wanted to kill.... To stab him now would be pointless—for she would not be stabbing the Captain Call she had hated for so long, but only the clothes and the fleshy wrappings of that man (459).

Her acknowledgment of Call as a man "not-Call" signals the third space as "a challenge to the limits of the self in the act of reaching out to what is liminal in the historic experience" (Bhabha 2006, xiii). Not a killer anymore, not a Texas Ranger, and certainly not the "salaried man" who was hired to kill her son, Call's body now emphasizes the "emptiness" or "arbitrariness" of the sign (Bhabha xi). As the arbitrary sign shifts across the open frame of signification, it marks the distance that lies between Maria's familiarity with the manhunter and the unknowability of the new man, "the old, sick man on the black horse" (459). As such, Maria can more easily approach him. McMurtry, both narratively and ideologically, has shrunk the ethical and moral gap that lies between Maria and Call. Notably, this meeting represents the first time Maria physically casts eyes on Call. When she finally does perceive with her own eyes the man himself, he has ceased to signify the myth. Call is only an old man dressed in the torn wrappings of the myth. The man Teresa's ears once perceived as a "king" has ceased to exist as well. Call as man-hunter and supreme executor of the myth is now a marker of the distance between an outdated history and a new narrative of accommodation. This moment in time and space is a bridge. The moment was first signaled by Lorena, who was made aware of it when she sawed off Call's leg with a nicked knife. Maria enunciates the time lag at the moment she understands that Call is not the same man. We find a similar course among major players in *Sleep Dealer*, discussed in chapter 6.

In the long epilogue that follows, Call's transformation is complete, as he turns the painful gaze of his own history to his body. He has broken with an outdated ideology and is well on the way to realizing an alternative to his bloody, violent history. Call concludes that on the morning of his injuries, the morning he wounded Joey—but did not kill him—it was his "untrustworthy eyes" that had "cost him himself: that was how he came to view it. Because of his untrustworthy eyes, he had been reduced to what he was now, a man with two crutches, a man who could not mount a horse" (544). Ironically, however, Call, in the end, has eyes only for Maria's child Teresa. Both Lorena and Clara Allen—the ranger Gus McCrae's former love interest—acknowledge Call "wouldn't last long without Tessie" (577); she remains his "sole attendant" (543). Only when Call looks at Teresa is he even alive: "[B]ut except for Teresa, he had no one. Even looking at the Captain, unless he was with Teresa, was painful. Often when he was looking at Teresa, Call had tears in his eyes. But otherwise, there was nothing in his eyes—he was an absence" (583). Call is an empty vessel. Having been stripped of the mythology, he remains only when his presence is mirrored back to him in the eyes of young Tessie, "who had not only Maria's look, but Maria's strength" (583). Call and Teresa's bond demonstrates a synthesis both physical and psychological. Their newfound attachment suggests a tactical subjectivity of cultural accommodation This stance challenges the written history—the myth—of the Southwestern frontier. Call's reintegration with the Other is further evidenced by his suggestion that the "little money" (580) he has managed to save be used to pay for Tessie's education at a special school for the blind. His future is now marked by the responsibility, indeed, the love, he feels for Teresa.

Despondent at first, in time, Call traverses the juncture between past and present. Crossing this point in time necessitates union with the Other, in this case, Teresa. In the end, there is

> a crack, a kind of canyon between the Woodrow Call sitting with Teresa on the train and the Woodrow Call who had made the campfire that morning. . . . [H]e could remember the person he had been, but he could not become that person again. That person—that Call—was back down the weeks, on the other side of the canyon of time. There was no rejoining him, and there never would be (565–66).

Call, a man who "lived somewhere back in memory, across a canyon, across the Pecos; that man had been blown away . . . on the plains of time" (574). Call moves from a "shadow" (38) of his former self, to an echo, to an "impostor" (574), and, finally, to an "absence" (583). Indeed, those aspects of the frontier mythology that Pilkington (1973) argues are major facets of McMurtry's ambivalence—"birth and death"—become synthesized in the body of Captain Call. By the novel's conclusion the limitless spaces of the Southwest have vanished; what is left in their stead is place, and a "shutting out" of the wild. The final line of the novel focuses on a life of domesticity: "Pea Eye shut the door of the oat bin, to keep out mice and snakes, and, at moments nervous, at moments relieved—at least she had called him *honey*— he followed his wife back to their house" (589).

A close reading of Call's movements from echo to absence paralleled by his strategic positioning not simply alongside, but as contained *within* Teresa's own blind eyes, her own psyche, obliges us to acknowledge transcendence and a new proposition. The old captain's attachment to Teresa underscores fixity, but more importantly, it represents a redefining of boundaries. No longer is Call bound to a vanishing mythology or to the vast, unsettled spaces of the frontier; instead, he will live out his days in the shelter of a secure domestic space at Pea Eye and Lorena's home with Teresa and a slew of kids. Not a home of his own, but a start.

CHAPTER 5

TOWARDS AN ETHICS OF PLACE IN TWO CHICAN@ CLASSICS

I n the previous chapter, we saw how a focus on history and memory disrupts the linear vision embedded within the frontier myth, especially as regards the precondition of vast spaces to be filled and destructive patterns associated with a spatial poetics. The cowboys in the border trilogy, like Captain Call in *Streets of Laredo,* forever remain haunted by a frontier myth that proves to be little more than wreckage and bones, "words of the dead" (McCarthy 1994, 411) that the old *gitano* enigmatically warns Billy Parham to heed. In these novels, the myth is a vestige by which characters construct a matrix of meaning that ultimately misrepresents worlds and ways of life either vanished or vanishing. The constraints of the "linearity of the road" keep Billy from fully contributing to and partaking in the cultural matrix that he learns about in the form of so many tales (Luce 1999, 205).

We find this pattern in McMurtry's first novel, *Horseman, Pass By* (1992), an elegiac story of the downfall of one ranch and one rancher in Texas that mirrors the wider decline of the myth in the Southwest by the mid-twentieth century. As emblems of the old west—a horse culture, self-sustaining family-owned cattle ranches, and long days of outdoor work that "keeps a man doing for himself" (106)—vanish, so too do the values associated with the myth fade. The novel resists closure, as readers are unsure whether the young protagonist, Lonnie Bannon, will follow in the footsteps of his old granddad, now dead, or the young vibrant Hud, his step-brother and supreme emblem of the New West antihero who will capitalize on and exploit the landscape by drilling for oil. When Lonnie leaves the ranch, despondent and unsure of his future, readers are left with the road metaphor and an inarticulate Lonnie, who doesn't "want to get into a long conversation about it" (179). *Horseman* ends on a note that echoes structures of feeling similar to Billy's, as the felt affective elements of the myth give way to emergent forms associated with place. Embryonic values and meanings of place are articulated by Jesse, a young, weary ranch hand following the footsteps of his cowboy father and aged beyond his years, like "an old loose horse" with "no paradise" to be found (148). Jesse warns Lonnie:

> You're better off to stop somewhere. . . . I could have myself, many a time. I had the chances any man has. I went all over this cow country, looking for the exact right place an' the exact right people, so once I got stopped I wouldn't have to be movin' agin, like my old man always done. But that's going at it all wrong. I shoulda just set down an' made it right wherever the hell it was (148).

The pastoral vision helped shape the historical quest by American Adams[1] like Jesse and Billy; but this vision necessitates a prerequisite rejection of place, especially in terms of the internal ordering of conditional forms of "permanence" as regards the flow of space and time, a condition central to Harvey's conception of place as discursive and symbolic (Cresswell 2015, 91–92). However, when the logic of linear time and boundless space is dissolved as a structure of feeling, the boundlessness of space further reveals the "unintended consequence of making space a means of control" (163). In the modern era, mobility can factor in the shaping of place when fixed to space by forms of capital. What is missing from Jesse's pronouncement is the simple fact that, as an Anglo male with no property to call his own, "setting down" in any one place was likely an impossibility without a legal, familial, or communal claim to ownership or control. We saw this pattern play out in John Grady's doomed quest. To "control" space in the American Southwest in the mid-nineteenth century necessitates capital, as was the case with elite Laredoans in the late nineteenth century. Capital, unlike place, is mobile; as such, the imposition of capital feeds the tension between the fixity of place and spatial mobility. Following from David Harvey, Cresswell considers how the power of capital combusts the "generalized crisis" of development as the physical landscape is reshaped and reconfigured such that prior places must necessarily be "devalued, destroyed, or redeveloped while new places are created" (93*)*. As structures of feeling associated with space shift and affective elements of consciousness drop away, pre-emergent meanings and values of place gain traction.

As we have seen, what follows from this pattern shapes an ethical gap, a liminal space of possibility that is also a bridge. This gap is a reference point by which major players ultimately embrace an understanding of how "geography informs power relations in a place marked by race and class struggles since its entrance into the Western imaginary" (Meléndez 2008, 196). As does Meléndez in her reading of Arturo Islas's *The Rain God*, which I discuss herein, we can read these shifts as "geographies of knowing" in terms of the way speciality concedes to temporality (196). Similarly, Captain Call's movement from manhunter and executor of the frontier myth to a man who can only know himself when reflected in the eyes of the Other—the young Teresa—by the novel's end, marks a time lag, what Emma Pérez (1999) refers to as an "interstitial moment" in history. Thus, what is also missing from Jesse's pronouncement is an understanding that places, by definition, are intentional sites of human existence. In the American Southwest, place embeds aspects, dispositions, and properties of Indigeneity and ethnic diversity that, as we witnessed in the border trilogy, effectively push through the frontier vision. In this chapter, we take a closer look at those places, seemingly devalued but hardly destroyed, that coalesce lost haunts as originary sites of belonging. The result is an ethical vision based in an understanding of rootedness and a deep commitment to what Cresswell (2015) refers to as the "resacralization of place" (95).

As regards the temporalities of everyday life, I turn again to Lefebvre, who chronicles how everyday life is made of repetitions and recurrences, basically of two different forms of time irreducible to each other. Simonson (2008) reads the connections he makes between time and space to discuss how, within his critique of everyday life, he locates a "double-sided" effort within the body itself that continually negotiates aspects of cyclical and linear time. Somewhat nostalgically, notes Simonson, Lefebvre associates cyclical repetitions with archaic societies where social life is attuned to seasons, generations, days and nights, and youth and age. Conversely, linear repetitions of time—again, felt and coded as an aspect of the body as lived in space—are mechanical, a "series of gestures, of blows of the hammer[,] . . . enframed, constrained and colonized by the space of the commodity and the territory of the state; it is the dominant temporality of modernity"

(8). Within the body, cyclical and linear time comingle; however, even as linear time encroaches on the cyclical, the latter never fully passes away, as private life and its symbols, like emotions and "affections," do not "submit to cumulative and linear processes" (8).

In the following discussion of two classic Chican@ novels of the American Southwest, I unpack comingled aspects of time as indexed by both the immediate landscape and bodies as lived in space to illustrate how a focus on place retains and maintains as palimpsest the stories and histories of Others that subsume and counteract dominant frontier narratives that ritualize and reenact space—such as McCarthy's border trilogy and Laredo's annual Colonial Ball and Presentation. The novels I discuss here have generally been read in terms of a Borderlands aesthetics that, by definition, accounts for cultural hybridity, *mestizaje*, belonging, and tropes further seeded in border theory. Recalling the Bordered frontier as a complex of intertwined tropes that continue to configure identity on the Borderlands into the twenty-first century, however, reminds us of the need to approach Borderlands texts from a position of inclusivity. In this chapter, I widen the lens to account for competing facets within frontier and Borderland imaginaries that converge as discursive registers within American Gothic.[2] Not surprisingly, conceptualizing a Southwestern landscape in gothic terms speaks to embedded forms of Indigeneity, Aztec and Mayan mythologies, and preconquest ways of living in the world that shatter spaciality. Further, an understanding of synchronic, mythological time in its circuity inexorably grounds the protagonists in these novels to move readers beyond the symbolic towards an understanding of the Borderlands as a complex and interactive cultural zone that prioritizes psychic, psychological, and metaphoric spaces and places of negotiation and belonging.

In this chapter, I introduce tropes related to American Gothic, which is quite different from European Gothic, as these narratives are deeply engaged with historical concerns—notably horrors such as Native American massacres and a legacy of American slavery that continue to haunt the stories we tell about ourselves, stories that make national identity possible. Gothic tropes highlight political and national concerns in order to subvert codes indexed to American mythologies that historically dramatize what Slotkin (1992) describes as its "moral consciousness" (5). Goddu (1997), who addresses various sites of historical horror such as Indian massacres and the means by which the legacy of slavery haunts American Gothic forms, foregrounds a reading of the Gothic as a distorted, rather than a disengaged, version of reality. American Gothic forms are not escapist, as has often been identified in relation to canonical British Gothic forms. Rather, the American Gothic is a regional, mutable, "uncertain" form obsessed with transgressing boundaries (3–5).

For Goddu, "specific sites of historical haunting, most notably slavery" sustain the Gothic's challenge in the US. In this light, she claims that American Gothic forms reveal sites of cultural contradiction that undermine narratives of American literary history to "unsettle[s] the nation's cultural identity" (10). These contentions are central to my argument. First, given that the American Southwest is a space of conflict and negotiation, a historically contested, postcolonial Borderland, Goddu's premise is fitting because the Southwest is a landscape steeped in the historical horrors not of slavery but of Native American massacres and the extermination of Indigenous peoples. Just as Native Americans in the American Southwest signify a ruined and conquered past, so too do the region's Indigenous cultures. Second, because "the Gothic tells of the historical horrors that make national identity possible" (10), yet which are often repressed within the highly mutable, transgressive Gothic mode, we can look to the Gothic mode to expose artificial and mythologizing foundations on which individual American identities are precariously balanced. Finally, in the American West, works linked to "frontier gothic" further break open repressed and silenced regional specters that can effectively expose the artificial and imaginary foundations on which American identities are precariously balanced.

The Gothic Texture of the Southwest: *Bless Me, Ultima*

American Gothic forms are haunted by race relations. The legacy of slavery in the nineteenth century and the various genocidal campaigns against Native Americans and Indigenous peoples both sustain and reveal sites of cultural contradictions that undermine American literary history and "unsettle the nation's cultural identity" (Goddu 1997, 10). The Gothic has a long history in American literature, generating fear and anxiety in readers and viewers. Its hauntings—sites of moral and mental terrors—habitually unsettle the very idea of America. If the country is built on national mythologies that underscore individual promise and faith in progress, American Gothic undermines these idealized myths by focusing on threats and anxieties related to race, class, gender, and the historical repression of dispossessed "Others."

The cruel reality of race relations, those unspoken and silenced histories of the Other, notably "the shadows surrounding civilized clearings" (14)

that haunt logocentric, linear narratives, comprise the jumping-off point for
Mogen, Sanders, and Karpinski. The chapters comprising *Frontier Gothic*
(1993) ferret out the gothic texture of a Southwestern landscape to penetrate place in terms of the superposition of worlds to compel our understanding of how the past continues in the present to abide parallel realities.
Where European Gothic works have historically focused on issues of class
and gender, American Gothic forms address inherent tensions of the optimism that entwines new-world ideals and values.

Scott P. Sanders (1993) argues for an understanding of the Southwest as
a landscape in which Indigenous, Euro Americans, and Mexican Americans
and Chican@s struggle "to realize their desires for a sure sense of cultural
identity and rootedness in a landscape which, with its gothic presence,
resists making of it a locale, a homeland where people, events, and places are
integrated" (55). Using gothic tropes and inclinations as a flashpoint that
effectively uncovers aspects of place moves us beyond the lineal dictates of
space to locate older visions, sacred centers, and a continuity of past and
present that displace the frontier depictions of McMurtry and McCarthy.
Gothic narratives call for forms of excavation to release the shadowy repetitions of history that major players have only *sensed* as structures of feeling but have not experienced, as in Arturo Islas's classic Chican@ text, *The
Rain God*. Still further, the layered consciousness that structures *Bless Me,
Ultima* is found not only within the dream sequences but in the superposition of plot time and mythic time that embeds an inclusive timelessness
that continues to shape the lived experiences of the present, as the young
protagonist's evolving consciousness suggests.

Where Goddu (1997) discusses Gothic forms that speak to historical
horrors that have shaped a national identity, Sanders turns to Gothic forms
that encase Southwestern classics like *Ceremony* (1977) and *Bless Me, Ultima*
(1972). Native American texts such as Leslie Marmon Silko's *Ceremony*
and N. Scott Momaday's *House Made of Dawn* (1968), texts in which the
gothic texture of the landscape figures as both a physical and figurative
reality that shapes and binds characters to primordial aspects of the landscape, are beyond the scope of this chapter. These novels, however, share
elements with *Bless Me, Ultima* and *The Rain God* in the ways that identity
remains inseparable from place to illustrate how patterns of remembering
and revering landscapes of origin uphold an ethical stance for navigating the
Borderlands via the political force of haunting. These connections reveal
Chican@ Borderlands texts as *necessarily* haunted by Indigenous ways of

being in the world to suggest that only when something is appropriately remembered can healing and social progress be made.

Bless Me, Ultima compels an understanding of the superposition of parallel realities that both shape and ghost against ethnic cultures in the Southwest. The coming-of-age story of Antonio Márez as he negotiates aspects of his mixed culture and identity, the novel's New Mexican landscape embeds a parallel reality and belief system. The New Mexican soil is alive with the plants, roots, and herbs that the old *curandera*, Ultima, knows and cultivates, especially as regards Tony's development. Indeed, near the novel's end, the landscape directly signifies reclamation, as illustrated by Ultima's bringing to justice the spirit of three wrongfully killed Comanche Indians who haunt the Téllez ranch. As spirits entombed in the cultural past that underlie the familiar locales around Tony's village of Las Pasturas are recovered, Ultima effectively "releases forces that have been unnaturally confined" (Sanders 1993, 62). Ultimately, her power is restorative, as she guides young Tony—who is torn between the vastly different life paths his parents dream for him—towards integration and a holistic vision of the human and natural world. In the novel, the gothic landscape offers an alternative to each of the narratives his parents offer. In time, Tony must learn to comprehend the *hold* that buried forms of knowledge yet have on him.

As divergent forms of spirituality and belief, signified in the novel by a "new" pagan god—the golden carp—and Tony's more entrenched daily instruction in his Spanish Catholic heritage vie for dominance within his waking consciousness, a continuity between disparate ways of knowing the world takes shape. In the end, Tony comes to understand that the silent "language of the earth" (263) is only one aspect of the "new religion" (261) that will shape his life. Heeding his father's words regarding those aspects of his Mexican, Indigenous, and Spanish heritage that he is now in a position to "reform" so as to "make something new" (261), Tony, at the novel's end, comes to a "mythic understanding and vision" (Lattin 1979, 629) that speaks to a newfound sense of rootedness and orientation. As a child, he believes his friend Cico when he tells Tony that he will "have to choose between the god of the church, or the beauty that is here and now," which Cico describes as "gods of beauty and magic, gods of the garden, gods in our own backyards" (251). Having learned and, indeed, experienced the magical, primal power of the land and soil beneath his feet, he concludes that "from my father and Ultima I had learned that the greater immortality is in the freedom of man, and that freedom is best nourished by the noble expanse of land and air and pure, white sky" (242).

As Vernon E. Lattin (1979) argues, Tony's burgeoning knowledge speaks to a broader pattern that shapes the Chican@ quest for unity and wholeness. Although the quest generally requires a rejection of Christian values and a return to Indigenous forms of belief that dissolve the logic of Western time and space, *Bless Me, Ultima* ends with the young hero able to synthesize seemingly incompatible frames of religion and spirituality. On the surface, Tony's reverence for the land can be compared to Billy Parham's pastoral vision. Tony's quest, however, is one of *true* return, as mythic wholeness for Tony is based in "a land vision that precede[s] the white conquerors" (Lattin 1979, 638). Billy's failure in *The Crossing* stems from the psychic distance between himself—a white male—and the mythic unity signified by the enduring quality of the wolf's mythic landscape. Conversely, Ultima instructs Tony in the ways of the New Mexican *llano*, how "even the plants had a spirit" (42), and how the mysteries held within the "groaning earth" could bring fulfillment and understanding (16). Because Billy has no tie to the wolf's history, neither embodied nor attained, knowledge of the wolf's landscape, recovery, and mythic wholeness—the things he desires to apprehend with his quest to return the she-wolf to her rightful home—can neither be had nor found. As a young Chican@ Tony has rightfully learned how to enfold aspects of the sacred history of his people into his daily life; as such, his quest culminates in a kind of racial and mythic unity that transcends the personal—especially when we consider the intimation that he will be a man of learning who may, in turn, educate others via lessons he has learned from Ultima. A pastoral vision much different from Billy Parham's, Tony's is based in ancient mythic memories, and so cannot be so easily quelled (Lattin 1979, 639).

The Desert Topography of *The Rain God*

In *The Devil's Highway* (2004), Luis Alberto Urrea describes the Southwestern desert as one that instills a sense of "placelessness," impermanence, and "transient memory" (108). Urrea grants the Southwestern desert a voice—it speaks in GPS coordinates and personal items both lost and found. As migrant walkers from Mexico emigrate to the US in search of a better life, they are devoured by the desert; their stories are sketchy, but their bones yet speak. Urrea's desert—desolation—signifies a place where the colonial and colonized intersect and overlay. Here, the ruins of ancient ancestral pueblos, long vanished, "still dot the ground . . . like ghost roads"

(7). Here, too, remain the footprints of "long-dead cowboys" (7). "Though the bones are gone," writes Urrea, "wagon ruts can still be found, and near these ruts, piles of stone still hide the remains of those who fell" (11). For Urrea, as Anaya, the Southwestern desert is a palimpsest in which reminders of an alternative literary hermeneutics is embedded. We find this pattern in Arturo Islas's Chican@ classic, *The Rain God.*

In many ways, *The Rain God* (1984) mirrors Arturo Islas's life on the US–Mexico Borderlands in the mid-twentieth century. Born to second-generation Catholic Mexican Americans and raised in El Paso, Texas within the conservative cultural and socioeconomic backdrop of the 1950s, Islas spent a lifetime struggling with his homosexuality and a bodily existence marred by recurring illness—themes the protagonist confronts in the novel. At the heart of *The Rain God* is the desert in which are found all of the souls that make up the Angel family. The Rain God, which serves as both the title of the book and the novel's final chapter, is metaphorically linked to the desert, where love and death continually merge. Miguel Chico, "the family analyst, interested in the past for psychological, not historical reasons," is the central character whose developing consciousness is tied to Islas's own (28). From the novel's onset, Miguel Chico longs to return to the desert; but his desire is not wistful. On the contrary, it is an urgent, ambiguous, and often phantasmagoric demand emanating from his own sick body that compels his return.

The novel embeds a Gothic narrative that calls for forms of self-excavation so as to release the unsettling repetitions of history that Miguel Chico has only *sensed* as a structure of feeling but has not experienced. The novel's focus on the heft of shadowy apparitions and a menacing desert landscape parallels the repressed psychological states and ambiguous relationships held by various characters in the novel. These include Miguel Chico's Uncle Felix and his son JoEl, although here I focus on Miguel Chico.[3] Gothic tropes such as hidden crimes, spectral forms of sin, and repressed fears and resentments call for a reading that turns inward, "away from society and towards the psyche" (Goddu 1997, 9). Notably, as Miguel Chico works through coming to terms with his fractured Borderlands identity, the gothic space of the desert first unravels and then nurtures a nightmarish space of renewal.

The novel spans the decades between the Mexican Revolution of 1910 to the late twentieth century. The first of six segments, "Judgment Day," introduces the Angel family as well as structurally foreshadows the final segment of the novel in which the family's matriarch, Mama Chona, dies. In this first segment, Miguel Chico, who at age thirty has undergone surgery that will leave him forever tied to a colostomy bag, muses on his childhood and make up, "his family . . . especially its sinners" (4). Thus are we introduced to two central themes of the novel: the narratives of the Angel family "sinners" and Miguel Chico's longing "to return to the desert of his childhood, not to the family, but to the place" (5). It is the pull of the desert as a place of origin that I focus on here.

When an adult Miguel Chico returns to the fictional town of Del Sapo on the Texas–Mexico border in the American Southwest, he confronts the trickery of a desert god that favors retribution. In the novel, the home represents a space of subjugation and alienation; the desert, to use José E. Limón's phrase from *Dancing with the Devil: Society and Cultural Poetics in Mexican-American South Texas* (1994), is "bedeviled," a colonized space that exemplifies gothic tropes and primordial imagery to illustrate how the past does not die, but remains a repository of memory and culture for Mexican Americans and Chican@s. Although the desert is associated with death, graveyards, terror, and bodily horrors, in the novel, it signifies a rupturing place of freedom tied to ancestral connections. Entrenched in the desert is the Rain God, a signifier of an originary worldview that first elicits and then directs Miguel Chico's emerging ethical vision for navigating the world in ways that promise healing, renewal, and a lifting of disruptive practices tied to a modernist, colonialist project in the American Southwest.

In *The Rain God*, the desert topography signifies cyclical time and memory. It is visceral and tied to Miguel Chico's need to reclaim an originary place both literal and spiritual. In the novel, the spatial poetics of the desert configure a space worked upon and etched over in terms of history and modernist practices that occluded Indigenous belief systems and ways of being. Upon this palimpsest Mexican myth and American ideologies contend for legitimacy. The space of the desert is a space of warring ideologies that mirrors Miguel Chico's own unease with his body. José David Saldívar (1997) reads *The Rain God* as a novel that recreates the topography of the US–Mexico Borderlands and the "social, gender, and sexual relations of its people" (74). He concentrates on the spatial, or what he calls the "topospatial," elements of the novel to illustrate how historicity and simultaneously spatial memories merge to suggest a reading of the desert landscape that attends to a "profound interaction of space and history, geography and psychology, nationhood and imperialism" that allows us to acknowledge space as a formative presence (79). Unaccounted for in Saldívar's topospatial reading is an equal consideration of place that effectively prioritizes the desert as a gothic storehouse of recovered Indigenous images that spur Miguel Chico's reentry into his estranged native culture. Additionally, Rosaura Sánchez (1998) situates Miguel Chico within a "subjective timeless frame" in which historical references are blurred and earlier social practices are "recalled and mapped out" in order to be finally expunged from his memory (116). She contends that the third generation of Angels—Miguel Chico's generation—fails to formulate an alternative to embedded patriarchal practices and ethnic and class prejudices. Neither Saldívar's nor Sánchez's reading considers how Miguel Chico, by the novel's end, comes to terms with the politics of haunting to embody a postmodern ethics of place that refuses the previous generation's systematic othering of the Indian.

La facultad as a Means to Apprehend Indigeneity

The Rain God roots its panoramic sense of place in a complex history linked to the nature of the Bordered frontier, as the desert enfolds a liminal site of memory and history. For Chican@s, Aztlán refers to the Mexican territories annexed by the US as a result of the Mexican American War of 1846–1848. In the late 1960s the Chican@ community named Aztlán as its homeland, instilling a sense of nation for a people threatened by assimilationist tendencies. This turn to history for Chican@s marked a new consciousness seated in the myths and legends of the Aztecs, a move that consciously and publicly recognized a Native American and Indigenous heritage. In seeking to define a character and "soul" that insists on the right to embed a communal, legal, and primordial place of origin into the psychological and spiritual consciousness of the community, Anaya (2017) argues that the naming of Aztlán helped "synthesize the Indo-Hispano cultures" of the American Southwest (233). For Anaya, this syncretism speaks to the need to foment a "new consciousness" that can lead to a "cultural renaissance" that embeds an ecological and spiritual awareness into the fabric of narratives that evoke Aztlán (37–38). Although Islas does not specifically name Aztlán, the Mesoamerican rain god Tlaloc is a signifier of primordial memories recoverable through memory and history. Just as Tony in *Bless Me, Ultima* synthesizes seemingly incompatible frames of religion and spirituality to transcend the personal and foment a kind of racial and mythic unity, so does Miguel Chico, in the final pages of *The Rain God*, reshape his fractured identity such that he is better poised to read the story of his life and of his culture's past correctly and meaningfully.

Tlaloc is associated with water, blood, life, and death in Aztec cosmology.[4] In the earliest chronicled descriptions, Tlaloc emerges as a god associated with the earth and the lower regions of the earth. Symbolically, the Rain God in Islas's novel is an allusion to a past Mesoamerican or Aztec way of life that has survived for both the Angel family and Chican@s in general; it is part and parcel of their identity, their *mestizaje*. Indigenous histories are the linchpin of a fluid Borderlands identity, as explained by Gloria Anzaldúa (2012). The names are ancient, and their roots run deep: Tlaloc, Cihuacoatl, Coatlicue.[5] The ancients, spirits unsettled and teeming, signify the traces of an abiding resistance to colonial domination and violence, and exist within a cyclical timeframe that disrupts a linear monologue of modernist, neoliberal practices. On the Borderlands, where Anzaldúa is rooted in the experiences and presence of ancestral spirits, *la facultad*, a "survival tactic" of those "caught between worlds," is a necessary, semi-psychic ability, a sixth sense that pierces the soul and deepens one's perceptions (61). *La facultad* naturally strengthens inside border dwellers who negotiate liminal, marginal spaces in their everyday realities. The desert topography, a composition that enacts cyclical time and memory, is therefore visceral and tied to embodiment.

Throughout *The Rain God*, Miguel Chico struggles to embody *la facultad*, as he yearns to construct an alternative discourse that will allow him to break free from a nationalist, hegemonic, modernist agenda. As the nonlinear, cyclical narrative jumps back and forth in time and space, a pattern emerges: nationalist hegemonic rule has not erased ancestral history and narrative; it has merely silenced these for a time. Similarly, the heterosexual, patriarchal norms espoused by the first generation of Angels and signified by Mama Chona in the novel ultimately reveal themselves to be little more than evanescent marks of censorship that have effectively closeted the abiding ghostly presences that signify longevity and recovery of history as a prelude to healing. In the novel, the home space perpetuates a homogenized national consciousness that disavows a sense of place necessary for Miguel Chico to come to terms with his homosexuality. The desert, however, embeds a subnational reality that compels his reactionary consciousness. The Southwestern desert, with its complex and layered history, encircles a space beyond the US and cut off from Mexico. Jelena Šesnić's (2007) comparative approach to Borderland contact zones illuminates how sites of ethnic localization give way to the transnational pull that ethnic citizens feel as they negotiate political realities within a space of "ghostly positionality" which extends across geopolitical, cultural, and generic boundaries (133). Her discussion of literary works on the Borderlands in terms of ethnic and minority "revision[s] of the national narrative" (134) evokes the gothic frontier.

In the novel, the Southwestern desert represents Miguel Chico's need to reclaim an originary space, both literally and spiritually. Complicating issues of ethnicity are "primordial sentiments" that Stuart Cochran (1995) parallels to "homing in" patterns that William Bevis (1987) asserts to be the most emblematic found in contemporary American Indian novels.[6] Bevis writes that in "Native American novels, coming home, staying put, contracting, even what we call 'regressing' to a place, a past where one has been before, is not only the primary story, it is a primary mode of knowledge and a primary good" (582). With this in mind, the desert is a dominant ideological strategy and structural device that both cements the family's history and revitalizes an essential connection, what Cochran calls an "inextricable mixture" in which the primordial becomes "a part of the culture and community that constructs the people and the land in a primordial nexus" (82). Gordon (2008) reminds us that we must acknowledge material and social effects that have sedimented back into the landscape. Doing so allows us to revere and ultimately cultivate the ghost alongside the utopian intimations that further arise in the reader as affect, as they too confront the loss and sublimated terrors that originate in the suppression of histories and silences. These structures of feeling that have been sedimented into the desert landscape remind us that, in Antonio Gramsci's terms, cultural hegemony is never total, as even totalizing systems are subverted by the inner dynamics by which new formations of thought emerge.

Remapping the Southwest: Critical Regionalism

Drawing from Arjun Appadurai's concept of the global production of locality, Šesnić (2007) discusses Borderlands literary productions in terms of localities "not drawn on any official map" but circulated in oral, written, and otherwise "commemorative, evocative, and memorial ethnic stories" (134). In articulating antagonistic relations between the ethnic and the national, her discussion of identity formation within liminal zones such as the American Southwest revises national narratives to underscore patterns of ethnic localization whereby localities are inscribed onto ethnic bodies. To arrive at this juncture, she evokes Williams's structures of feeling, articulations I have discussed as linked to Gordon's politics of haunting. To retain the dynamics of the "in-between, being in the nation-state but not entirely of it" (135), Šesnić further echoes the claims of Stuart Cochran, who conceptualizes primordial forms of affiliation as those marked by ties to the land, soil, and place.

Recalling Gordon's (2008) comprehension of structures of feeling as expressive of those presences that signify "the tangled exchange of noisy silences and seething absences," that shape expressions of haunting (200), reminds us to look beyond such shapes to discover their forms and reference points. Such absences are articulated by Anzaldúa as a layered consciousness of *mestizo* subjects who must penetrate the psychic recesses of cultural histories compulsively concealed under the façades of systems of power such as capitalism, colonial histories, and social marginalization. Anzaldúa (2012) claims the serpent as the symbol of truths discredited by colonialism and patriarchal structures to conceptualize downward descent as a path to knowledge. Her theory of "entering into the serpent," the title of chapter 3 in *Borderlands/La Frontera*, illustrates the means by which she recovers the symbolic resonance of Indigenous deities effectively driven underground during the post-conquest era in Mexico. The author's descent into the Earth—signified by the serpent's belly—unites the lost pieces of herself, fragments of flesh and spirit rent asunder by institutionalized religion, white rationality, and a culture that keeps transgressors in rigidly defined roles. Underground, in a swirl of cyclical time that inches backward while anticipating the future, she renews the value of the old gods. Anzaldúa's "entry" into the "body of the Earth Serpent" signifies a metaphorical journey that reconfigures sacred and Indigenous paths to knowledge (56). She feeds the old gods, nourishes them as does Islas. Just as the lifeblood of *Borderlands/La Frontera* is primal, hopeful, and apocalyptic in that what is revealed to readers is nothing short of a different way of being in the world, so too does *The Rain God* invite us to engage the shadow side of what lies beyond and beneath the resonance of the present.

Cresswell (2015) notes how political geographer Peter Taylor discusses nation-states as abstractions of space that further embed emotional qualities related to place and place-making. Regions, broadly speaking, exist somewhere between the scale of the nation and the local. Regions mark "locational designations" (144), but how do the complex entanglements of history and geography factor into the enactment of place at the regional level? Recalling the discussion in chapter 2, critical regionalism is a strategy that de-centers the imperatives of the nation-state and conceptualizes polyglot areas in terms of their sociocultural fullness. As such, it is one way to uncover ways of life—including symbols and metaphors of resistance— that have been effectively pushed to the recesses of memory by nation-state imperatives and impulses. Butler and Spivak (2007) discuss how critical regionalism can move us "over and under" abstract structures of the nation in ways that usher redress (100). These national structures of feeling are endorsed by Mama Chona, who refuses to associate herself with anything Mexican or Indian because she believes such to be "somehow impure" (27). As Gramsci reminds us, structures of feelings appear within the gaps of official discourse. Such forms of social experience are elusive, transient, and not fully articulated; as such, they must be inferred.

Critical regionalism's interest in place stems from a faith in continuity and the ways that place fosters "the shaping of life" rather than focusing on the ways and means by which ideologies "packaged . . . from above" continually mark personal and collective identities (Butler and Spivak 2007, 96). Significantly, it insists on the "value of honoring the best impulses of the past" and aligns with burgeoning forms of analyses that seek to unburden national identity as a unified hegemonic discourse (96). In Islas's novel, the meaning of Tlaloc, the mythical pre-Columbian Mexican deity central to Indigenous belief, has been subverted in the face of nationalism and modernity. A critical regionalist approach allows us to dialogue within and across transnational and local forms of culture and resistance with equal significance. On the US–Mexico border, this is especially apt as demographic extensions result from a dynamic and fluid US–Mexico Borderlands space. As *The Rain God* is concerned with a specific desert landscape within a broad historical time frame, a critical regionalist approach allows us to break open the historical antecedents of a uniquely Chican@ landscape that predates the surface-level nationalist imaginary espoused by Mama Chona and central to Miguel Chico's struggle of identity throughout the novel. His need is not to exorcise but integrate the past in a way that is transformative, introspective, and aligned with an expulsion of both personal and collective guilt.

When we prioritize place in such a way that foregrounds the Angel family's essential connection to a land that internalizes their Borderland origins into a collective ethos further realized through cross-cultural tensions, we uncover the roots of the desert as a generative site of ethnic identity. It is here where we locate what Nora (1989) refers to as "the repetition of the ancestral" (7), those collectively remembered values compulsively neglected by modernity in the campaign for a national memorial consciousness that "maintains by artifice and by will a society deeply absorbed in its own transformation and renewal, one that inherently values the new over the ancient, the young over the old, the future over the past" (12). It is precisely the "subjective timeless frame" to which Rosaura Sánchez (1998) alludes that I believe lends Miguel Chico the opportunity to recall a specific, geographical, ancestral site in such a way that place—the Southwestern desert—becomes a generative site of ideology. The desert unites the novel's six separate segments; it is more than "a secondary motif and strategy" (126). Rather, it encapsulates the central strategy by which Miguel Chico learns to read the story of his life and of his culture's past correctly and meaningfully. In the end, it is the protagonist's primal connection to the Mesoamerican rain god that coalesces the forces of retribution and redemption within his own body such that he can finally make peace with desires that have haunted him from childhood.

Integrating the Indian as Other: The Monster in the Closet

Miguel Chico's eventual embrace of his Indigenous identity repudiates a public, nationalist narrative and field of vision imbricated within the cultural baggage of American modernity. Underscoring the phenomenological experience of the desert as a nightmarish place of renewal where he works through personal, familial, and historical trauma grants a shape to abstractions of state structures. In this way, he carves an emergent politics from "spectral forms of sin" to suggest how facing such terrors can serve as a "prelude to healing" (Wickelson 2013, 99–100).

In his discussion of Sandra Cisneros's *Caramelo*, Paul Wickelson draws on the work of William Veeder to describe how elements of gothic and place in Borderlands texts complicate the uncanny repetitions of history by integrating elements of remembrance and resistance. Furthermore, John J. Su (1998) argues that one's identification with place in the postmodern novel directs the individual and provides an "ethical orientation" (597) within what he calls "narratives of return" (608). Identification with places of origin and past traditions, however, is key to internalizing ethical principles and the politics of belonging associated with place; thus embedding an ethical vision within postmodern narratives requires attention to "places of origin to find a basis for belief" (592). Laredoans, as we have seen, have historically disidentified with place, as such a sense of existential displacement is manifest in the narratives of the WBCA. I discussed this pattern of disidentification in Guálinto Gómez, the doomed anti-hero of *George Washington Gómez*. In this novel, Guálinto is a would-be hero who ultimately disidentifies with his past, resulting in his continued fragmentation of self and identity. Much like the women of the Princess Pocahontas Council in Laredo, Guálinto "polices" the Indian in his history, a gesture of dispossession that Anzaldúa (2012) cautions against in *Borderlands/La Frontera* (44). So too does Mama Chona, the matriarch of the Angel clan in *The Rain God*. Both Guálinto and Mama Chona point towards a generation of Mexican Americans who found it necessary to disidentify with a pre-Columbian belief system as they effectively internalized a myth of pure Spanish descent:

> The snobbery Mama Chona and Tia Cuca displayed in every way possi-
> ble against the Indian and in favor of the Spanish in the Angels' blood was
> a constant puzzlement to most of the grandchildren. In subtle, persistent
> ways, family members were taught that only the Spanish side of their her-
> itage was worth honoring and preserving: the Indian in them was pagan,
> servile, instinctive rather than intellectual, and was to be suppressed, the
> Indian in them denied (142).

The rendering of Indian as Other embeds a layered gothicism in *The Rain God* where Euro American and Chican@ cultural forms contend for legitimacy. A hermeneutics that uncovers the multi-layered history ensconced in the gothic geology of the desert allows us to conceptualize the desert as "a locale, a homeland where people, events, and places are integrated" (Sanders 1993, 55). Only when Miguel Chico understands the desert as homeland, storehouse of memory, and place of integration will an ethical stance in a region that both historically and today lacks a unified ethos be manifest. In this way, *The Rain God* is a postmodern novel that uses American gothic forms and motifs of haunting to illustrate how the past does not die but, rather, remains in the gaps between memory and history.

Integration of Indigeneity is central to *The Rain God*. Early in the novel, Miguel Chico recalls childhood trips to the cemetery to visit his dead friend, Leonardo. These memories cement the idea of the Rain God as both giver and taker: "[L]ove and death came together for Miguel Chico and he was not from then on able to think of one apart from the other" (19). At the novel's end, when Miguel Chico actually *feels* the Rain God come into Mama Chona's hospital room just as her death approaches, the Rain God is unequivocally—and importantly for Miguel Chico—one of both life and death. With the entrance of the Rain God into the room, he is finally able to drop the hand of Mama Chona, the hand that she has so tightly held—both literally and figuratively—throughout the novel. Mama Chona is dead, but the old ways, the ways of the Rain God, will forever remain with the Angel family, and especially Miguel Chico, in the desert and in their blood.

Miguel Chico's longing for and terror of the desert manifests his unease surrounding the uncanny repetitions of colonial and hegemonic forms of erasure; these fears, complicated by a spectral landscape governed by the Rain God, haunt him throughout the novel. The protagonist's need to "shape himself . . . free of the influence and distortions" (28) of the cultural and moral imperatives signified by Mama Chona is reified by his desire to penetrate the ghostly aspects of an absence encapsulated in the specter of the Rain God. In confronting the trace of this absence, Miguel Chico effectively reinscribes a genealogy of silenced and disqualified forms of knowledge. Finding those shapes that describe absences captures the "paradox of tracking through time" and across the forces that make their mark by being there and not, by both absence and presence (Gordon 2008, 6). In *The Rain God*, the "shape" of absence is signified by the monster of Miguel Chico's nightmare in the final section of the book, titled "The Rain God."

Miguel Chico's final dream in the novel represents his need not to exorcise the past but to integrate racial memories of a collective past to effectively redirect his future. If, as Sánchez (1998) posits, the "home is truly the cave where the monster resides" (122), then the desert, the place that "calls" Miguel Chico to return home, becomes a place of synthesis and, more importantly, renewal. Sánchez maintains that Miguel Chico longs for the desert of his childhood with resentment and concludes that Miguel Chico's near-death experience at the novel's onset compels him to come to terms with the past so as to be free of it, thus mirroring Islas's necessity to achieve freedom from past hierarchical structures. Conversely, I read the monster in the closet as an invitation for Miguel Chico to make contact, to embrace the shadow of what lies beyond the resonance of the present era and develop a sense of historical accounting distinct from the postmodern hypervisibility of the present. If we link the politics of an accounting that insists upon a moral and ethical reckoning with ancestral places that shape and direct personal and communal efforts, then we evoke a structure of feeling that Gordon (2008) insists is "perhaps the most appropriate description of how hauntings are both transmitted and received" (18).

As a child, part of Miguel Chico's "instruction was to accompany Mama Chona on her visits to her sister and her daughters, where, she told them, they would learn proper manners" (161). Additionally, he acknowledges that "[m]uch of the children's knowledge of the family's history as well as its scandals came from these visits" (161). History, then, revolves around familial narratives, but it is a vision of the Rain God entering Mama Chona's hospital room that finally gives Miguel Chico the courage to drop her hand. Only when he feels the Rain God come into the room where Mama Chona lies dying can he say: "Let go of my hand, Mama Chona. I don't want to die" (180). Coming to terms with his double—the monster of his dreams, the "manipulator and the manipulated," the "victim and the slayer," "the loved and the unloved," the "judge and the advocate" (159)—signifies Miguel Chico's moral and ethical reckoning by superposing the strange onto the familiar.

Sánchez (1998) argues that the monster in Miguel Chico's dream symbolizes both family and patriarchy. She reads Miguel Chico's plunge off the bridge with the monster of his nightmare as "his decision to commit suicide with his violator . . . to end the silence and begin writing the story of his family and thus of himself" (120–21). However, if we read the monster as Miguel Chico's "dark double," as does Manuel de Jesús Vega, we decode this symbolic act of descent as a type of conquest in which Miguel Chico finally comes to grips with his sexuality.[7] I believe that Miguel Chico's decision to take the monster with him represents his need to integrate the past in such a way that life and death become linked through time and history, and, more importantly, remembrance and return. With Miguel Chico's dream, the logic of space and time is dissolved such that he can experience wholeness and continuity of past and present. Miguel Chico is both analyst and historian who understands the burden of history as well as the necessary impetus to embrace the "historical imagination." Mario J. Valdés writes,

> Every aspect of the present is grounded in a past of its own, and the very birth of understanding is the imaginative reconstruction of what came before. . . . The aim of the historical imagination is to utilize the fullest spectrum of perception as the starting point for the building of the past through which it has come to be. It is therefore a return to the headwaters of present experience (quoted in Márquez 1994, 4).

Thus, upon awakening from his dream, Miguel Chico's primary mode of knowledge is his need not to banish the dead, but "to make peace with his dead, to prepare a feast for them so that they would stop haunting him. He would feed them words and make his candied skulls out of paper" (160). He conjures a traditional feast, the yearly Mexican holiday of the Day of the Dead, not as an act of merely honoring his dead ancestors, including the Rain God, but to "feed them words" (160), to recall them yearly, and to rewrite their often-neglected histories as well as his own from a new vantage point. As Chela Sandoval (1991) writes of those who act in opposition to hegemony: the struggle, which both begins and ends with the body, brings "into view a new set of alterities and . . . demands that oppositional actors claim new grounds for generating identity, ethics, and a political activity" (9). Miguel Chico's yearly act of homage fortifies his disinterred faith in alternate forms of knowledge and further links an Anzaldúan epistemology of recovery to broader efforts of belonging and justice.

Following Gordon, Martha J. Cutter (2012) argues that understanding haunting as a political force is crucial for both healing and social progress. She writes that understanding and "claiming the disremembered and unaccounted for events, bodies, and identities that haunt US history is vital to social progress" (5). Tlaloc, then, is a force of both retribution and redemption. As "Lord of the Underworld, superior of the souls of the ancestors," he sits in judgment on sinners (Klein 1980, 197). Miguel Chico's "sin," however, emerges as his homosexuality.[8] The struggle with and eventual mastery over the monster of his nightmare signifies a psychic integration with his double in terms of both judgment and a final act of contrition. This symbolic act allows Miguel Chico to ghost back against the silenced and erased voices of the past in an effort to move beyond the cultural scripts that have haunted him as well as previous generations of Angels in the present day. To achieve congruity and possibly coherence, Miguel Chico must legitimate his relationship to the past; he does this by integrating communal memory and communal values onto his body in the form of his closeted monster. By the novel's end, he has the resources and the capital that come with embracing the past—in the novel expressed by the deep references wrenched from the depths of time and geology and inscribed in the desert landscape—to move beyond fragmentation and shame toward remembrance and healing.

Just as American Adams like John Grady Cole and Billy Parham leave home in search of a new life, the individual shapes his or her ultimate reality, and so an individual consciousness serves as the vehicle of that reality. This trajectory results in the failure of such characters to adequately apprehend place. Conversely, in this chapter, we see how longstanding signifiers of place embed fields of gravity more powerful than one's individual will. *Bless Me, Ultima* and *The Rain God* suggest how moving beyond the self towards those experiences and worldviews that recommend a wider transpersonal self, where identity is "not a matter of finding one's self but of finding a self that includes a society, a past, and a place" (Bevis 1987, 585), is key to a sense of unity, rootedness, and an ethics of place. Additionally, tapping the aesthetics of American Gothic tropes and foregrounding a critical regionalist perspective allows us to remap the Southwest as a mythopoetic site that abides parallel cultural realities and speaks to the inclusive timelessness of place.

CHAPTER 6

COMING TO CONSCIOUSNESS ON THE BORDERLANDS AND THE RESTORATION OF ETHICS

U p to now, I have discussed how an understanding of the politics of haunting and the state of being haunted as an avenue to discerning spectral traces within colonized landscapes shifts the focus to modern forms of dispossession, exploitation, and repression for Borderlands subjects. A further sensitivity to the gothic texture of the American Southwest brings those silenced and suppressed histories of the Other to the forefront in ways that effectively ghost against nationalist values and ideologies to suggest how a return to Indigenous forms of belief can manifest a sense of wholeness or mythic unity for subjects who are consequently better poised to read the story of their life and their culture's past correctly, meaningfully, and with an eye towards what Walter Mignolo (2007) calls "delinking" from dominant, often bifurcating, Western epistemologies. De-linking fractures the hegemony and "politics of knowledge organizing the darker side of modernity" (459) that systematically refuses to recognize difference and the possibilities linked to other ways of knowing and being in the world. Importantly, de-linking "changes the terms and not just the content of the conversation" as a goal is to "de-naturalize concepts and conceptual fields that totalize" given realities (459). The objective, then, is not to just manipulate or overturn dominant frontier narratives to focus aspects of the Bordered frontier, but to imbue a sense of restoration and moral obligation while concurrently recovering parallel realities and histories that remain outside the institutions of official knowledge and public memory.

In this chapter, I discuss Alex Rivera's sci-fi film *Sleep Dealer* (2008) in terms of restorative moves within postmodern narratives that illustrate how the coming back of time restores an ethics of place on the Borderlands that is sustainable and speaks to the ways that place and ethics are intimately connected in the Mexican American ethos.[1] Mexican Americans' attachment to place is described by Devon Peña (2005): "[O]ur neighborhood, our hometown or village, the land around us if you will—is as important to our sense of who we are as the common cultural bonds of language, religion, history, food, music, and dress" (xxvii). In *Sleep Dealer* we see how structures of feeling that embed the presence of the past in our everyday lives can dismantle fragmenting, modernist frameworks to free individuals to act on behalf of community and habitat. In the film the coming back of time restores the promise of a sustainable future independent of dominant myths of progress. In anchoring the natural environment to the transformation, or reconstruction, of identity of major players, *Sleep Dealer* reconstitutes a land ethic that counters what Mick Smith (2001) calls "enclosures" of modern economic, legal, or otherwise institutionalized frameworks. A reconstitution of ethics seated within a spatio-temporal paradigm counters such enclosures and "explicitly recognizes the importance of locality and context" and further strengthens "a *sensus communis*, a practical moral sense of the needs and value of our fellows and surroundings that is constitutive of genuine self-identity" (20–21). The goal is to embed an ethics of place, "grounded in the geography of our lives" (6) such that individuals and, subsequently, entire communities begin to dissolve the machinery of totalizing discourses of modernity "indelibly associated with the artificial, the unnatural, and the colonizing" (5). The extension of ethics to land relations in *Sleep Dealer* substantiates pre-emergent structures of feeling crucial to place and place-making. Conversant with Williams, we see how meanings and values "actively lived and felt" dissolve as pre-emergent forms associated with premodern forms of traditional environmental knowledge take shape in the minds and hearts of major players. The result is a new reality and way of being in the world that entwines place and memory in the context of history.

Latin@ Speculative Productions

Scholars suggest that since at least the 1970s, Latin@ cultural productions have engaged speculative and utopic tropes and genres to underscore projects of social and cultural emancipation in their efforts to reclaim and reconceive the future.[2] These efforts contribute to ongoing debates surrounding US structures of racism, historical genocide wrought by projects of modernity, and the complex ways colonized subjects seek to liberate the imagination as a tool of social justice. Speculative works written from the point of view of Indigenous peoples or those who write from a postcolonial or postmodern perspective impart a democratizing lens by which to theorize cultural and material productions that excavate, alter, and create new narratives of identity and belonging. In *Sleep Dealer*, recovery of landscape is directly tied to memory, embodied knowledge, and the transformation of identity that speaks to wider patterns of social dreaming and utopic hope. The film links issues of land use and radical ecology to illustrate how emergent structures of feeling compel "affective elements of consciousness and relationships" to foment an "interrelated continuity" with the past as the social experience of main characters is illustrated as process rather than fixed (Williams 1977, 132).

Sleep Dealer begins with Memo Cruz, a young man who lives with his family in the fictional town of Santa Ana del Rio, Oaxaca, as he recalls the days before the horrible tragedy that forced him to seek work in the sleep dealers of Tijuana. His memories are structured around his father, the *milpa* (cornfield) his father owned and worked, and a huge dam built and operated by an American conglomerate based in San Diego, California. Memo dreams of a world outside of dusty Santa Ana, where the most striking indication of a future twenty-first century is the hi-tech dam built and controlled by Del Rio Water, the US-based company that secures its investment via remote drones and paramilitary might. The company virtually holds the community hostage, charging outrageous amounts for water and hiking up prices on a whim. By night, Memo hacks into the global network using a homemade device. One evening, he stumbles upon the transmission of a security force seeking "aqua-terrorists" in the area of Santa Ana. He shuts down his radio, but it's too late. Unknown to him, his home has become the target of a terrorist intercept. The next day, a drone plane flown by a remote pilot, Rudy in San Diego, annihilates the family home, killing Memo's father. Guilt-ridden, Memo leaves his hometown and migrates to Tijuana to earn money so that the surviving members of his family may live. On the bus ride to Tijuana, Memo meets Luz, a brilliant, yet struggling, writer who sells other people's memories as stories via the global network. She talks to Memo on the long bus ride into Tijuana and downloads his memory via "TruNode," described as "the world's number one memory market." She does not tell Memo that she has used his memory. To her surprise, the memory sells and the unknown buyer prepays for more memories. The buyer wants to know why Memo is in Tijuana and where his family is—notably his father. So begins the strangely intimate triangle that propels the highly original, socially minded plot of *Sleep Dealer*.

In this future dystopia where the Mexico–US border is sealed by brute military force, Mexican workers telecommute from Tijuana—"The City of the Future"—and transmit their labor while connected to the global economy via their bodies' nervous systems. *Maquiladoras*, called "sleep dealers" by workers because they toil until they collapse, have become virtual factories. Here, human bodies fitted with nodes are plugged in like so many manikins and drained of their labor (figure 6). This system of virtual labor provides the United States with "all the workers it wants without the immigrants"—the American Dream in a dystopic nutshell.

In an earlier essay, I focus on dehumanizing labor practices and Donna Haraway's cyborg metaphor to show how the film's three main characters, Memo, Rudy, and Luz—intermittent cyborgs—destabilize the boundaries between humans and the natural environment to illustrate the metaphoric potential of individual responsibility that must attend an escalating environmental crisis of the Mexico–US border. Additionally, I discuss how the trio inaugurates tangible, egalitarian social change in the Borderlands.[3] This chapter marks a return to the decolonizing mode of inquiry illustrated in chapter 1 and further positions the theories of Gloria Anzaldúa to show how modernist practices of landscape exploitation in the Borderlands merge with acts of recovery and shifts in consciousness. In the film, Memo's recovery of a history that has effectively been rendered ghostly mobilizes his coming to consciousness in an Anzaldúan sense. The connective tissue that binds *Sleep Dealer* to *Lone Star* becomes clear when we bear in mind how a modern infrastructure has effectively hegemonized Indigenous forms of an earlier self-sufficient land-owning culture by shifting the power structure

Figure 6: "Cybraceros" connect to the virtual net through their nervous systems in *Sleep Dealer* (2008). Courtesy of Alex Rivera.

as it relates to water. In *Sleep Dealer*, however, a premodern way of life that has literally had its lifeblood (water) impounded and apprehended is liberated when Memo, Rudy, and Luz destroy the dam. Through the use of the master's own tools they decolonize the landscape and release the mythical and historical forces that have been sedimented into the landscape as structures of feeling. When the trio explode the dam, they liberate an earlier self-sufficient and sustainable way of life effectively held hostage by the capitalization of a natural resource on the Borderlands.

As scientists and citizens from all walks of life have become increasingly aware, we are on the cusp of a global environmental crisis of progressively limited natural resources where access to clean water and sustainable landscapes threaten the existence of entire communities. Policies steeped in environmental racism and environmental marginalization of native cultures along the Mexico–US Borderlands in the twenty-first century often focus on the impacts and effects of NAFTA. In *Sleep Dealer*, the Bracero Program, the agricultural guest worker initiative prompted by the US demand for manual labor during World War II that began in 1942 and ran through 1964, is the catalyst that indicts a destructive American capitalist system at the expense of its wage earners. The antagonist here is not technology, unchecked industrial development, or even the environmental damage that the passage of NAFTA in 1992 brought to the Borderlands. Rather, as Miguel Lopez-Lozano (2008) has argued of dystopian works, governmental systems that continue to "instrumentalize" human beings "for the ends of the dictatorial state or the needs of the market" are clearly implicated (19).

The film disrupts twenty-first century projects of modernization that systematically contribute to the erasure of poor, marginalized communities via dehumanizing labor practices.[4] It both contributes to readings herein that indict modernist systems which fail to account for place, memory, and history, as well as speaks to the ways projects of hope can challenge the living present to enact egalitarian change in the Borderlands.

Where works like *The Rain God* and *Bless Me, Ultima* delineate an alternative hermeneutics of ethnic identity and belonging, *Sleep Dealer* moves along a similar trajectory to show how a return to ethics and personal responsibility "interrupts the abstractions of the state structure" (Butler and Spivak 2007, 100). Drawing together strands from previous chapters in combination with an understanding of the differences between what Mick Smith (2001) describes as "the *moral architecture* of modernity and the anarchic, postmodern *ethics of place* that characterizes radical environmentalism" (151, italics in original) moves us towards an understanding of how we might move beyond the tensions that spatial mobility and capital wrest from the permanence of place. Just as elite Laredoans have preserved their capital investment in a disingenuous narrative through the perpetual devaluation of precapitalist encumbrances of geography, so too in *Sleep Dealer* has Del Rio Water deliberately abnegated natural geographical configurations that once rooted Indigenous ways of knowing and being to premodern, sustainable modes of being and production. Contextualizing the movements of the main characters in the film within a decolonial framework dissolves the machinery of the totalizing discourse signified by the dam in a way that links an ethics of place to a Borderlands bioregion.

Borderlands as Bioregion

During the first few minutes of the film, the audience is confronted with one of the most pernicious lessons of George Orwell's *Nineteen Eighty-Four*: "Who controls the past, controls the future: who controls the present controls the past."[5] The scene takes place at sundown and is filtered by the warm orange glow of the Mexican desert. It combines expansive long shots with close-ups to fuse the characters' emotional state to the landscape. Two men stand before their small cornfield, preparing to water the few rows by hand; a warm breeze rustles the plants. The younger man, Memo, asks his father why their family remains in the rural town of Santa Ana, Mexico.

Memo: Hey, Pop, can I ask you . . . Why are we still here?
Father: Well, let me ask you. . . . Is our future a thing of the past?
Memo: (Laughs)
Father: You think it's funny?
Memo: Well, yeah. That's impossible.
Father: No. We had a future. You're standing on it. When they dammed up the river, they cut off our future.[6]

Memo's baseball cap, baggy jeans, and basketball jersey accentuate his youth and his distance from his Mexican culture. His father, darker and sun ravaged, wears the traditional attire of a farmer: long-sleeved cotton shirt, boots, and a straw cowboy hat. Memo is too young to recall the change in land use exemplified by Del Rio Water. His father, however, recognizes Del Rio Water as the basis of a power shift that altered the local community from a land-owning culture of self-sufficient Mexican farmers to a class of poor, landless laborers. In this way, the scene narratively and visually establishes a central conflict between competing narratives entwined in the power shift that has transformed their community's economic and cultural status. The modern narrative framed by Del Rio Water alienates the community from place, history, and memory; the premodern narrative espoused by Memo's father harks to a reckoning with the instrumentality of a haunted landscape that can move the rural village "beyond fragmentation, toward forms of remembrance and coherence" (Cutter 2012, 6). Significantly, the scene both foreshadows and parallels the film's final sequence in which Memo comes to terms with his own history as well as how his future, and that of his entire community, can become "a thing of the past."

Bioregions have a unique cultural identity, often spanning the borders of two or more countries, and are small enough for local residents to consider home. Lawrence Buell (2005) writes, "a bioregion or ecoregion is a geographical area of similar climate where similar ecosystems and groups of species are found on similar sites" (135). Notably, argues Buell, bioregions encompass "a domain of consciousness" as well as a "focus of citizenly allegiance that challenges conventional political boundaries" (135). Smith (2001) looks to Jim Cheney's landmark essay on postmodern environmental ethics to argue that an understanding of bioregions and the means by which these shape the "ecological self" bring to bear a view of expanded notions of place that include nature as an active agent in the construction of our communities. The result is an "anchoring" of place to the narratives that shape our values and our lives.[7] This position provides us with a trajectory to better understand how communities like Laredo, in enacting dominant myths of progress dependent on artifice and an abstraction of space, effectively estrange entire communities of place memories. Place memories, for Cresswell (2015), speak to the ways that places "contain" experience. For the most part, however, he concludes that places of memory generally serve to "commemorate the winners of history" (122). This becomes obvious when we think of public places like state capitols, museums, and monuments around the globe that commemorate *particular* views of history and social life. Indeed, until quite recently places of memory have not often served to commemorate the poor, women, the dispossessed, or other minority figures, as such are often bound within painful or otherwise shameful memories. As such, Cresswell concludes that "the question of which memories are promoted and which cease to be memories at all is a political question" (123), a fact made evident by the specious narrative surrounding Laredo's annual George Washington's Birthday Celebration.

Priscilla Solis Ybarra (2009) positions a central concern of Anzaldúa's as the exploitation of the Borderlands bioregion when she argues that her "environmental awareness helped her see the human crisis in [the] region as well as how the land's exploitation relates to injustices in the human community" (185). Anzaldúa (2012) positions the Mexico–US border as a distinctive bioregion in *Borderlands* when she likens the South Texas landscape to a coiled serpent: "I know Earth is a coiled Serpent," she writes. "Forty years it's taken me to enter the Serpent, to acknowledge that I have a body, that I am a body and to assimilate the animal body, the animal soul" (48). In the section titled "El retorno," she returns home to "watch the curling, twisting serpent, a serpent nailed to the fence where the mouth of the Rio Grande empties into the Gulf" (111). Anzaldúa characterizes the river as "a serpent nailed to the fence." The river is not merely a symbol of the natural environment unnaturally staked. Rather, it is the means by which she asserts the interdependence and reciprocity between humans and nonhuman nature. Her depiction leaves us with a vision of the region and its people nailed to the unnatural built environment of a border fence that cuts and separates rather than heals and unites. By fusing her physical body with the body of the earth, she compels an understanding of the complex nature of her ecological and spatial awareness. This stance further reveals how a master narrative in which the colonization of a natural resource directly relates to broader human injustices in the Borderlands.

Under the threat of "Anglo terrorism," writes Anzaldúa, she and others living in a Borderlands of constant transition remain "separated from our identity and history" (30), an idea that directly parallels the *milpa* scene. Memo's father tells him, *"no sabes ni quién eres"* (you don't even know who you are). With these words, he unknowingly sets in motion Memo's eventual pursuit of his identity, a search that begins with the sleep dealers of Tijuana and ends in ecological revolution as well as Memo's understanding of his father's implication of a "future that is a thing of the past." Initially, Memo does not comprehend how one's future can be a "thing of the past." His father's pronouncement, however, is an admonishment of Memo's desire to erase the history ensconced in his father's traditional environmental knowledge. The conversation at the *milpa* ends with Memo's father asking him if he would like to see the family *milpa* destroyed, to which Memo answers *"exacto."* This exchange is directly related to the change in land use exemplified by Del Rio Water, and the shift from a self-reliant land-owning culture signified by his father. The floundering *milpa* signifies Memo's cultural inheritance—at this point in the film, nothing more than a ghostly nuisance. Importantly, his father grows beans and corn, staples that thrive symbiotically, foregrounding the inextricable linkages between humans and the natural environment. This symbiotic relationship is a cornerstone of Mexican traditional environmental knowledge, which underscores communal expressions of identity and is "a particular form of place-based knowledge" that harks to the Mayan concept of *in lak ech* ("you are my other self") (Peña 2005, 53, 198).

Anzaldúa (2012) describes the Mexico–US border as a landscape in "a constant state of transition" where "the only 'legitimate' inhabitants are those in power, the whites and those who align themselves with whites" (25–26). As described, the historical exploitation of the landscape directly parallels Anzaldúa's *mestiza* consciousness. As she details how the land has endured centuries of ill treatment by various and shifting political regimes, Anzaldúa merges the land's abuse with the mistreatment of its native inhabitants: "Our psyches resemble the bordertowns and are populated by the same people" (109). Any emancipatory, consciousness-raising struggle, she insists, is first inner, and then played out in the outer terrains. Integration within the material body may be achieved by un-covering, re-membering, and re-appropriating what she calls the *desconocimientos* of an internal colonialism born from the shame and terrorism of cultural tyranny in the Borderlands. *Desconocimientos* are shadows, ghostly and as yet "unacceptable attributes and unconscious forces that a person must wrestle with to achieve integration" (Anzaldúa 2002, 309). Acts of recovery—whether of history, memory, or culture—reside within the material body as well as the body of the earth. She insists: "Every essay, fiction, poem I write is grounded in the land, the environment, the body, and therefore in the past/ancestors. Every piece enacts recovery" (2009a, 292). When we link ideas of recovery to an ecological ethic that positions the Mexico–US Borderlands as a bioregion, the utopian pulse of the film is manifest.

Coming to Consciousness on the Borderlands

Memo's emergent consciousness, like Anzaldúa's, is directly tied to the Earth. For Anzaldúa (2002), "The snake is a symbol of awakening consciousness—the potential of knowing within, an awareness and intelligence not grasped by logical thought" (540). In *Sleep Dealer*, Memo "awakens" when he puts his "history through a sieve" (Anzaldúa 2012, 104) and relearns to embrace his Indigenous ties to the landscape. Anzaldúa maintains that when this is done, we reinterpret history through the use of new symbols and the shaping of new myths. Moreover, we can trace the trajectory of those who aim to communicate such a rupture with the goal of reconstructing individual identities so as to work to "transform the small 'I' into the total Self" (104–5). The total Self is achieved only as it is contained within a viable relationship to the terrain. Transformation, emergence, and renewal occur—just as consciousness does—*within*; such changes, however, are reflected in, and reflective of, outer terrains. This trajectory is evident in *Sleep Dealer*, as Memo's conscious rupture with an oppressive cultural tradition of disposable labor (*maquiladora*, or cyber-*maquiladora* work) that estranges his physical body from the actual work he performs ends with the successful destruction of the dam. The dam is a signifier of the machine, but it also represents a rupture in time; it has symbolically detached his entire community from its prior self-determining, precolonial landowning and farming heritage.

Memo "awakens" when he embraces the wilted Indigenous landowning culture of his father. In "Speaking across the Divide," Anzaldúa (2009a) suggests that the promise of psychic integration rests in the recovery of an Indigenous landscape. This idea of "the interconnectedness of people and nature and all things, an awareness that people [are] part of nature and not separate from it" (282) undergirds Anzaldúa's theory of *nepantla*, the Nahuatl word meaning "in-between space." In Anzaldúan thought (2002), *nepantla* is a liminal, transitional space, a zone of possibility where you're two people, split between before and after. . . . In *nepantla* you are exposed, open to other perspectives, more readily able to access knowledge derived from inner feelings, imaginal states, and outer events, and to "see through" them with a mindful, holistic awareness (544).

For Anzaldúa (2009c), only when we come to grips with our *deconocimientos*—ignored knowledge from the past—can we rethink the borders of our bodies and identities to engage strategic acts of reparation. Memo confronts his personal *desconocimientos* to transform what he initially believes comprises the prescribed limits of his body. Rudy, too, signifies a process of coming to consciousness, as described briefly herein. The decolonizing movements of both Rudy and Memo directly result in a decolonized landscape. Once Memo and Rudy come to terms with their personal *desconocimientos*, they are empowered to "become sentinels, bearers of witness, makers of historias" (248).

Testimonio and Crossing Over

Sleep Dealer opens with a series of fluid images and swirls of supersaturated colors. Slowly moving hands, eyes, and the electric blue tendons that connect Memo's nervous system to the virtual network flash across the screen and bleed into the gauzy, hallucinatory images of his mind. Here a procession of women in peasant garb drifts by, and there stands his father amidst the arid desert landscape of his home. These are Memo's memories, and they float dreamily across the screen, a mirror of his mind's eye. A heartbeat links the images, and now we hover, as we might in Rudy's drone. The images fade, as does Memo's voice, and the first realistic frame is of water pouring from a glass. His mother is making tortillas, and we have slipped with Memo from his present as a cyber-*maquiladora* worker into the past, to a time when his father was alive.

Shaped by Memo's memories, the events in *Sleep Dealer* are related in the past tense to viewers, making the film a visual *testimonio*. In the introduction to *Telling to Live* (2001), The Latina Feminist Group situates testimonies, or life stories, as "critical in movements for liberation in Latin America, offering an artistic form and methodology to create politicized understandings of identity and community" (3). Mohanty (2003) affirms that the "primary purpose" of *testimonio* is to "document and record the history of popular struggles, foreground experiential and historical 'truth' which has been erased or rewritten in hegemonic, elite, or imperialistic history, and bear witness in order to change oppressive state rule" (81). The *testimonio* strategy is to speak from "*within* a collective, as participants in revolutionary struggles, and to speak with the express purpose of bringing about social and political change" (81, italics in original). In Latin American women's writings, *testimonios* produce complicity in the reader as they offer the potential to move beyond the fissures of public and private spheres. Thus, Mohanty argues, they are about building relationships between the *testimonio*'s subject and the receiver of his or her story in order to invite and precipitate change (82).

Sleep Dealer is told in the form of Memo's *testimonio* to emphasize the significance of recorded history as a basis for the constitution of memory. It foregrounds questions of ideology politics, social reality, and counter-visions of history. Because it is "by, for, and about" brown bodies resisting via an oppositional politics, it is closely aligned with earlier Chican@ films, which Rosa Linda Fregoso (1993) has persuasively argued "developed within the context of the Chicano Power Movement's struggle of anti-racism," and encompass efforts for equality, self-determination, human rights, and social justice (xvii). However, its emphasis on water rights, disembodied workers, and disposable labor practices that continue to threaten the livelihood of marginalized communities foregrounds broader, universal themes that have become increasingly tied to our globalized world. Additionally, the film "questions the promises of science, technology, and humanism" as it reflects the diasporic experiences of Mexicans and Mexican Americans, thus aligning it with works Catherine S. Ramírez has called Chicanafuturism.[8] For all of these reasons, I suggest that *Sleep Dealer* effectively pushes the "for" aspect of Fregoso's trinity; this film is "for" anyone who is, first, troubled by the dehumanizing labor practices of today's global market economy, and, second, hopeful about the power of individuals to enact change.

The *testimonio* format supplies an intertextual mode of storytelling to focus the relation of past to present, but it is also meant to rouse, perhaps incite, an audience's thinking. What does it mean to have a history without a past? What happens when the flow of capital, ideas, images, and technologies operates within a culturally schizophrenic landscape where one person's community becomes another person's prison? These are just two of the urgent questions that feed the humanistic pulse of *Sleep Dealer*. Yet, like all serious science fiction, *Sleep Dealer* is idea-based, and so it delivers more questions than answers.

In the final minutes of the film, Memo approaches Luz with the proposition that they join forces with Rudy. Initially, Luz cannot comprehend Memo's position. However, Rudy is only able to confront Memo after he has come to terms with his own *desconocimientos*. His words echo an earlier conversation between Luz and Memo in which she relates the story of her own crossing of what she calls an "invisible border." This echo of the word "crossing" solidifies Memo's belief in Rudy, and Luz's faith in Memo:

> Luz: You want me to plug him in?
> Memo: Yes.
> Luz: This is crazy. He's a killer.
> Memo: He's here because of you, because of your stories.
> Luz: That doesn't mean we have to help him.
> Memo: Luz—Think about it. Remember what you told me about crossing to the other side?
> Luz: Yes.
> Memo: That's what he did. He crossed over. All we have to do is help him.

A postmodern figure who alternates between the organic and technological body, Rudy eventually comes to terms with the subject–object duality that holds him prisoner within an ideology of fixed borders. In the film's first half, Rudy's gaze is bifurcated (figure 7). From above, as a cyber soldier and in his drone, he is hypnotized by a corporatized, ideological system in which the Other (Memo's father, the man behind the misbegotten terrorist intercept) signifies "terrorist." Rudy views Memo's father in much the same way Maria Garza views Woodrow Call before she actually sets eyes on him as just an old man who wears the torn wrappings of the Texas Ranger but no longer performs the role. Rudy is a weapon, a cog in the corporate machine. As a cyber worker, where his labor power "is jacked in, tuned out, and systematically drained of its value by an invisibly remote ruling class" (Clover 2009, 8), he is disembodied mind from flesh; he signifies what Daniel Dinello (2005) and others have called a "technologist vision," one facet of which is to elevate technology to divine status.[9] In *Sleep Dealer* this is fitting because Rudy "plays God" when he obeys a disembodied directive and opens fire from above on Memo's father, an innocent man helplessly crawling from the wreckage of his obliterated home.

In the film, Rudy—much like Captain Call in *Streets of Laredo*—inhabits a third space, a place in time that exists "in-between the violent and the violated, the accused and the accuser, allegation and admission" (Bhabha 2006, x). This site is a contact zone of opportunity where Rudy effectively, and in Memo's words, "crosses over." Anzaldúa (2012) uses the term "cross over" to describe the Coatlicue state, a kind of "way station" where one kicks a

Figure 7: Rudy Ramirez, drone pilot, Del Rio Water company is featured on the reality show, *Drones!* in *Sleep Dealer* (2008). Courtesy of Alex Rivera.

hole out of "the old boundaries of the self" to become truly vigilant, "that which abides[,] ... [a] thousand sleepless serpent eyes blinking in the night, forever open" (71, 73). Rudy is an American citizen who virtually crosses into Mexico as part of his job as a drone pilot for Del Rio Water. Only after he decides to track Memo down does he physically cross into Mexico. And although *Sleep Dealer* is presented in Spanish with English subtitles, Rudy and his parents speak English.[10] As Sandoval (1999) describes in "New Sciences," a white male [read: Rudy]—indeed, *any* citizen subject existing under first-world conditions of transnationalization—may act in opposition to and beyond a dominant ideology when engaging the tactics of a differential consciousness, a strategy of oppositional consciousness embedded within US feminist theoretical tracts. Note that this is the same trajectory we see Sam Deeds following in *Lone Star*.

Rudy first appends Memo's father to the signified: terrorist. But he increasingly desires to *own* his actions. In time, he chooses responsibility in order to "enact recovery" (Anzaldúa 2009a, 292). His physical and psychical search leads him to disclose a narrative that will push him from a state of objectification to identification. In the linkages among perception, bodily sensation, and intellectual comprehension, Rudy eventually comes to acknowledge and subsequently apprehend the signified—the concept "terrorist" in the *form* of Memo's father—as "empty." This is an example of "sign reading," a technology of the oppressed in Sandoval's methodology. In this case, sign reading emerges as a tool of survival and, ultimately, transformative change.

Ecological Revolution on the Borderlands

Only when Rudy is externally removed from his cyber body is he able to take what Anzaldúa (2012) calls an "evolutionary step forward" to "become the quickening serpent movement" (103) where transformation can occur. Rudy's "performative utterance"—to borrow a term from Homi Bhabha (2006)—in a bioregional Borderlands space, transforms the three actors into "agents of a new hybrid national narration" (Ikas 1984, 129). This is achieved as the triad moves from what Donna Haraway deems the "standpoint of the subjugated"—whereby subaltern peoples put into practice the cyborg skills they must necessarily develop as "outsider identities," through what Sandoval terms a "rhetoric of resistance" (1999, 255, 257). These moves are performed within the third space, via a technology of differential consciousness. As such, their collective performance "occurs in a register permitting the networks themselves to be appropriated as ideological weaponry" (260).

Sandoval (1991) defines differential consciousness as a "topography of consciousness in opposition . . . which identifies nothing more and nothing less than the modes the subordinated of the United States (of any gender, race, or class) claim as politicized and oppositional stances in resistance to domination" (11). For Sandoval, differential consciousness is a powerful strategy of oppositional consciousness because it is mobile, "a kinetic motion that maneuvers, poetically transfigures, and orchestrates while demanding alienation, perversion, and reformation in both spectators and practitioners" (3). In *Methodology of the Oppressed* (2000), Sandoval examines the juncture that connects the disoriented first-world citizen-subject who longs for a new sense of identity and redemption in a postmodern space alongside forms of oppositional consciousness as developed by subordinated or colonized Western citizen-subjects (9). Of Haraway, Sandoval (1999) writes: "[H]er cyborg feminism is capable of insisting on an alignment between what was once hegemonic feminist theory with theories of what are locally apprehended as indigenous resistance, 'mestizaje,' US third world feminism, or the differential mode of oppositional consciousness" (253).[11]

Sleep Dealer embraces an ecological, decolonizing approach to individual and collective history by reasserting the idea of nature and the natural world as historical actor. In the end, both Rudy and Memo understand that they can never go home.[12] When Rudy comes to terms with his *desconocimientos*, he dislocates his techno-body from his cultural body, thereby marking the distance from a corporatized, master narrative of colonization in which he can easily absolve himself of any responsibility. In confronting and finally apprehending an ideology deprived of true historical meaning, his consciousness is "interrupted." This positions him to bridge or transcend "horizons for translating and communicating the multiple elements and experiences of the self and the other that are simultaneously present and thought to interact in a contact zone" (Ikas 2009, 130). When he finally locates Memo, he does so to effect justice; he holds out his arms to Memo, displaying the implanted nodes that connect him to the virtual network, and says, "I'll do anything." This is not an empty gesture; it is an invitation to action. Memo comprehends this when he tells Luz that Rudy has "crossed over." These moments in time and space are bridges. Rudy's disembodied action of killing Memo's father can mean something in the new space of his body only when he can connect, or bridge, that initial action to a subsequent action of reparation. For Anzaldúa (2009a), "Once *conocimiento* (awareness) is reached, you have to act in the light of your knowledge" (292). By the film's end, Rudy makes a conscious decision to perform an action—push the button and destroy the dam—contrary to the "machine," signified by Del Rio Water. But he is only able to do this when he becomes the conscious operator of his own flesh. "In our very flesh," writes Anzaldúa (2012), "(r)evolution works out the clash of cultures" (103).

A New Story of Hope and Sustainability

Sleep Dealer is a critical dystopia that shows how memory—individual and cultural—must form "part of a social project of hope" (Baccolini 2004, 521). Significantly, Baccolini argues that a utopian outlook sustains the critical dystopia: "It is in the acceptance of responsibility and accountability, often worked through memory and the recovery of the past, that we bring the past into a living relation with the present and thus begin to lay the foundations for utopian change" (521). Additionally, as an audience engages *Sleep Dealer* via *testimonio*, we enter a third space of cultural critique and political confrontation, as the potential of memory as a form of cultural resistance coalesces wide-ranging possibilities for local responses to broader ideas of environmental racism and issues of social justice on the Borderlands. By according sustainable ecological principles a place in the narrative of cultural and historical memory, the film moves from a confining, post-industrial, corporatized model where natural resources are managed and controlled for profit towards a more sustainable paradigm where, in order to thrive, we actively, and in the spirit of mimesis, "make ourselves

Figure 8: Drone pilot Rudy Ramirez destroys the Del Rio Dam via drone with the help of Memo and Luz. *Sleep Dealer* (2008). Courtesy of Alex Rivera.

'like' the environment, not as object, but in the deepest sense of visceral remerging with the earth" (Merchant 1989, 267).

Environmental historian Carolyn Merchant (1989) maintains that ecological revolutions are major transformations in human relations with non-human nature that arise from changes, tensions, and contradictions that develop between society's mode of production and its ecology, as well as between its modes of production and reproduction. These dynamics, she adds, "support the acceptance of new forms of consciousness, ideas, images, and worldviews" (2). As part of her organizational framework, she demonstrates how forms of consciousness are power structures. "When one worldview is challenged and replaced by another during a scientific or ecological revolution," writes Merchant, "power over society, nature, and space is at stake" (22). In *Sleep Dealer*, the complex actions entwined in Rudy's and Memo's coming to consciousness culminate in an ecological revolution, a revolution in which a natural resource—water—bound, capitalized, and corporatized for profit, is effectively liberated and redirected to run its natural course, thereby immediately impacting non-human nature alongside the Indigenous economy (figure 8).

I believe that when Gloria Anzaldúa (2012) attests, "[l]ike the ancients, I worship the rain god and the maize goddess, but unlike my father I have recovered their names" (112), she is speaking of an ancient, continuous story that *mestizas/os* must recover on their way towards a new consciousness. In

Sleep Dealer, this is a consciousness directly seated in a recovery of history and cultural memory by the main characters, Rudy and Memo. Their *conocimientos* are situated in a Borderlands ethics of knowledge and landscape that reaches its apex in a synthesis of Indigenous, Mexican, and Anglo cultures. Anzaldúa's struggle, the struggle of the *mestiza*, culminates in return and rebirth, and the final image she presents us with in her *Borderlands* chapter, "*La conciencia de la mestiza*," is one of sowing and planting in her homeland terrain in the American Southwest. "Growth, death, decay, birth," she writes. "The soil prepared again and again, impregnated, worked on. A constant changing of forms, *renacimientos de la tierra madre*" (113). *Sleep Dealer* ends similarly, with Memo watering the seeds of his own small *milpa* on the edge of Tijuana. His final words hark to a "history with a past" and a commitment to fight for a sustainable future where diversity and difference are central values. "But maybe there's a future for me here," says Memo. "A future with a past. If I connect . . . and fight."

CONCLUSION

I t was many years later, as a graduate student, that I made the connection between my father's need to reclaim a past tied to La Tinaja de Lara and my mother's conviction that she was doing the work of history as a member of the Princess Pocahontas Council. In many ways, *The Haunted Southwest* began as an attempt to ghost back against the discourse of loss she and the other women on the council are partly responsible for perpetuating. The collective hallucination that is the Washington's Birthday Celebration incapacitates and splinters social and public memory. And so, the city remains haunted by the parallel realities of Mexican, Chican@, and Mexican American cultural forms that yet inhabit the landscape and underlie the everyday. In disidentifying with place, the main performances of the WBCA and the Princess Pocahontas Council do little to oblige Laredo's citizenry to act on behalf of place, biosphere, or habitat.

In *Lone Star*, we see how the false public narrative surrounding the mythic sheriff Buddy Deeds catalyzes his son's confrontation with his own contrived history such that he is finally able to discern the truth behind both the murder of Charlie Wade and his own disquieting childhood. Likewise, in Laredo, the circulation of public narratives that made it possible to silence factual environments of memory like La Tinaja perpetuate forms of historical and cultural disidentification with place to the detriment of inclusivity and diversity for *all citizens* who call this locale their home. Stories that remain buried beneath the ragged edges of the Bordered frontier challenge neocolonial practices that continue to marginalize entire cultures and fragment identities on the Borderlands, especially in terms of structures of feeling that presuppose the social being as living and felt rather than fixed. Postmodern works like *Sleep Dealer*, *Bless Me, Ultima*, and *The Rain*

God further speak to the ways that dominant systems of belief influence, explain, and factor into the social consciousness of individuals as they are lived. As the "produced institutions" of the past crumble, so too do embryonic pre-emergent structures of feeling take shape (Williams 1977, 128).

If a contrived history of Laredo continues to be celebrated publicly—as it certainly will—what is *not* being celebrated? For example, what can the stories of dispossession that began to resurface in the 1980s as a result of the Asociación de Reclamantes tell us about the varied cultural and native forms or prior living arrangements in the area? Could the narratives of *mestizos* of Spanish blood who were born in the US and who later established the earliest *ranchos* in the area surrounding Los Dos Laredos shatter the false public memories that surround the WBCA? Can such narratives effectively liberate early cultural forms from the gothic experience rendered along the frontiers of discourse in the Southwest? Laredo as a case study encapsulates a central position of *The Haunted Southwest*. The point is not how or why misleading and illusionary narratives gain the traction necessary to silence *actual* historical realities, but how to confront the ghostly aspects, those traces and absences, that remain as both structures of feeling and parallel realities ensconced in the landscape itself, for only a reckoning with all stories on the Bordered frontier will yield those bridges that both bind and separate the past from the present. Further, a decolonial stance that engages values and processes that reject Western epistemologies in order to make space for Indigenous practices that have survived colonizing structures breaks down the destructive spatial poetics of the American frontier with the goal of reintegrating place and place-making processes of Indigenous practices that have survived colonization and that preserve a land ethic nourished by premodern forms of knowledge.

The neoliberal modernist turn of our eyes and hearts to the immediate promises of power and profit, claim the editors of *Arts of Living on a Damaged Planet* (2017), regularly outpaces the biorhythms of life in a given geographical space.[1] Ghosts, they argue, are uncanny signifiers of indeterminate environmental and biological disruptions, those assemblages of the dead that remind us that we live in an "impossible present—a time of rupture, a world haunted with the threat of extinction" (G6). This pattern is exemplified by the destructive environmental effects of investment capital in *Sleep Dealer*, an arrangement only hinted at in *Lone Star*. Ghosts and hauntings, claim the authors of *Damaged Planet*, speak to possibilities and strategies that stretch beyond the bifurcating commitments of modernity and towards more sustainable futures *for the planet* as opposed to the select few. Although the essays focus generally on the natural, biological, and ecological sciences and the complex designs of animal, human, and environment that shape our present in the Anthropocene, the heart of *Damaged Planet* is an understanding of how "the debris of capitalist waste, the unspectacular lives of discarded things" (G3) come together with the living. The goal is to de-link from dominant myths of progress that, in the second half of the twentieth century, neither privilege an ethics of place nor anchor the immediate natural environment in the construction of community.

Mark Turner, author of *The Literary Mind* (1998), reminds us that stories are a central organizing principle of experience and knowledge. Stories shape the way we view our world before anything else, and the language we adopt gives structure to how we think about our world.[2] I began this book with my father, a *mestizo* who remained haunted throughout his lifetime by the stakes of imperial ghosting laid bare by systematized corresponding structures of feeling shaped by a frontier mythos in the American Southwest—a ruling mythology of infinite space to be possessed and capitalized. His story mirrors my own and is complicated by other facts based in my mother's lineage, which have been traced to early Mexican pioneers who settled Texas under New Spain in the early decades of the nineteenth century.[3] As a tenth-generation *tejana*, I, too, remain haunted by a lack of sure-footedness inseparable from a culture of amnesia where moral certainty and a connection between place and ethics seems impossible. I am haunted by what cannot be forgotten, by what must always be remembered. Only when we create living environments appropriate to our pasts will the signifiers of haunted landscapes be mitigated.

When essential foundations for belief are once more treasured, no longer hemmed or entombed in the cultural past, earlier practices and relationships with the landscape held by Chican@s, Mexicans, and Mexican Americans on the border can be understood in their own right and as parallel realities. Denaturalizing a complex term like "landscape" within the Bordered frontier positions us to delink from ruling, bifurcating Western epistemologies that create blind spots in the historical record. This is a path taken by Priscilla Solis Ybarra (2016), who writes about Mexican American and Chican@ environmental writing in terms of community, non-possessiveness, and humility, aspects that surround what she calls "goodlife writing." By bringing ethnic studies and mainstream environmental studies into conversation, she breaks down the mainstream Western dichotomy between humans and

nature to accommodate Indigenous practices and narratives that have survived colonial practices to preserve and adapt traditional environmental
knowledge. In this sense, she proposes a more nuanced understanding of
environmentalism—and, correspondingly, landscape—that is invested in
building bridges between strands of knowing that posit mutually beneficial relationships between humans and the natural world. Goodlife writing
embeds traditions of community, non-possessiveness, and humility that
have never succumbed to modernist values.[4]

Because historical ghosts speak of denials, erasures, and unresolved
spaces of national violence, shifting the focus from the individual level to
the social further speaks to erasures at the wider societal level. Films like
Lone Star and postmodern narratives of the Bordered frontier such as those
of haunted cowboys discussed herein call out for a reckoning and an understanding of how identity in the Southwest continues to be haunted by a
cultural script that is inapt in terms of sustainability—for the language of
the frontier is an artifice rooted in a tenuous reality and scripted for the few.
The Southwest Borderlands encompass and entwine fluid sites of cultural
exchange and negotiation where the contradictions and challenges of a still
extant frontier mythology lies hidden just beneath the surface of the landscape itself. Exposing the frontier's underbelly brings to the forefront the
silenced and buried histories of the Bordered frontier. The stories of the
places, spaces, and peoples of the Southwest cannot be seen as linear narratives. Rather, like works in progress, the stories entwined in the spaces
and places along the Southwestern Borderlands encompass works of the
imagination, constantly reinventing themselves and, therefore, the history
and people who yet inhabit the landscape. What is unabated, what is eternal
in the American Southwestern mythology, is a sense of place. Hidden certainly, but not lost, and waiting to be reclaimed.

EPILOGUE

Since my college days, my greatest solace, my most perfect moments of peace, come when I ride my mountain bike over the rough terrain and through the *senderos* of my uncle's ranch off Highway 359 in Laredo. I am not a runner like my father, but like him, I require those connections with "the old earth itself" to feel grounded to a landscape that is more than terrain, more than property or real estate. I love this place. Each thing that shoots up from the forever-parched earth sticks, needles, or prickles the skin. The thorns and spines that flourish here compel one to look and tread closely. Rushing through the natural landscape is not just dangerous, it is impossible. Along the dusty, unpaved road to the ranch, I pass a small *colonia* complete with its own ballroom. I feel rooted on the ranch. What grounds me is the sameness of the dusty gravel under my feet, the constancy of the syrupy, bitter smell of mesquite. From the high ridges of this place, I can see the mountains of Mexico; but I also see the new landfill and a number of new fracking sites. If I use my binoculars, I can spot a new detention center and ICE facility.

Growing up on the Texas border meant that I grew up juggling conflicting ideologies and ways of being in the world. In Laredo, which straddles its Mexican "sister city" Nuevo Laredo to the south and an expansive frontier to the north, east, and west, this was not difficult to do. By the time I was seventeen, I was driving *al otro lado* into Nuevo Laredo without a thought that I was entering another country; it was all the same to me. The border was intrinsic to my worldview, and it was entwined in an expansive Texas landscape where people, goods, and ideas moved fluidly. The International Bridge that connected Laredo to Nuevo Laredo was just another road.

Almost everyone I came in contact with seemed to exist comfortably on both sides of more than one culture and language. Like the works in *The Haunted Southwest* that detail the varied complexities of the Bordered frontier, the daily lives of many, if not most, Borderlands citizens encompass, and indeed flit between, Mexico and the United States. But what will always hold me is the singular resonance of the old earth that kept my father running all those years, for it is here that ghostly forces—those ancient, continuous stories, ancestral and primal—make their mark by both being there and not.

The last time I visited Laredo, I took my mountain bike with me; I always do. I don't need an excuse to ride at the old ranch on Highway 359. But I found a new lock on the gate. Determined to ride, I suited up and rode along the barbed-wire fence. I knew what I was looking for. After riding east for about half a mile along the southernmost fence line skirting the ranch, I found it: a crawlspace where the fence had been loosened and lifted up carefully to permit entry. I crawled through and dragged my bike after me. I've seen these crawlspaces all my life; the Mexicans traversing the landscape in the dead of night make them. The ranchers fix the cuts in the fence, and Mexicans pursuing the American Dream, or a job, or a chance to reconnect with family members who have successfully made the journey, cleave through them. It's all part of the same cycle. Sometimes I find evidence of their journeys: discarded wrappers, bits of foil, empty water bottles caked in dirt. When I make my way to Frog Pond and the little *cabaña* where my uncles like to cook *fajitas* on Sundays, I sometimes notice that Epifanio, the rancher, has surreptitiously left several gallon water jugs by a grove of mesquite trees. One day I asked Epifanio, who was born in Nuevo Laredo, but who has legally lived and worked on the ranch in Laredo for over twenty years, about the jugs. A quiet man of few words, he smiled and softly said, *"Están para los que cruzan el río, los que tienen tan poco"* (They are there for those who cross, for those who have so little).

In the twenty-first century, the myth of the frontier is linked to the ongoing experiences of globalism and imperialism. In Laredo, the mythos is alive and well, as evidenced by the increasing extravagances of the yearly Laredo George Washington's Birthday Celebration. So too does the frontier myth of unlimited space and American exceptionalism continue to produce and reproduce emblems of social memory and places of memory that generally serve to commemorate the "winners" of history. But one thing is certain. If myths, as Sara Spurgeon (2005) reminds us, "are what we wish history had been—a compressed, simplified, sometimes outright false vision of the past but a vision intended to serve a specific purpose in the present" and subsequently consign "a specific shape to the future" (3), a major reason to reconstruct the past—and study history—is to effectively re-vision the future by re-orienting the shapes that structure that future. Overturning a frontier mythos in the Southwest effectively splinters its hegemony and breaks open haunted sites, locales, and subsumed pathways to knowledge. Just as "illegal" Mexicans will continue to cut holes in fence lines along the Bordered frontier, so too will their stories continue to slip through.

I mentioned Turner's *Literary Mind* earlier, and I turn again to his writing to comment on what is perhaps the most pernicious quality of haunting and ghostly matters—hauntology. The French philosopher Jacques Derrida first introduced the concept in *Specters of Marx* (2006).[1] A fluid and difficult idea to conceptualize, hauntology is a postmodern theory and lens of enormous scale that, in a sense, deconstructs the living present to unfasten virtual traces, or spaces of spectrality that defy any sharp distinction between "the real and the unreal, the actual and the inactual" that mark the opposition between what is present and what is not (12). Hauntology is about the aesthetics that we imitate, rather than those we create; it refers to the emotional residue of the past that is extant in our future conceptions. For example, the Colonial Ball and Presentation sponsored by the WBCA that I discussed in chapters 2 and 3 continually re-presents a narrative first instituted by the Red Men and later perpetuated by the Society of Martha Washington—a storied performance that effectively restructured Laredo's capitalist economy in terms of "commerce-friendly images of nation and nationality" via repetition and a "meticulously crafted sense of decorum" (Peña 2020, 8). If we recall how the IORM fraternity brothers sought to "claim" Laredo for the United States through a performance that belonged neither to the present nor the past but some "implied 'timeless' era" (Fisher 2014, 11), then we must also acknowledge how the WBCA's continued performances in the present reify a nineteenth-century colonialist narrative as a condition of modernity "in which life continues, but time has somehow stopped" (6). This illumes Fisher's impression of "the slow cancellation of the future," a structure of feeling borrowed from Franco "Bifo" Berardi.[2]

What disconcerts both Berardi and Fisher as regards our neoliberal milieu is the continuity of persistent forms like the performances of the WBCA within our cultural productions. Such "postmodern anachronisms" (13) on the surface may *appear* modern or innovative, but because they remain embedded in established neoliberal projects and archaic and overworked visions of the future, they merely refurbish antiquated paradigms; the effect is the disappearing of radically *alternative* futures. It is this element of stasis, of potential futures that cease to exist, that Memo Cruz's father in *Sleep Dealer* cautions against. When one is deprived of the resources to even *imagine* a "lost" future—as was Memo—then we are (seemingly) made incapable of moving beyond the uneasy compromises of our present capitalist economy. To further illustrate, Jake Dionne (2019) notes how the future in *Sleep Dealer*, which is marked by a high-tech border wall, is also a future that signifies the persistence of racial hierarchies[3] (figure 9). *Sleep Dealer*'s future is an anachronism; what *appears* modern and technologically advanced is not, it's merely a rehabilitated paradigm that is "managed" much in the same way as it is maintained in the present—through a metaphor-laden reality television show called "Drones," a show that first thrills Memo and then horrifies him by displaying his father's cold-blooded murder. The future dam in the film, like the technologically updated Mexico–US checkpoint Rudy moves through, has had its stasis merely "buried, interred behind a superficial frenzy of 'newness'" (Fisher 2014, 6). In short, there's nothing new or radical in the towering dam or the automated checkpoint: they remain as haunted emblems of coloniality.

In many ways, such stagnation signifies a failure of a wider moral imagination. Specters, however, remain beyond terminal time; they are ghostly reminders that there exist cultural forms and ways of being yet adequate to our contemporary experience—but these must be harnessed from present cultural moments in which time has folded back on itself. Specters and ghosts are resources that mark the shape of things both there and not, appearing at random or at will, but hardly inert in a world where the presence of the past is all around us. Hauntology explores these impasses with the goal of shaping posterities which insist that there are futures beyond our present reality—beyond what we've been conditioned to expect out of our present social constructs.

Throughout the pages of *The Haunted Southwest*, I have aimed to locate and then trace specters and ghosts that occupy the in-between spaces that haunt the living present and undermine its contemporaneity in the American Southwest. In the twenty-first century, the deliberate cancellation of a future that persists to shape recognizable cultural and social forms inadequate to our multicultural present is being met by communities of difference across the US and, indeed, the globe. Many of these communities

Figure 9: The technologically updated US–Mexico border checkpoint in *Sleep Dealer* (2008)—a haunted emblem of coloniality—is eerily familiar. Courtesy of Alex Rivera.

are moving beyond recognizing truths that have been denied them for generations; they are building conceptual coalitions and mobilizing against unsustainable, untruthful narratives, icons, and technologies—towards restoration.

As I write this, while the pandemic that is Covid-19 continues to seethe outside our doors, collective values appear to be shifting. Inchoate structures of feeling reminiscent of the Civil Rights era are fomenting on a massive scale. Citizens *en masse* are taking to the streets in efforts to reshape the American landscape, as evidenced by the public destruction of Confederate monuments and colonial emblems of public memory that reify racism and whiteness as the only legitimate sources of power. Frustrated and disillusioned by a status quo bent on preserving forms of power at their expense, citizens of all races, nationalities, ethnicities, and classes are seeking to recoup a sense of agency for themselves and their communities. As citizens *choose* to no longer validate stories that glorify racism and colonial paradigms, the silenced subtext of accurate, factual, and self-determining narratives of a truly multicultural and shared history are given impetus to bubble up and out of our American communities. These new stories recognize and reaffirm the accomplishments of the poor, the dispossessed, and other minority figures to the American story. As new conversations of social, racial, and ethnic justice take shape, so may the ghostly remnants of haunted forms that refuse silence one day be justly honored and revered.

Perhaps, like the outdated monuments of Euro American superiority, the myth of the American frontier will one day be like so many ruins and bones. And although the wreckage of the frontier and its abiding mythology will likely never entirely subside from the American ethos, it appears that the markers and artifices of countless tenuous narratives of history are giving way to more truthful representations of place memory that, perhaps, can dissolve the machinery of those totalizing discourses and specters of modernity that are inherently destructive. Remapping forgotten, lost, silenced, or otherwise invisible histories shifts and blurs a nationalist agenda that left its multicolored players beneath the surface of things, subordinate and struggling for breath. Widening the frame of interpretation in ways that expose frontier narratives as Borderlands stories in disguise reifies a place for ethics alongside the uncanny repetitions of history and paves the way to an understanding of landscape as it is shaped by an inclusive timelessness and a superposition of worlds still extant.

ACKNOWLEDGMENTS

A s an academic, I am indebted to previous scholarship as well as countless others who have so generously lent that most precious of resources—their time and encouragement. I express my thanks here to those who have helped me see beyond the limits of the present, and those who continue to inspire me to do "work that matters."

There are many people who have been key to the realization of this book, which began as a dissertation project when I was a graduate student at the University of Texas at San Antonio. At UTSA, I had the opportunity to work alongside an incredible group of women, exemplary scholars in every sense. Thank you, Norma E. Cantú, Linda Townley Woodson, Sonia Saldívar-Hull, and Gabriela González for your guidance, support, and dedication. A special note of thanks goes to Norma E. Cantú, who has been mentor extraordinaire, friend, and touchstone throughout my academic career; I aspire to reach the level of grace and generosity you model as a thinker and human being. Thank you also to Reina Vargas and Bridget Drinka in the Department of English at UTSA for your help in all matters academic and administrative.

The seeds of this book germinated during my time at UTSA but came to fruition at Texas Tech University, where I have continued to receive the invaluable support of friends, colleagues, and students, as well as the financial support necessary to present my work at national and international conferences. At Tech, Sara Spurgeon gifted me with the occasion to spend two incredible days with Larry McMurtry and Dianna Ossana, which galvanized my desire to further unpack Western mythogenesis. And it was here too that I met Cristina García, who encouraged me to incorporate creative elements into my scholarly writing. I must also acknowledge Joe Moreno, Special Collections Librarian at the Laredo Public Library, the staff at Texas

A&M International University, David Lintz, Director of the Red Men Museum and Library in Waco, and Christina Davila-Villarreal at the Webb County Historical Foundation for their generous assistance with some of the research on this project. I am indebted to the trustees of the Lamar Bruni Vergara Educational Fund for Graduate Students at Texas A&M International University, and the Humanities Center at Texas Tech, which helped fund this project. Thanks also to Sylvia Santos, Yolanda Villarreal, Violeta Benavidez, Cordelia Valdez, and all the members of the Princess Pocahontas Council. At TTU Press, I thank Travis Snyder for his initial support of this project. Thanks also to Joanna Conrad, Katie Cortese, Christie Perlmutter, Hannah Gaskamp, and Barbara Hoyt for their design and editorial assistance throughout the many stages that this manuscript has gone through to reach publication. My gratitude also extends to the anonymous readers of this project for their extensive critiques and enthusiasm; and a very special thank you to John Morán Gonzalez for his initial review of this book.

There are many friends and colleagues that I have benefited from knowing and learning from during the years I worked on this book, and I would be remiss not to thank them for contributing to my development as a teacher, scholar, and lifetime student. I only hope that I don't leave anyone out, and, likewise, I take full responsibility for any shortcomings in this book. Through personal correspondence and at various conferences I attended, I've had the great fortune to talk through ideas with outstanding scholars like José E. Limón, Rolando Hinojosa, Kenneth M. Roemer, Alex Rivera, Norma Alarcón, Lyman Tower Sargent, María Herrera-Sobek, and Frederick Luis Aldama. Colleagues Cathryn Merla-Watson, B. V. Olguín, Candace de León-Zepeda, Micah Donohue, David J. Vásquez, Alex Hunt, Brian Still, Yuan Shu, Bruce Clarke, Allison Whitney, Kent Wilkinson, Diane Warner, Ian Hancock, Gary Reger, Jada Ach, Margaret Cantu, Linda De Roche, Esther De-Leon, Linda Heidenreich, Ire'ne Lara Silva, William Brannon, Leonard Engel, Bob Evans, Matthew Wanat, C. Alejandra Elenes, Josie Méndez-Negrete, Murray Leeder, and Stephen Tatum have provided support and encouragement throughout my career. I have been fortunate to have students like Kerry Fine, Monica Montelongo-Flores, Kazutaka Sugiyama, Sarah Cuevas, Martin Benitez, Jamesa Brown, Iracema Quintero, and Bernadette Russo; these and so many others have made it a pleasure to be a professor.

I owe a special debt of gratitude to my wonderful family, in particular my partner Julie Ann Carlton, for bearing with me and continuing to support my (sometimes erratic) writing moods and aspirations through the years. This book is dedicated to my parents, Minerva Cantú Barrera (1940–2021) and Ramiro Barrera Jr. (1941–2014). Thanks, Mom, for gifting me your love of reading and lifelong learning, and thank you, Dad, for opening my eyes to the mysteries of the earth, and so, to worlds beyond.

The following permissions have been generously granted: *Quarterly Review of Film and Video* has granted permission to reprint portions of chapter 1 that appeared in my previous article entitled "Border Theory and the Politics of Place, Space, and Memory in John Sayles's *Lone Star*," vol. 27, no. 3 (2010): 210–18; *Western American Literature* has granted permission to reprint portions of chapter 4 that appeared in my previous article "Written on the Body: A Third Space Reading of Larry McMurtry's *Streets of Laredo*," vol. 48, no. 3 (2013): 233–52; Grey House Press has granted permission to reprint portions of chapter 4 that appeared in the "Critical Readings" section of *Critical Insights: Southwestern Literature*, edited by William Brannon and titled "The Haunted Frontier: Cormac McCarthy's *Border Trilogy*," 2016, 186–200; *Chicana/Latina Studies (MALCS)* has granted permission to reprint portions of chapter 6 that appeared in my previous article entitled "Cyborg Bodies, Strategies of Consciousness, and Ecological Revolution on the México-US Borderlands," vol. 14, no. 1 (2014): 28–55; UCLA Chicano Studies Research Center Press has granted permission to reprint portions of chapter 6 that appeared in my previous chapter, "*Becoming Nawili*: Utopian Dreaming at the End of the World," in *Altermundos: Latin@ Speculative Literature, Film, and Popular Culture*, edited by Cathryn Merla-Watson and B. V. Olguín, 2017, 393–405; and Lexington Books has granted permission to reprint portions of chapter 5 that appeared in "Desert Haunting: A Gothic Reading of Arturo Islas' Classic *The Rain God*," a chapter I authored in *Reading Aridity*, edited by Gary Reger and Jada Ach, 2020, 67–86.

APPENDIX

For Your Information only.

General Land Office

AUSTIN, TEXAS 78701
BOB ARMSTRONG, COMMISSIONER

May 5, 1972

Mr. Cándido Barrera
Box 33 Los Saenz Sta.
Roma, Texas 78584

Dear Mr. Barrera:

Our records show that Manuel Barrera is the original grantee of the tract "La Teraja de Lara" which comprised 25,684 acres located in Jim Wells County. On September 28, 1836, the grantee was put in possession of the tract, he having occupied it in 1833. It was patented to the original grantee on May 8, 1819. There is no copy of the original title in the General Land Office. We do have the patent which may be copied for $2.00, and a file. The file consists of four instruments and a jacket. The fees for copies are $1.00 for the jacket, $4.00 for the field notes, $2.00 for the tax collector's certificate, $3.00 for the deputation of F. A. Blucher as tax collector, and $9.00 for the decree of the court confirming the title to five leagues and twenty labors of land.

We were unable to find a grant known as "Rio de las Nueces Lot No. 20." We did find a title to land in Wilson County. On August 12, 1830, Manuel Barrera petitioned for four leagues of land at the "Rancho de las Cabras Viejas." On April 20, 1831, Governor Letona conceded to the petitioner three leagues and a labor of land. This title consists of ten pages, eight of which are written in Spanish, one in English and a plat. Unfortunately, this is only a part of the original. The testimonio of this title, dated November 29, 1833, for three leagues of land is complete. There are no records for the balance in this office. The testimonio consists of twenty-six pages, twenty are in Spanish. It contains a copy of the original title, the field notes, and various instruments certifying as to the authenticity of signatures and documents. Both of the above-mentioned instruments may be copied for $1.00 per page, or a total of $36.00.

We made a careful search of our records and found that porciones 67 and 108 in Starr County were granted to Mrs. Maria Bartola and Francisco Antonio Villareal respectively.

We do not have any information on claim numbers, the value of the land or the description of it as recognized by the different reclamations and treaties between the United States and Mexico. We only have the documents concerning the original grant. Any subsequent transactions are filed in the County Deeds Records in the county where the land is located. Perhaps the county tax collector assessor may be able to inform you on the value of the land.

Page 2
Mr. Ramiro Barrera

The fee for the "Index to Spanish and Mexican Land Grants" is $5.00.

Please let us know if you wish to obtain copies of any of the above. Your copies will be prepared and mailed immediately on receipt of the respective fees.

Sincerely yours,

Matilde S. Rosales

Matilde S. Rosales
Spanish Archives

Letter from Matilde S. Rosales in the General Land Office to Ramiro Barrera Sr., attesting to the Barrera family ownership of the tract "La Tinaja de Lara." Dated May 5, 1977, written while Bob Armstrong was commissioner of the General Land Office.

NOTES

Prologue

1. My father, Ramiro Barrera Jr., was named "Athlete of the Year" in 1985 by the *Laredo Morning Times*. See Salo Otero, "Moreno, Barrera: Coach, Athlete of Year," *Laredo Morning Times*, January 1, 1984, 1B. The photo, titled "Jogging Weather," was taken by *Laredo Times* photographer Jerry Lara and appeared in the *Laredo Morning Times* on December 12, 1989. The photo, taken on East Del Mar Blvd. in Laredo, illustrates the open world of my adolescence less than two miles from my family's home. From this road, my father and I would ride around a nearby pig farm and several natural ponds on our motorcycles. Today, Del Mar Blvd. is a bustling corridor bursting with commerce in the form of endless strip malls, housing, and other developments.

Preface

1. See Arturo Longoria, *Adios to the Brushlands* (College Station: Texas A&M University Press, 1997). A trained biologist and former investigative reporter, Longoria laments a vanishing habitat that once covered nearly four million acres of the Rio Grande Valley. He links loss of landscape to the death of his grandfather and further reports on early public policies and private actions that reduced the brushland to less than five percent of its former extent.

2. I employ the capital "B" in "Borderlands" throughout *Haunted* to evoke an Anzaldúan conception of the Borderlands that moves beyond the geopolitical space of the Texas/Mexico border, to encompass a range of psychic, spiritual, and metaphoric meanings and further signal transformational spaces of potentiality and possibility; use of the lowercase "b" refers to the region on both sides of the US–Mexico border. For more, see Gloria E. Anzaldúa,

Borderlands/La Frontera: The New Mestiza, 4th ed. (San Francisco: Aunt Lute, [1987] 2012); AnaLouise Keating, ed., *The Gloria Anzaldúa Reader* (Durham, NC: Duke University Press, 2009).

3.   The novels that comprise the tetralogy were published over a period of thirteen years. In order of publication, they are *Lonesome Dove* (1985), *Streets of Laredo* (1993), *Dead Man's Walk* (1995), and *Comanche Moon* (1998). The novels were not published in the order in time in which the story occurs. *Dead Man's Walk* and *Comanche Moon*, respectively, are prequels to *Lonesome Dove*, and *Streets of Laredo* is the sequel to *Lonesome Dove*.

4.   For more on how Mexico and the US are visualized as racially derived, yet distinct, adjoining national spaces, see María Josefina Saldaña-Portillo, *Indian Given: Racial Geographies across Mexico and the United States* (Durham, NC: Duke University Press, 2016).

5.   Chapter 5 of Saldaña-Portillo's *Indian Given* (see n4) presents a historical and legislative account of mapping Aztlán in the Southwest. For a broader study of the historic and continued meaning surrounding Aztlán as a unifying force and rallying symbol of Chicano unity and consciousness, especially as it was conceptualized as a key aspect of the Chicano movement of the 1960s and 1970s, see Rudolfo Anaya, Francisco A. Lomeli, and Enrique R. Lamadrid, eds., *Aztlán: Essays on the Chicano Homeland*, rev., exp. ed. (Albuquerque: University of New Mexico Press, 2017).

6.   "Survivance" was first used in the context of Native American Studies by Anishinaabe scholar Gerald Vizenor to describe the continuance of Native stories in terms of survival, endurance, and resistance. For more, see Vizenor, *Manifest Manners: Narratives on Postindian Survivance* (Lincoln, NE: Bison Books, 1999), and Vizenor, ed., *Survivance: Narratives of Native Presence* (Lincoln: University of Nebraska Press, 2008).

Introduction

1.   For more on the early Spanish, French, and British-American colonial history before the era of liberal nationalisms in the US Southwest region, see Walter Prescott Webb, *The Great Plains* (Boston: Ginn and Company, 1931); Laura Gómez, *Manifest Destinies: The Making of the Mexican American Race* (New York: New York University Press, 2007); Martha Menchaca, *Recovering History, Reconstructing Race: The Indian, Black and White Roots of Mexican Americans* (Austin: University of Texas Press, 2001).

2.   Limerick emphasizes patterns of conquest and so argues that other states exhibiting the same patterns of competition over legitimacy of language,

culture, religion, and property, such as Iowa, Missouri, Arkansas, Louisiana, and Alaska, can also be included in her definition of the West as place.

3. For more on the historical borderlands, see John Francis Bannon, *Spanish Borderlands Frontier, 1513–1821* (New York: Holt Rinehart and Winston, 1970) and Jack D. Forbes, "Frontiers in American History," *Journal of the West* 1 (1962): 63–73. For more regarding José de Escandón and the Spanish border province of Nuevo Santander, a topic I take up in chapters 2 and 3, see Jerry Thompson, *Sabers on the Rio Grande* (Austin: Presidential Press, 1974) and Gilberto Miguel Hinojosa, *A Borderlands Town in Transition: Laredo, 1755–1870* (College Station: Texas A&M University Press, 1987).

4. Broadly, *perceived space* refers to spatial practices that include the built environment and the interrelationships between institutional practices and daily routines or experiences. *Representations of space* are linked to relations of production, that is space as conceptualized and constructed by urban planners, scientists, engineers, and so on. *Lived spaces* move us beyond conceived and perceived space to more broadly account for symbolic aspects of space, often existing contrary to public rhetorics of representational space.

5. In *Myth and the History of the Hispanic Southwest* (Albuquerque: University of New Mexico Press, 1998), David J. Weber writes that Herbert Eugene Bolton, whom he calls the "founder of the Borderlands school, recognized at an early date the wisdom of applying Turner's thesis to Spanish-American frontiers" (35). Furthermore, although "the Bolton school offered a valuable balance to the chauvinism of the Turnerians, who had come to see the term 'frontier' as synonymous with the Anglo-American frontier" (37), Weber nonetheless concludes that "Bolton's extraordinary academic progeny concerned itself more with archival research and the reconstruction of the particulars of the past than with theory in general or with the impact of the frontier on Mexican society or institutions in particular" (38).

6. Alurista, the nom de plume of Alberto Baltazar Urista Heredia, is generally credited with popularizing the term "Aztlán" in a poem presented during the Chicano Youth Liberation Conference in Denver, Colorado, March 1969. For more, see Anaya, et al., eds., *Aztlán: Essays on the Chicano Homeland* and Rafael Pérez-Torres, *Movements in Chicano Poetry: Against Myths, Against Margins* (New York: Cambridge University Press, 1995).

7. Ramirez contends that H.R. 4437 (the Sensenbrenner Bill), passed at the end of 2005 by the US House of Representatives, but not the Senate, "would have transformed undocumented workers into felons" (50).

8. Specifically, Ramirez focuses his study on two short stories (Viramontes's

"Cariboo Café" and Daniel Chacón's "Godoy Lives") to discuss how each demonstrates what he describes as a "borderlands ethical stance" that moves beyond national laws and borders. For more, see Pablo A. Ramirez, "Toward a Borderland Ethics: The Undocumented Migrant and Haunted Communities in Contemporary Chicana/o Fiction," *Aztlán: A Journal of Chicano Studies* 35, no. 1 (Spring 2010): 49–67.

9. See J. L. Ruiz, H. Galán, H. Cisneros, M. Moreno, and S. R. Ulibarri, *Chicano! Quest for a Homeland*, in *Chicano! The History of the Mexican American Civil Rights Movement* (Los Angeles: NLCC Educational Media, 1996).

10. At its inception in 1898, the festivities were called the Washington's Birthday Celebration. In 1923, the Washington's Birthday Celebration Association (WBCA) was created to oversee all events included in the celebration. For example, the Border Olympics were added in 1933; the Mr. South Texas award in 1952; a Youth Parade in 1972; the Señor International Event in 1977; and the Jalapeño Festival and Princess Pocahontas Council in 1979. For more, see Stanley Green, *A History of the Washington Birthday Celebration* (Laredo, TX: Border Studies Publishing, 1999).

Chapter 1

1. The Black Seminoles established small, albeit thriving, communities along the borders of the Indian Territory, Coahuila, and Texas—what is today the Southwest Texas–Mexico border. Often called "buffalo soldiers," the Black Seminoles of Brackettville, Texas, Kinney County, referred to in *Lone Star* are likely the descendants of nineteenth-century soldiers stationed at the US Army base, Fort Clark. The story of the Black Seminoles from the early nineteenth century through the twentieth century in Texas has been well documented by Ian F. Hancock. For more on the Black Seminoles of Texas, see Hancock's "Gullah West: Texas Afro-Seminole Creole," in *Further Studies in Lesser-Known Varieties of English*, eds. Jeffrey P. Williams, Edgar W. Schneider, Peter Trudgill, and Daniel Schreier, 236–64 (New York: Cambridge University Press, 2015) and *The Texas Seminoles and Their Language* (Austin: University of Texas African and Afro-American Studies Research Center, 1980). Other works include Sara R. Massey's *Black Cowboys of Texas* (College Station: Texas A&M University Press, 2000); Kevin Mulroy's *Freedom on the Border: The Seminole Maroons in Florida, the Indian Territory, and Coahuila, and Texas* (Lubbock: Texas Tech University Press, 1993); Sherman W. Savage's "The Negro Cowboy of the Texas Plains," *Negro History Bulletin* 24 (April 1961); Doug Sivad's *The Black Seminole Indians of Texas* (Boston: American

Press, 1984); and Quintard Taylor's *In Search of the Racial Frontier: African Americans in the American West, 1528–1990* (New York: W.W. Norton & Co., 1998).

2. The name "Karen" is a pejorative slang term for an angry, entitled, and often racist middle-aged white woman who uses her privilege to police other people's behavior. Stereotyped as having a blond bob haircut, in 2020 "Karen" went viral as a label used to call out white women who were captured in videos engaging in what are widely seen as racist acts.

3. Pilar's exchange with the angry parents early in the film sets the stage for freeing history, but Chican@s are not the only ethnic group struggling to define their identity in Frontera. Freedom for African Americans in Frontera further echoes Emma Pérez's articulation of a decolonial imaginary that reflects a third space that does not fully represent liberation, but, rather, a transitory space of possibilities not yet realized. (See Pérez, *The Decolonial Imaginary: Writing Chicanas into History* (Bloomington: Indiana University Press, 1999.) Through its reliance on revisionist methods of identity politics, *Lone Star* demonstrates how colonialist impulses in Frontera silenced a history of African Americans from the landscape because it did not fit into the neat, white-centered mythology of the township. However, African Americans actively work to create what Peréz theorizes as a "postcolonial imaginary" so as to re-mythologize the history of the west from the African American point of view. For more, see Cordelia Barrera, "Border Theory and the Politics of Place, Space, and Memory in John Sayles's *Lone Star*," *Quarterly Review of Film and Video* 27 (2010): 210–18.

4. See chapter 5, "The Silencing of the Lambs," of Rodolfo F. Acuña's *Assault on Mexican American Collective Memory, 2010–2015* (Lanham, MD: Lexington Books, 2017), in which he introduces Hollywood films detailing the Battle of the Alamo to conclude how "[h]istory resembles the Alamo remakes; it fits a national purpose and perpetuates its illusions" (136).

5. Delmore Payne's father is Big Otis, the proprietor of "The Big O." Otis has earned the honorary title "mayor of Darktown." When his grandson, Chet, visits him for the first time, Otis shows him around the "museum" of Black Seminole and border artifacts he displays in a back room of his bar. Otis recounts the story of the Texas Seminoles who once worked alongside the predominantly white US cavalry as scouts. The artifacts and photos that Otis displays inform the history that "continues to live in the present" through the local Army base, a military presence in the border region that dates back to the mid-nineteenth century, as well as through Otis himself. For more, see Tomás

F. Sandoval, "The Burden of History and John Sayles' *Lone Star*," in *Westerns: Films Through History*, ed. Janet Walker, 71–85 (New York: Routledge, 2001), 72.

Otis makes the point that in Frontera, history has always been "fuzzy" and ambiguous, reminding viewers that an individual's "place" is a type of cognitive map that is nonetheless fluid and so can be contested at the political, cultural, social, and, finally, individual level. It is only when Chet "connects" with his Black Seminole forebears by way of material culture that he can finally envision a future in which he can move beyond victimhood to personhood. Historical amnesia has, to use Hayden White's term, lifted the "burden of history" (Sandoval, "The Burden," 121) and paved the way towards a new consciousness. Confronting material artifacts of his Seminole past allows Chet to treasure those ghostly aspects and begin to fill in the shape of those absences. Significantly, though, many of the characters in *Lone Star* proactively *choose* which aspects of their past they will actively engage while forging present-day identities faithful to individual historical circumstance.

In addition, Ian Hancock argues that Black Seminoles retained an ethnic identity in the area based in part on their linguistic distinctiveness. The African American presence in the film focuses on the historical presence of Black Seminoles in a specific geographical site. As such, further discussion must rightly focus on a sociolinguistic history that touches on African American multilingualism to show how African Americans often acquired and utilized various European and American Indian languages while intermingling or serving as cultural mediators between whites and American Indians as guides, or scouts, and interpreters. This discussion is beyond the scope of this work. For more information, see Hancock and Mark L. Lauden, "African-Americans and Minority Language Maintenance in the United States," *The Journal of Negro History* 85, no. 4 (2000): 223–40.

6. A few examples serve to illustrate the racial divide that has historically fragmented African Americans, Mexicans, and Anglos in Texas. Research shows African Americans along Texas borders were generally the targets of bitter, racist tactics. In 1886, a sign reading "Nigger, don't let the sun go down on you in this town" was posted just outside De Leon, Comanche County (Elliott Young, "Red Men, Princess Pocahontas, and George Washington: Harmonizing Race Relations in Laredo at the Turn of the Century," *The Western Historical Quarterly* 29, no. 1 (1988): 63). Conflicts between Black soldiers at Fort McIntosh in Laredo and Mexicans erupted three times in 1899. Texas Army commander Colonel McKibben concluded that "the trouble at

Laredo is due primarily to race prejudice between Mexican residents and the soldiers, and the association of these soldiers with Mexican women" (Young, "Red Men," 64). In *Anglos and Mexicans in the Making of Texas 1836–1986* (Austin: University of Texas Press, 1987), historian David Montejano observed a propensity for whiteness among upper-class Mexicans along the border. He argues that Texas Mexicans occupied a transitional position in the racial hierarchy—if they had enough money or married Anglos they had the moral and material qualifications to become "American" (251–52); the same did not apply to either American Indians or Blacks.

Chapter 2

1. For more, see Arnoldo De León, *They Called Them Greasers: Anglo Attitudes toward Mexicans in Texas, 1821–1900* (Austin: University of Texas Press, 1983), and Américo Paredes, *With a Pistol in His Hand: A Border Ballad and Its Hero* (Austin: University of Texas Press, 1971).

2. The following was obtained from David Lintz, director of the Red Men Museum and Library in Waco, Texas, on April 14, 2021, via e-mail to the author. It is transcribed directly from the Long Talk of the Great Sachem (Records of the Fourth Council of the Great Council of Texas, August 1898): "WASHINGTON'S BIRTH-DAYS The one hundred and seventy sixth return of the natal day of the father of his country, our George Washington, was a red letter day for Redmanship in Texas. Yaqui Tribe No. 59 celebrated that day in their hunting-ground in the City of Laredo. Their success was truly wonderful. Never before in this reservation has the day been so honored either in magnitude or grandeur. On the banks of the Rio Grande river, the extreme boundary where only a few hundred feet from the foreign soil of a sister republic the American flag was seen on every house top, and the visitors who trailed from the center of our reservation to the famed city on Monterey, Mexico, joined the assembled throng to honor the day and show their good will to our Order. All honor is due to the citizens of Laredo and their sister city on the opposite side of the river for their generous assistance in making the day one long to be remembered with pleasure by all. Yaqui Tribe has done much for the Order in celebrating the day and the ten thousand assembled to see for the first time the reproduction of the first overt act by the 'Sons of Liberty' for this country and to hear the address on the life and character of our Washington. Laredo is truly a Red Man's city. All honor to her and Yaqui tribe."

3. The city ordinances, minutes, and deeds books provide an early example

of post-annexation politics. On February 27, 1872, the first English entry by a Laredo city alderman who recorded the proceedings and events of the city council meetings was entered into the official Laredo Minutes (Laredo Minutebook A. May 15 1867–October 13, 1877). Notably, this admission in the Laredo Minutes concerns the sale of tracts of land in Laredo. It is noteworthy that this first English entry is a "double" entry. The English entry, which is found on page 46 of this book, is a duplicate entry of a Spanish entry from page 42 of the same book. For reasons unknown, the unnamed alderman felt it necessary to translate the Spanish entry found on page 42 to English on page 46. A further noteworthy element of the English entry on page 46 is the fact that the introduction of aldermen was not altered and remains in Spanish. Only the text regarding the sale of city lots was translated to English. The translated text on page 46 reads:

"At the meeting of the board of aldermen it was resolved that from and after the first day of March 1872 the [unintelligible word] of city lots shall be ten dollars each in gold and that not over two lots shall be sold to one person [*sic*] But if anyone may desire to have a larger number he may make his application and the board will decide if his petition be granted"

The Laredo City Ordinance books, vols. 1 and 2, which date through September 5, 1873 are recorded in Spanish. There is no book with entries between September 5, 1873 and January 1, 1874. The entirety of Laredo Ordinances, vol 2, January 5, 1859 to September 1873 is documented in Spanish. The next ordinance book in the sequence, Ordinances, vol. 3, January 1, 1874 to June 29, 1883 is entirely in English. The city's books of deeds are recorded in Spanish through July 13, 1869. The deeds books show a gap between July 13, 1869 and November 1872 as well. The volume titled "Deeds Nov. 1872 to June 1888" contains, about mid-way, the first entry for deeds in English. This entry is dated January 30, 1874. This volume reveals a gap between December 1, 1873, for which the deed entry is in Spanish, and the first English entry on January 30, 1874. Once more, it is noteworthy that this volume details a seemingly abrupt shift from the Spanish language to English. Significantly, this first entry in English also concerns the sale of land tracts in Laredo:

"The State of Texas, the County of Webb know all men by these presents [*sic*] that the corporation of the City of Laredo for and in consideration of the fencing and improving—to M. Botello have granted bargained sold and conveyed and do by this presents [*sic*] grant bargain and sell and convey until the said Maxamalliano [*sic*] Botello a certain tract of land situated on the west side of the Arroyo Chacon and within the corporation limits to have and to hold the same tract of land for a term of five years free of rent provided he fences and improves the same. Attested by Hugh James, Secretary and Benavidez Mayor. Jan. 30, 1874."

These three collections of books, which encompass the earliest Laredo City Council minutes and records, reveal abrupt shifts in two of the three sets. Both the deed books and the minutes books shift unexpectedly in mid-volume from Spanish language entries to English entries. The ordinance books, although they contain no language shift mid-way, show an almost four-month gap between volume 3, which is recorded in English, and volume 2, which is recorded in Spanish. The change in public records, then, is as follows: The City Council Minutes moved to English language usage first, on February 27, 1872; the City Ordinances followed suit on January 1, 1874; and the first volume of deeds books in English was recorded beginning January 30, 1874.

4. Lorraine Whitoff Laurel, comp., "Samuel Mathias Jarvis," Webb County Historical Society Records, Laredo, Texas, n.d. "Sanborn Maps 1874–1894," Luciano Guajardo Historical Collection. Norma Elia Cantú also refers to these name changes in her 1995 address, "The Streets of Laredo: Myth and Reality of a Legendary Site," Conference on Barrios and Other Ethnic Neighborhoods in the U.S., Université Paris VII, Paris, France, 1995.

5. In 2021, for the first time in its 124-year history, the WBCA postponed the annual celebration due to the Covid pandemic; the website states that the WBCA will resume its operations in full beginning January 2022. See https://www.wbcalaredo.org/

6. David Lintz verified that Charles M. Barnes was one of eighty-seven members of the Natchez Tribe #4, instituted in San Antonio, Texas in 1896. Barnes held the position of chief of records and sachem of the tribe (perhaps the first sachem), terms of which lasted only six months. Additionally, Barnes served as great representative for Texas. Barnes ran for great senior sagamore (first vice president for Texas) in August 1897 and lost. After this date, his name does not appear in the State Proceedings, although he is still listed as a past sachem for Natchez Tribe #4.

7. See Raúl Homero Villa, *Barrio-Logos: Space and Place in Urban Chicano Literature and Culture* (Austin: University of Texas Press, 2000).

Chapter 3

1. There is no "set" number of participants in the yearly presentation, but there are generally thirteen to seventeen young women presented as part of the

Princess Pocahontas Court. The members of the court are determined in two ways. First, young women—all high school seniors—with mothers who have been active members in the Princess Pocahontas Council for at least three years are eligible to be presented in the February event, as well as join in any other court events. Additionally, each Laredo high school selects one female senior to represent the school. Young women from participating high schools are nominated and selected by their classmates. The young women being presented select the young men who serve as their escorts.

2. *Las Marthas* details the long year of preparation for the 2011 Colonial Ball and Pageant by following two young women. The first is legacy daughter Laura Garza Hovel, who traces her history to Laredo's founder, Tomás Sánchez. The other is a first-generation invited guest, Rosario Guadalupe Reyes, originally from Nuevo Laredo, and whose family moved to the US when she was a child. As we are invited into their homes and family lives, astute viewers perceive that although the two attend the same private high school in Laredo, they embody vastly different perspectives regarding their motivations, hopes, and aspirations. For example, Rosario, who had a *quinceañera*, shares a long list of self-imposed accomplishments that speak to community service efforts and her dedication to youth leadership in her community. Laura's story spends time detailing her genealogical inheritance and changes to her legacy dress. (A legacy dress is one that has been passed down from an earlier debutante.) Perhaps most telling is an emotional truth that makes itself known during the final dress rehearsal. When Rosario openly cries (either out of fatigue or sheer disenchantment), Laura suggests it is due to her position as a non-legacy invitee. Where Rosario is "so scared . . . of not doing it right," Laura wonders aloud if Rosario has been "trained" to do all that community service. Such moments of class consciousness, as Saldaña-Portillo relates in the film, illustrate how the event signals a critical juncture in these young women's lives, as it marks "a sense of differentiation . . . a time that begins to set them apart from one another."

3. I wish to indicate here that I in no way mean the conclusions I present in chapters 2 and 3 of this study to be disparaging. My mother, Minerva Cantu Barrera, worked alongside the women of the PPC for many years. I know many of these women personally and consider many of them to be dear friends. In fact, the council has honored my mother's long legacy with the PPC by dedicating their 2022 program to her memory, a beautiful gesture that my family and I will cherish for years to come. Similarly, I was socialized and educated alongside countless young men and women who performed throughout the

years in both the Colonial Ball and Princess Pocahontas Pageant. Many of my closest friends, cousins, and all three of my brothers performed in these ceremonies. As regards my own participation in the PPC Pageant of 1984, although my ambivalence remains, I have many fond memories.

4. For example, in *¡Viva George! Celebrating Washington's Birthday at the US–Mexico Border* (Austin: University of Texas Press, 2020), Elaine Peña shapes her ethnographic study of the event as a type of anthropological history to disclose key civic, religious, and economic imperatives behind the yearly celebration, which she describes as a "border enactment." Moving beyond site-specific features of the celebration, she delves into how the success of the yearly celebration "depends on the strength of sustained bilateral communication and cross border relationships" between Laredoans and Mexicans (7).

5. For further reading on the Removal Era of American Indians, see Richard White's *The Middle Ground: Indians, Empires, and Republics in the Great Lakes Region, 1650–1815* (New York: Cambridge University Press, 1991); Benedict Anderson's *Imagined Communities: Reflections on the Origin and Spread of Nationalism*, rev. ed. (London: Verso, 1991); and Roy Harvey Pierce's *Savagism and Civilization: A Study of the Indian and the American Mind* (Berkeley: University of California Press, 1998).

6. Although Pierre Nora's work focuses primarily on French identity and memory, his study of collective memory and the construction of memory as it applies to nationalist aims and public consciousness is central to key aspects of this chapter, namely the idea that there is no "place" for the past in modern societies due to both metaphoric and physical disassociation with *milieux de mémoire*, or "true" environments of memory. See Nora, *Realms of Memory: The Construction of the French Past*, 3 vols., ed. Lawrence D. Kritzman, trans. Arthur Goldhammer (New York: Columbia University Press, 1996–1998).

7. See Patricia Nelson Limerick's *Something in the Soil* (W.W. Norton, 2000), in which she discusses at length—notably in her chapter titled "Haunted America"—the ways that the Western landscape, the actual soil beneath one's feet, still "bears witness to the violent subordination of Indian people" (33).

Chapter 4

1. The quote is taken from José E. Limón's book in progress, *The Streets of Laredo: Modernity and Its Discontents*, parts of which he most generously shared with me. A Laredo native, Limón has written extensively on the folklore, literature, and cultural politics of the US–Mexico Borderlands and Greater Mexico. For more on Laredo's economy and political structure during the post–Civil

War period, see Jerry Thompson's *Tejano Tiger: Jose de los Santos Benavides and the Texas–Mexico Borderlands, 1823–1891* (College Station: Texas A&M University Press, 2017). For more on the business and economic history of Laredo, including commercial relations between Mexico and the US, see John A. Adams, *Conflict and Commerce on the Rio Grande: Laredo 1755–1955* (College Station: Texas A&M University Press, 2008).

2. For more, see Cordelia E. Barrera, "Written on the Body: A Third Space Reading of Larry McMurtry's *Streets of Laredo*," *Western American Literature* 43, no. 3 (Fall 2013): 233–52.

3. On October 29, 2020, José E. Limón gave a talk at West Texas A&M University in conjunction with the Center for the Study of the American West (CSAW). In this talk, he discusses the nineteenth-century cowboy as a "conscript of modernity," a phrase he indicates was derived from anthropologist David Scott's *Conscripts of Modernity: The Tragedy of Colonial Enlightenment* (Durham, NC: Duke University Press, 2004). For Limón the folk song, "The Streets of Laredo," which he reminds us is often called "the most famous American cowboy ballad," exposes a contradiction between the cowboy and modernity. This contradiction, he suggests, is in large part based on our own ambivalence regarding modernity and the town/city as its most discernible presence. The following is from his talk: "But we also know that in the face of modernity, the cowboys had to die metaphorically, and yet we grieve his loss through the song's vivid images but also in the lento tempo and aspirating vowels of the tune even as we accept modern progress, grudgingly perhaps." His talk can be found at West Texas A&M CSAW home page: https://www.wtamu.edu/museum/csaw/past-events.html

Chapter 5

1. In *The American Adam: Innocence, Tragedy, and Tradition in the Nineteenth Century* (Chicago: University of Chicago Press, 1959), R.W.B. Lewis describes the American Adam as a figure of "heroic innocence and vast potentialities," overcrowded with illusion. The imagery attached to such men is entwined in myth and a spirit of adventure. There is a moral posturing that accompanies such men, one of "promise and possibility." Yet this "Adamic myth" is highly susceptible to challenge (1).

2. I capitalize the term "Gothic" when referring to the literary tradition, including its forms.

3. For a broader discussion on the haunted aspects of the desert landscape in the novel, see Cordelia Barrera, "Desert Haunting: A Gothic Reading of Arturo

Islas' *The Rain God*, in *Reading Aridity*, edited by Gary Reger and Jada Ach, 67–86 (Lanham, MD: Lexington Books, 2020).

4. The symbolic associations related to Tlaloc are various and complex. In addition to these associations, Esther Pasztory and Cecilia Klein discuss further associations that include weapons of war, fertility, the symbol of the earth as crocodile, relationships to mirrors, clairvoyance, and divinity. See Pasztory, *The Iconography of the Teotihuacan Tlaloc*, Studies in Pre-Columbian Art and Archaeology no. 15 (Cambridge, MA: Harvard University Press, 1974); and Klein, "Who Was Tlaloc?" *Journal of Latin American Lore* 6, no. 2 (1980): 155–204.

5. For more on the complex relationship between the significance of Cihuacoatl, a motherhood and fertility goddess described by Gloria Anzaldúa as the "dark guise" of Tonantzin driven underground by the Azteca-Mexica, see chapter 3 of *Borderlands/La Frontera*, "Entering into the Serpent." In "Who Was Tlaloc?", Klein links early Tlaloc figures to Cihuacoatl in terms of the date-glyph "4 Ollin" to connote a possible end to the present fifty-two–year temporal cycle; in this respect, she concludes Tlaloc signifies an "end" to the present time period.

6. See William Bevis, "Native American Novels: Homing In," in *Recovering the Word: Essays in Native American Literature*, ed. Brian Swann and Arnold Krupat, 580–620 (Berkeley: University of California Press, 1987). For more on "primordial sentiments" that map ties to land, soil, and place, see Stuart Cochran, "The Ethnic Implications of Stories, Spirits, and the Land in Native American Pueblo and Aztlán Writing," *MELUS* 20, no. 2 (Summer 1995): 69–91.

7. For more on a reading of *The Rain God* in terms of Islas's homosexuality as a construct that shapes the novel, see Manuel de Jesús Vega's "Chicano, Gay, and Doomed: AIDS in Arturo Islas' *The Rain God*," *Confluencia* 11, no. 2 (Spring 1996): 112–18.

8. Interesting, but beyond the scope of this essay, is Klein's reference to a stone relief found at Templo Mayor at Tenochtitlan, which she indicates "strongly suggests" a "possibly bisexual aspect of the deity" ("Who Was Tlaloc?", 162). Specifically, she refers to a two-headed Tlaloc stone relief that shares aspects, including breasts, the Ollin sign, and a skull-and-crossbones skirt of the old earth goddess, Ilamatecuhtli-Cihuacoatl.

Chapter 6

1. Alex Rivera is not Mexican American nor from the Southwest; he was born in

New York City. His father is a Peruvian immigrant, and his mother was born in the United States.

2. For more, see Cathryn Josefina Merla-Watson and B. V. Olguin, eds., *Altermundos: Latin@ Speculative Literature, Film, and Popular Culture* (UCLA Chicano Studies Research Center Press, 2017) for a comprehensive study of Latin@ and Chican@ futurist speculative fiction.

3. See Cordelia E. Barrera, "Cyborg Bodies, Strategies of Consciousness, and Ecological Revolution on the US–Mexico Borderlands," *Chicana/Latina Studies (Mujeres Activas en Letras y Cambio Social)* 14, no. 1 (Fall 2014): 28–55. Additionally, note that in this final chapter, I invert the more commonly used term "US–Mexico" to read Mexico–US. This overturning serves two purposes. First, it challenges the hierarchy of writing the US first, and second, it underscores the fact that the film's perspective is viewed from Mexico primarily, rather than from the US.

4. For more regarding Chicano and Mexican writers who employ utopian or dystopian rhetoric, see Miguel López-Lozano's *Utopian Dreams, Apocalyptic Nightmares: Globalization in Recent Mexican and Chicano Narrative* (West Lafayette, IN: Purdue University Press, 2008), in which he discusses the work of authors such as Carlos Fuentes, Alejandro Morales, Carmen Boullosa, and Homero Aridjis in terms of dystopian science fiction.

5. I am indebted to López-Lozano for his intuitive use of Orwell's quote in the introduction to *Utopian Dreams, Apocalyptic Nightmares.*

6. *Sleep Dealer* was produced in Spanish with English subtitles. Specific passages quoted throughout this chapter are taken directly from the film's English subtitles so that the English text remains consistent.

7. In *An Ethics of Place: Radical Ecology, Postmodernity, and Social Theory* (New York: State University of New York Press, 2001), Mick Smith situates radical ecological theory as a challenge to myths of progress that justify artifice and abstract space. Radical environmentalism is beyond the scope of the present study. I follow, however, from Smith's privileging of ethics, specifically an ethics of place and the means by which an ethics of place can accord meaning to and shape a postmodern stance that accounts for rootedness and connection to embedded forms of knowledge that places a greater emphasis on the non-human world. For more on Smith, see Jim Cheney's "Postmodern Environmental Ethics: Ethics as Bioregional Narrative," *Environmental Ethics* 11 (1989): 11–34.

8. For more, see Catherine S. Ramírez's "Afrofuturism/Chicanafuturism: Fictive Kin," *Aztlán: A Journal of Chicano Studies* 33, no. 1 (2008): 185–94.

9.   See Daniel Dinello's *Technophobia: Science Fiction Visions of Posthuman Technology* (Austin: University of Texas Press, 2005).

10. Rudy is a Mexican American who has roots in the machine; he tells us that both his father and mother before him served in the military. It is his legacy and a marker of his cultural identity. When Rudy visits his parents after he has had time to assimilate the consequences of the aqua terrorist episode in which he killed Memo's father in cold blood, he asks his father whether he has ever had "doubts," referring to his father's own military career. Specifically, as he sits at the dinner table with his parents, Rudy adds, "I didn't think I would. Most of the time I don't feel anything." The conversation, comprised of close-up shots of Rudy, his father, and his mother, is significant both narratively and visually. The close-up shot of Rudy's father is framed by a painting of *The Last Supper*, suggesting the singular power of a militarized weapons system and the projection of a masculinist gendering of technology that is both omnipotent and iconic. The painting is further attached to a colonial legacy of Christianity that obscures the spiritual order of Indigenous peoples, a key aspect of the film central to Memo's awakening consciousness that harks back to the requisite recovery of history and cultural memory by Anzaldúa's Borderland subject.

11. See Chela Sandoval's "New Sciences: Cyborg Feminism and the Methodology of the Oppressed," *Cybersexualities: A Reader on Feminist Theory, Cyborgs, and Cyberspace*, edited by Jenny Wolmark (Edinburgh: Edinburgh University Press, 1999), 247–63.

12. In the film, we learn much about Rudy's and Memo's home life, as we meet both sets of parents and are invited into each of their homes. When we first meet Luz, however, she is traveling by bus. We know she was once a university student, and that she now lives alone in an apartment. At the film's conclusion, we can only assume that she stays with Memo.

Conclusion

1.   See *Arts of Living on a Damaged Planet: Ghosts and Monsters of the Anthropocene*, ed. Anna Tsing, Heather Swanson, Elaine Gan, and Nils Bubandt (Minneapolis: University of Minnesota Press, 2017). This book is organized around two themes: ghosts and monsters. The distinction between the two themes is noted by a G or M, which correspond to the distinct sections of the book.

2.   See Mark Turner, *The Literary Mind: The Origins of Thought and Language* (New York: Oxford University Press, 1998).

3. A relative of mine, Jose Antonio Lopez, self-published a family history titled, *The Last Knight: Don Bernardo Gutierrez de Lara, a Texas Hero* in 2008 (Bloomington, IN: Xlibris, ISBN: 978-1-4363-1500-5). This account details the journey of my mother's side of the family from Guerrero, Mexico to Texas beginning about 1816. Additionally, in the interest of full disclosure, there are other claims to La Tinaja de Lara. One of these includes the family of Gabriela González, also of Laredo, Texas.

4. For more, see Priscilla Solis Ybarra's *Writing the Goodlife: Mexican American Literature and the Environment* (Tucson: University of Arizona Press, 2016). Four values comprise what Ybarra calls "goodlife writing": simplicity, sustenance, dignity, and respect. Ybarra recasts mainstream literary ecocritical traditions that often fail to account for a US legacy of colonization and racism. The author engages tensions of modernity, human-to-human power hierarchies, issues of decoloniality, and local ways of knowing to introduce how literary ecocriticism may be understood via a decolonial lens. *Goodlife* begins in the second half of the nineteenth century and moves through examples from contemporary Mexican American and Chican@ literature and popular culture.

Epilogue

1. Jacques Derrida's *Specters of Marx: The State of the Debt, the Work of Mourning & the New International* (New York: Routledge, 2006) is based on two lectures he delivered on April 22 and 23, 1993, at the University of California, Riverside. Broadly, Derrida locates the metaphysical link between Marxist thought as it has shaped a long legacy, a kind of spectrality that continues to haunt generations of scholars, mainly as a failure to properly read Marx and, rather, invest—often in name only—all of the various ideological pursuits to which Marxism has been attached in the twentieth century. In engaging directly with Marx's texts, Derrida considers complex relations between virtuality and discourses of reality. In contrast to Mark Fisher, *Ghosts of My Life: Writings on Depression, Hauntology, and Lost Futures*, E-book (Alresford, UK: Zero Books, 2014), in *Specters of Marx* we do not find what Avery Gordon describes in *Ghostly Matters: Haunting and the Sociological Imagination* (Minneapolis: University of Minnesota Press, 2008) as a "motivated distress at the claim of history's end" (210, n7). Significantly, Fisher popularized Derrida's concept of hauntology to comment on popular trends, specifically music and film, and the shift to post-Fordist economies of the late 1970s. In so doing, he explored what he saw as a late–twentieth-century impasse, that

is, he had effectively "given up" on the future. In *Capitalist Realism: Is There No Alternative?* (Alresford, UK: Zero Books, 2009), he described the sense that, in our failure to imagine a radically different future, capitalism was the *only* viable economic and political system. This failure to imagine a coherent alternative to capitalism in a way "cancelled" certain futures, even creating "lost futures," as it systematically deprived artists of the resources (and even the imagination) to produce anything really "new" or revolutionary. A prolific documentarian of disappointed futures and tragedies wrought by late-stage capitalism, Fisher's work, like his well-known blog K-Punk (his alias) continues to influence a generation of scholars and citizens who, like him, mourn the loss that real, and radically different, social transformation can bring.

2. See Franco "Bifo" Berardi, *After the Future* (Oakland, CA: AK Press, 2011).

3. See Jake T. Dionne, "Viewing *Sleep Dealer* as Teoria Povera in the Trump Era: Rhetorical Coloniality, Reality Television, and Water Dispossession," *Present Tense: A Journal of Rhetoric in Society* 8, no. 1 (2019), http://www.presenttensejournal.org/volume-8/viewing-sleep-dealer-as-teoria-povera-in-the-trump-era-rhetorical-coloniality-reality-television-and-water-dispossession/, accessed April 20, 2020.

WORKS CITED

Acuña, Rodolfo F. *Assault on Mexican American Collective Memory, 2010–2015*. Lanham, MD: Lexington, 2017.

Adams, Anna. "Forget the Alamo: Thinking about History in John Sayles' *Lone Star*." *The History Teacher* 40, no. 3 (2007): 339–47.

Adams, John A. *Conflict and Commerce on the Rio Grande: Laredo 1755–1955*. College Station: Texas A&M University Press, 2008.

Allen, Paula Gunn. "Bringing Home the Fact: Tradition and Continuity in the Imagination." In *Recovering the Word: Essays on Native American Literature*, edited by Brian Swann and Arnold Krupat, 563–79. Berkeley: University of California Press, 1987.

———. *Pocahontas: Medicine Woman, Spy, Entrepreneur, Diplomat*. New York: Harper, 2003.

———. *The Sacred Hoop: Recovering the Feminine in American Indian Traditions*. Boston: Beacon Press, 1986.

Alonzo, Armando C. *Tejano Legacy: Rancheros and Settlers in South Texas, 1734–1900*. Albuquerque: University of New Mexico Press, 1998.

Anaya, Rudolfo. *Bless Me, Ultima*. New York: Warner, 1995.

———. "A Homeland without Boundaries." In *Aztlán: Essays on the Chicano Homeland*, rev. ed., edited by Rudolfo Anaya, Francisco A. Lomeli, and Enrique R. Lamadrid, 31–42. Albuquerque: University of New Mexico Press, 2017.

Anaya, Rudolfo, Francisco A. Lomeli, and Enrique R. Lamadrid, eds. *Aztlán: Essays on the Chicano Homeland*. Rev. ed. Albuquerque: University of New Mexico Press, 2017.

Anchondo, Carlos. "Cristina Ibarra." *Latino Leaders* 15, no. 6 (2014): 40.

Anderson, Benedict. *Imagined Communities: Reflections on the Origin and Spread of Nationalism*. Rev. ed. London: Verso, 1991.

Anderson, Eric Gary. *American Indian Literature and the Southwest: Contexts and Dispositions*. Austin: University of Texas Press, 1999.

Anzaldúa, Gloria. *Borderlands/La Frontera: The New Mestiza*, 4th ed. San Francisco: Aunt Lute, 2012.

———. "Let Us Be the Healing of the Wound, the Coyolxauhqui Imperative: *la sombra y el sueño*," 303–17. In *The Gloria Anzaldúa Reader*, edited by AnaLouise Keating. Durham, NC: Duke University Press, 2009b.

———. *Light in the Dark/luz en lo oscuro*. Edited by AnaLouise Keating. Durham, NC: Duke University Press, 2015.

———. "now let us shift . . . the path of conocimiento . . . inner work, public acts." In *This Bridge We Call Home: Radical Visions for Transformation*, edited by Gloria E. Anzaldúa and AnaLouise Keating, 540–76. New York: Routledge, 2002.

———. "Speaking across the Divide." In *The Gloria Anzaldúa Reader*, edited by AnaLouise Keating, 282–94. Durham, NC: Duke University Press, 2009a.

———. "(Un)natural bridges, (Un)safe spaces." In *The Gloria Anzaldúa Reader*, edited by AnaLouise Keating, 243–48. Durham, NC: Duke University Press, 2009c.

Arreola, Daniel D. "Forget the Alamo: The Border as Place in John Sayles' *Lone Star*." *Journal of Cultural Geography* 23, no. 1 (2005): 23–42.

———. *Tejano South Texas: A Mexican American Cultural Province*. Austin: University of Texas Press, 2002.

Baccolini, Rafaella. "The Persistence of Hope in Dystopian Science Fiction." *PMLA* 119, no. 3 (2004): 518–21.

Bannon, John Francis. *Spanish Borderlands Frontier, 1513–1821*. New York: Holt Rinehart and Winston, 1970.

Barker, Joanne. "Looking for Warrior Woman (Beyond Pocahontas)." In *This Bridge We Call Home: Radical Visions for Transformation*, edited by Gloria Anzaldúa and AnaLouise Keating, 314–25. New York: Routledge, 2002.

Barr, Alan P. "The Borders of Time, Place, and People in John Sayles's *Lone Star*." *Journal of American Studies* 37, no. 3 (2003): 365–74.

Barrera, Cordelia. "Border Theory and the Politics of Place, Space, and Memory in John Sayles's *Lone Star*." *Quarterly Review of Film and Video* 27 (2010): 210–18.

———. "Cyborg Bodies, Strategies of Consciousness, and Ecological Revolution on the US–Mexico Borderlands." *Chicana/Latina Studies (Mujeres Activas en Letras y Cambio Social)* 14, no. 1 (Fall 2014): 28–55.

———. "Desert Haunting: A Gothic Reading of Arturo Islas' *The Rain God*." In *Reading Aridity in Western American Literature*, edited by Gary Reger and Jada Ach, 67–86. Lanham, MD: Lexington Books, 2020.

———. "Written on the Body: A Third Space Reading of Larry McMurtry's *Streets of Laredo*." *Western American Literature* 43, no. 3 (Fall 2013): 233–52.

Barrera, Mario. *Race and Class in the Southwest: A Theory of Racial Inequality*. Notre Dame: University of Notre Dame Press, 1979.

Barrera, Minerva. "The Princess Pocahontas Pageants 1980–1998." In *A History of the Washington Birthday Celebration*, edited by Stanley Green, 215–30. Laredo: Border Studies Publishing, 1999.

Bennett, Patrick. *Talking with Texas Writers: Twelve Interviews*. College Station: Texas A&M University Press, 1980.

Berardi, Franco. *After the Future*. Oakland, CA: AK Press, 2011.

Bevis, William. "Native American Novels: Homing In." In *Recovering the Word: Essays on Native American Literature*, edited by Brian Swann and Arnold Krupat, 580–620. Berkeley: University of California Press, 1987.

Bhabha, Homi. *The Location of Culture*. New York: Routledge, 2006.

Bloom, Harold, ed. *Bloom's Guides: Cormac McCarthy's* All the Pretty Horses. New York: Chelsea House Publishers, 2004.

Brady, Mary Pat. *Extinct Lands, Temporal Geographies: Chicana Literature and the Urgency of Space*. Durham, NC: Duke University Press, 2002.

Buell, Lawrence. *The Future of Environmental Criticism: Environmental Crisis and Literary Imagination*. Oxford: Blackwell Press, 2005.

Busby, Mark. "Into the Darkening Land: The World to Come." In *Modern Critical Views: Cormac McCarthy*, edited by Harold Bloom, 141–67. New York: Chelsea House Publishers, 2002.

Butler, Judith, and Gayatri Chakravorty Spivak. *Who Sings the Nation-State? Language, Politics, Belonging*. Kolkata: Seagull Books, 2007.

Campbell, Neil. *Post-Westerns: Cinema, Region, West*. Lincoln: University of Nebraska Press, 2013.

Cant, John. *Cormac McCarthy and the Myth of American Exceptionalism*. New York: Routledge, 2008.

Cantú, Norma Elia. *Canícula: Snapshots of a Girlhood* en la Frontera. Albuquerque: University of New Mexico Press, 2015.

———. "The Streets of Laredo: Myth and Reality of a Legendary Site." Conference on Barrios and Other Ethnic Neighborhoods in the U.S. Université Paris VII, Paris, France, 1995.

Cheney, Jim. "Postmodern Environmental Ethics: Ethics as Bioregional

Narrative." *Environmental Ethics* 11 (1989): 11–34.

Chicano! History of the Mexican American Civil Rights Movement (Quest for a Homeland). Video. NLCC Educational Media, 1996.

Clover, Joshua. "The Future in Labor." *Film Quarterly* 63, no. 1 (2009): 6–8.

Cochran, Stuart. "The Ethnic Implications of Stories, Spirits, and the Land in Native American Pueblo and Aztlán Writing." *Varieties of Ethnic Criticism*, special issue of *MELUS* 20, no. 2 (1995): 69–91.

Comer, Krista. *Landscapes of the New West: Gender and Geography in Contemporary Women's Writing*. Chapel Hill: University of North Carolina Press, 1999.

Cooper-Alarcón, Daniel. "All the Pretty Mexicos: Cormac McCarthy's Mexican Representations." In *Cormac McCarthy: New Directions*, edited by James D. Lilley, 141–52. Albuquerque: University of New Mexico Press, 2014.

Cresswell, Tim. *Place: An Introduction*. 2nd ed. West Sussex: Wiley Blackwell, 2015.

Currie, Mark. *About Time: Narrative, Fiction and the Philosophy of Time*. Edinburgh: Edinburgh University Press, 2007.

Cutter, Martha J. "Editor's Introduction: The Haunting and the Haunted." *MELUS* 37, no. 3 (2012): 5–12.

Davis, Robert E. *History of the Improved Order of Red Men and Degree of Pocahontas 1765–1988*. Waco, TX: R.E. Davis, 1990.

de Certeau, Michel. *Heterologies: Discourse on the Other*. Minneapolis: University of Minnesota Press, 1986.

De León, Arnoldo. *They Called Them Greasers: Anglo Attitudes toward Mexicans in Texas, 1821–1900*. Austin: University of Texas Press, 1983.

Deloria, Philip. *Playing Indian*. New Haven, CT: Yale University Press, 1998.

Dennis, Dion. "Washington's Birthday on the Texas Border." *CTTheory.Net*. e036, February 2, 1997. https://journals.uvic.ca/index.php/ctheory/article/view/14834. Accessed January 17, 2020.

Derrida, Jacques. *Specters of Marx: The State of the Debt, the Work of Mourning & the New International*. Routledge Classics. New York: Routledge, 2006.

Dinello, Daniel. *Technophobia: Science Fiction Visions of Posthuman Technology*. Austin: University of Texas Press, 2005.

Dionne, Jake T. "Viewing *Sleep Dealer* as Teoria Povera in the Trump Era: Rhetorical Coloniality, Reality Television, and Water Dispossession." *Present Tense: A Journal of Rhetoric in Society* 8, no. 1 (2019). http://www.present-tensejournal.org/volume-8/viewing-sleep-dealer-as-teoria-povera-in-the-trump-era-rhetorical-coloniality-reality-television-and-water-dispossession/

Ellis, Jay. *No Place for Home: Spatial Constraint and Character Flight in the Novels of Cormac McCarthy*. New York: Routledge, 2006a.

———. "What Happens to Country in *Blood Meridian*." *Rocky Mountain Review* 60, no. 1 (2006b): 85–97.

Fisher, Mark. *Capitalist Realism: Is There No Alternative?* Alresford, UK: Zero Books, 2009.

———. *Ghosts of My Life: Writings on Depression, Hauntology, and Lost Futures*. E-book. Alresford, UK: Zero Books, 2014.

Fitz, Brewster E. *Silko: Writing Storyteller and Medicine Woman*. Norman: University of Oklahoma Press, 2004.

Forbes, Jack D. "Frontiers in American History." *Journal of the West* 1 (1962): 63–73.

Fregoso, Rosa Linda. *MeXicana Encounters: The Making of Social Identities on the Borderlands*. Berkeley: University of California Press, 1993.

Goddu, Teresa A. *Gothic America: Narrative, History, and Nation*. New York: Columbia University Press, 1997.

Gordon, Avery. *Ghostly Matters: Haunting and the Sociological Imagination*. Minneapolis: University of Minnesota Press, 2008.

Green, Stanley, ed. *A History of the Washington Birthday Celebration*. Laredo, TX: Border Studies Publishing, 1999.

———. *Laredo Neighborhoods. The Story of Laredo, No. 18: An Oral History of 1200–1300 San Jorge*. Laredo, TX: Border Studies Publishing, 1993.

Gutiérrez, David G. "Significant to Whom? Mexicans Americans and the History of the American West." *The Western Historical Quarterly* 24, no. 4 (1993): 519–39.

Hancock, Ian F. "Gullah West: Texas Afro-Seminole Creole." In *Further Studies in Lesser-Known Varieties of English*, edited by Jeffrey P. Williams, Edgar W. Schneider, Peter Trudgill, and Daniel Schreier, 236–64. Cambridge: Cambridge University Press, 2015.

———. *The Texas Seminoles and Their Language*. Austin: University of Texas African and Afro-American Studies Research Center, 1980.

Hancock, Ian F, and Mark L. Lauden. "African-Americans and Minority Language Maintenance in the United States." *The Journal of Negro History* 85, no. 4 (2000): 223–40.

Harvey, David. *Spaces of Hope*. Berkeley: University of California Press, 2000.

Hinojosa, Gilberto Miguel. *A Borderlands Town in Transition: Laredo, 1755–1870*. College Station: Texas A&M University Press, 1987.

Huhndorf, Shari M. *Going Native: Indians in the American Cultural Imagination*.

Ithaca, NY: Cornell University Press, 2001.

Ikas, Karin. "Crossing Into a Mexifornian Third Space." In *Communicating in the Third Space*, edited by Karin Ikas and Gerhard Wagner, 123–45. New York: Routledge, 2009.

Islas, Arturo. *The Rain God*. Palo Alto, CA: Alexandrian Press, 1984.

Juarez, José Roberto. "San Agustín Plaza." Keynote speech. Webb County Historical Commission San Agustín Plaza Restoration Project. Laredo, TX, May 19, 2001.

Kapchan, Deborah A. "Common Ground: Keywords for the Study of Expressive Culture." *The Journal of American Folklore* 108, no. 430 (1995): 479–508.

Klein, Cecilia. "Who Was Tlaloc?" *Journal of Latin American Lore* 6, no. 2 (1980): 155–204.

Klein, Kerwin Lee. *Frontiers of Historical Imagination: Narrating the European Conquest of Native America, 1890–1990*. Berkeley: University of California Press, 1997.

Kollin, Susan. "Genre and the Geographies of Violence: Cormac McCarthy and the Contemporary Western." *Contemporary Literature* 42, no. 3 (2001): 557–88.

Kristeva, Julia. *Powers of Horror: An Essay on Abjection*. Translated by Leon Roudiez. New York: Columbia University Press, 1982.

Las Marthas. Video. Directed by Cristina Ibarra, Women Make Movies and PBS *Independent Lens*, 2014.

Latina Feminist Group. *Telling to Live: Latina Feminist* Testimonios. Durham, NC: Duke University Press, 2001.

Lattin, Vernon E. "The Quest for Mythic Vision in Contemporary Native American and Chicano Fiction." *American Literature* 50, no. 4 (1979): 625–40.

Laurel, Lorraine Whitoff, comp. "Samuel Mathias Jarvis." Webb County Historical Society Records. Laredo, TX, n.d.

Lawrence, D. H. *Studies in Classic American Literature*. New York: Penguin, 1971.

LDF online. Laredo Development Foundation. June 10, 2020. http://www.ldfonline.org/

Lefebvre, Henri. *The Production of Space*. 1st ed. Hoboken, NJ: Wiley-Blackwell, 1992.

Lewis, R.W.B. *The American Adam: Innocence, Tragedy, and Tradition in the Nineteenth Century*. Chicago: University of Chicago Press, 1959.

Lich, Lera Patrick Tyler. *Larry McMurtry's Texas: Evolution of a Myth*. Waco,

TX: Eakin Press, 1988.

Limerick, Patricia Nelson. *The Legacy of Conquest: The Unbroken Past of the American West.* New York: Norton, 1987.

———. *Something in the Soil: Legacies and Reckonings in the New West.* New York: W.W. Norton and Co., 2000.

Limón, José E. "Border Literary Histories, Globalization, and Critical Regionalism." *Twenty Years of American Literary History: The Anniversary Volume,* special issue of *American Literary History* 20, no. 1/2 (2008): 160–82.

———. "Tex Sex-Mex: American Identities, Lone Stars, and the Politics of Racialized Sexuality." *American Literary History* 9, no. 3 (1997): 598–616.

Lone Star. Directed by John Sayles. Video. Castle Rock Entertainment, 1996.

Longoria, Arturo. *Adios to the Brushlands.* College Station: Texas A&M University Press, 1997.

López-Lozano, Miguel. *Utopian Dreams, Apocalyptic Nightmares: Globalization in Recent Mexican and Chicano Narrative.* West Lafayette, IN: Purdue University Press, 2008.

Luce, Dianne C. "The Road and the Matrix: The World as Tale in *The Crossing.*" In *Perspectives on* The Crossing, edited by Edwin T. Arnold and Dianne C. Luce, 195–219. Jackson: University Press of Mississippi, 1999.

Magowan, Kim. "Blood Only Means What You Let It: Incest and Miscegenation in John Sayles's *Lone Star.*" *Film Quarterly* 57, no.1 (2003): 20–31.

Márquez, Antonio C. "The Historical Imagination in Arturo Islas's *The Rain God and Migrant Souls. MELUS* 19, no. 2 (1994): 3–16.

McCarthy, Cormac. *All the Pretty Horses.* New York: Vintage International, 1992.

———. *Cities of the Plain.* New York: Knopf, 1998.

———. *The Crossing.* New York: Knopf, 1994.

McCarthy, Cormac. *All the Pretty Horses.* New York: Vintage International, 1992.

McClintock, Anne. "Imperial Ghosting and National Tragedy: Revenants from Hiroshima and Indian Country in the War on Terror." *PMLA* 129, no. 4 (2014): 819–29.

McMurtry, Larry. *Horseman, Pass By.* New York: Pocket Books, 1992.

———. "The Southwest as Cradle of the Novelist." In *The American Southwest: Cradle of Literary Art,* edited by Robert W. Walts and John Graves, 22–42. San Marcos: Southwest Texas State University Press, 1979.

———. *Streets of Laredo.* New York: Simon and Schuster, 1993.

Meléndez, Theresa. "El Contrabando de El Paso: Islas and Geographies of Knowing." In *Critical Mappings of Arturo Islas's Fictions,* edited by Frederick Luis Aldama, 193–207. Tempe: Bilingual Press, 2008.

Menchaca, Martha. *Recovering History, Reconstructing Race: The Indian, Black and White Roots of Mexican Americans*. Austin: University of Texas Press, 2001.

Merchant, Carolyn. *Ecological Revolutions: Nature, Gender, and Science in New England*. Chapel Hill: University of North Carolina Press, 1989.

Merla-Watson, Cathryn Josefina, and B. V. Olguin, eds. *Altermundos: Latin@ Speculative Literature, Film, and Popular Culture* (Aztlan Anthology). Los Angeles: UCLA Chicano Studies Research Center Press, 2017.

Mesnil, Marianne. "Place and Time in the Carnivalesque Festival." In *Time Out of Time: Essays on the Festival*, edited by Alessandro Falassi, 184–96. Albuquerque: University of New Mexico Press, 1987.

Mignolo, Walter. "Delinking: The Rhetoric of Modernity, the Logic of Coloniality, and the Grammar of De-Coloniality." *Cultural Studies* 21, nos. 2–3 (2007): 449–514.

Mogen, David, Scott Patrick Sanders, and Joanne B. Karpinski. *Frontier Gothic: Terror and Wonder at the Frontier in American Literature*. Rutherford, NJ: Fairleigh Dickinson University Press, 1993.

Mohanty, Chandra Talpade. *Feminism without Borders: Decolonizing Theory, Practicing Solidarity*. Durham, NC: Duke University Press, 2003.

Montejano, David. *Anglos and Mexicans in the Making of Texas, 1836–1986*. Austin: University of Texas Press, 1987.

Moraga, Cherríe. *Loving in the War Years: lo que nunca pasó por sus labios*. Brooklyn: South End Press, 1983.

Moreno, Joe R. "The Paso de Jacinto Crossing on the Rio Grande, 1746–2006." *Journal of South Texas* 19, no. 2 (2006): 152–64.

Morris, Pam, ed. *The Bakhtin Reader: Selected Writings of Bakhtin, Medvedev and Voloshinov*. London: Edward Arnold, 1994.

Nething, Margaret. "Pocahontas: The Early Years." In *A History of the Washington Birthday Celebration*, edited by Stanley Green, 211–15. Laredo, TX: Border Studies Publishing, 1999.

Nickell, Pat Smith. "Postmodern Aspects in Larry McMurtry's *Lonesome Dove, Streets of Laredo, Dead Man's Walk*, and *Comanche Moon*." PhD diss., Texas Tech University, 1999.

Nixon-Mendez, Nina. "Historic District/Landmark Board Communication." Laredo Public Library Special Collection, Laredo, TX, August 29, 1995.

———. Memo to Alfredo Castillo regarding "Information Requested on Bruni Plaza," November 30, 1994. Laredo Public Library Special Collection, Laredo, TX.

Nixon-Mendez, Nina, and Jerry Thompson. "Jarvis Plaza." Laredo Public Library Special Collection, Laredo, TX.

Nora, Pierre. "Between Memory and History: *Les Lieux de Mémoire.*" *Memory and Counter-Memory*, special issue of *Representations*, no. 26 (1989): 7–24.

———. *Realms of Memory: The Construction of the French Past.* 3 vols. Abridged. Translated by Arthur Goldhammer and edited by Lawrence D. Kritzman. New York: Columbia University Press, 1996–1998. Originally published as *Les Lieux de Mémoire.* Paris: Éditions Gallimard, 1984–1992.

Owens, Barcley. *Cormac McCarthy's Western Novels.* Tucson: University of Arizona Press, 2000.

Paredes, Américo. *George Washington Gómez: A Mexicotexan Novel.* Houston: Arte Público Press, 1990.

———. *With a Pistol in His Hand: A Border Ballad and Its Hero.* Austin: University of Texas Press, 1971.

Pasztory, Esther. *The Iconography of the Teotihuacan Tlaloc.* Studies in Pre-Columbian Art and Archaeology, no. 15. Cambridge, MA: Harvard University Press, 1974.

Paz, Octavio. *The Labyrinth of Solitude: Life and Thought in Mexico.* New York: Grove Press, 1961.

Peña, Devon G. *Mexican Americans and the Environment: Tierra y Vida.* Tucson: University of Arizona Press, 2005.

Peña, Elaine A. *¡Viva George! Celebrating Washington's Birthday at the US–Mexico Border.* Austin: University of Texas Press, 2020.

Pérez, Emma. *The Decolonial Imaginary: Writing Chicanas into History.* Bloomington: Indiana University Press, 1999.

Pérez, Héctor. "Voicing Resistance on the Border: A Reading of Américo Paredes's *George Washington Gómez. MELUS* 23, no. 1 (1998): 27–48.

Pérez-Torres, Rafael. *Movements in Chicano Poetry: Against Myths, Against Margins.* New York: Cambridge University Press, 1995.

Pierce, Roy Harvey. *Savagism and Civilization: A Study of the Indian and the American Mind.* Berkeley: University of California Press, 1998.

Pilkington, William T. *My Blood's Country: Studies in Southwestern Literature.* Fort Worth: Texas Christian University Press, 1973.

Ramirez, Catherine S. "Afrofuturism/Chicanafuturism: Fictive Kin." *Aztlán: A Journal of Chicano Studies* 33, no. 1 (2008): 185–94.

Ramirez, Pablo A. "Toward a Borderland Ethics: The Undocumented Migrant and Haunted Communities in Contemporary Chicana/o Fiction." *Aztlán: A Journal of Chicano Studies* 35, no. 1 (2010): 49–67.

Ricoeur, Paul. *Memory, History, and Forgetting.* Translated by Kathleen Blamey and David Pellauer. Chicago: University of Chicago Press, 2006.

Robertson, Robert. "Glocalization: Time-Space and Homogeneity-Heterogeneity." In *Global Modernities,* edited by Mike Featherstone, Scott Lash, and Roland Robertson, 25–44. Thousand Oaks, CA: Sage, 1995.

Rodríguez, Richard T. "Glocal Matters: A Response to José E. Limón." *American Literary History* 20, no. 1/2 (2008): 183–86.

Rosaldo, Renato. "Imperialist Nostalgia." *Memory and Counter-Memory,* special issue of *Representations,* no. 26 (1989): 107–22.

Ruiz, J. L., H. Galán, H. Cisneros, M. Moreno, and S. R. Ulibarri. "Chicano! Quest for a Homeland." In *Chicano! The History of the Mexican American Civil Rights Movement.* Los Angeles: NLCC Educational Media, 1996.

Ryan, Jack. *John Sayles, Filmmaker: A Critical Study and Filmography.* 2nd ed. Jefferson, NC: McFarland, 2010.

Saldaña-Portillo, María Josefina. *Indian Given: Racial Geographies across Mexico and the United States.* Durham, NC: Duke University Press, 2016.

Saldívar, José David. *Border Matters: Remapping American Cultural Studies.* Berkeley: University of California Press, 1997.

Saldívar, Ramón. *The Borderlands of Culture: Américo Paredes and the Transnational Imaginary.* Durham, NC: Duke University Press, 2006.

Sánchez, Rosaura. *Chicano Discourse: Sociohistoric Perspectives.* New York: Newbury House Publishers, 1983.

———. "Ideological Discourses in Arturo Islas's *The Rain God.*" In *Criticism in the Borderlands,* edited by Héctor Calderón and José David Saldívar, 114–26. Durham, NC: Duke University Press, 1998.

Sanders, Scott. "Southwestern Gothic: On the Frontier Between Landscape and Locale." In *Frontier Gothic: Terror and Wonder at the Frontier in American Literature,* edited by David Mogen, Scott P. Sanders, and Joanne Karpinski, 55–70. Rutherford, NJ: Fairleigh Dickinson University Press, 1993.

Sandoval, Chela. *Methodology of the Oppressed.* Minneapolis: University of Minnesota Press, 2000.

———. "New Sciences: Cyborg Feminism and the Methodology of the Oppressed." In *Cybersexualities: A Reader on Feminist Theory, Cyborgs, and Cyberspace,* edited by Jenny Wolmark, 247–63. Edinburgh: Edinburgh University Press, 1999.

———. "Third World Feminism: The Theory and Method of Oppositional Consciousness in the Postmodern World." *Genders* no. 10 (1991): 1–24.

Sandoval, Tomás F. "The Burden of History and John Sayles' *Lone Star*." In *Westerns: Films Through History*, edited by Janet Walker, 71–85. New York: Routledge, 2001.

Savoy, Lauret. *Trace: Memory, History, Race, and the American Landscape.* Berkeley, CA: Counterpoint, 2016.

Sayles, John. *Men with Guns & Lone Star.* London: Faber and Faber, 1998.

Scott, David. *Conscripts of Modernity: The Tragedy of Colonial Enlightenment.* Durham, NC: Duke University Press, 2004.

Šesnić, Jelena. *From Shadow to Presence: Representations of Ethnicity in Contemporary American Literature.* Amsterdam: Rodopi Press, 2007.

Silko, Leslie Marmon. "Landscape, History, and the Pueblo Imagination." In *The Ecocriticism Reader: Landmarks in Literary Ecology*, edited by Cheryll Glotfelty and Harold Fromm, 264–75. Athens: University of Georgia Press, 1996.

Simonson, Kirsten. "Bodies, Sensation, Space and Time: The Contribution from Henri Lefebvre." *Geografiska Annaler: Series B, Human Geography* 87, no. 1 (2016): 1–14.

Sivad, Doug. *The Black Seminole Indians of Texas.* Boston: American Press, 1984.

Sleep Dealer. Directed by Alex Rivera. Park City, UT: Maya Entertainment, 2008.

Slotkin, Richard. *The Fatal Environment: The Myth of the Frontier in the Age of Industrialization, 1800–1890.* Cambridge: Atheneum, 1985.

———. *Gunfighter Nation: The Myth of the Frontier in Twentieth-Century America.* Cambridge: Atheneum, 1992.

Smith, Mick. *An Ethics of Place: Radical Ecology, Postmodernity, and Social Theory.* New York: State University of New York Press, 2001.

Soja, Edward W. "History, Geography, and Modernity." In *The Cultural Studies Reader*, 2nd ed., edited by Simon During, 113–25. New York: Routledge, 1999.

———. *Postmodern Geographies: The Reassertion of Space in Critical Social Theory*, 2nd ed. London: Verso, 2011.

Soja, Edward W., and B. Hooper. "The Spaces That Difference Makes." In *Place and the Politics of Identity*, edited by M. Keith and S. Pile, 183–205. New York: Routledge, 1993.

Solis Ybarra, Priscilla. "Borderlands as Bioregion: Jovita González, Gloria Anzaldúa, and the Twentieth-Century Ecological Revolution in the Rio Grande Valley." *MELUS* 34, no. 2 (2009): 175–89.

———. *Writing the Goodlife: Mexican American Literature and the Environment.* Tucson: University of Arizona Press, 2016.

Spurgeon, Sara L. *Exploding the Western: Myths of Empire on the Postmodern Frontier.* College Station: Texas A&M University Press, 2005.

Su, John J. "Haunted by Place: Moral Obligation and the Postmodern Novel." *Locations of Culture: Identity, Home, Theory,* special issue of *The Centennial Review* 43, no. 3 (1998): 589–614.

Swartz, Mimi. "Once Upon a Time in Laredo." *National Geographic* 210, no. 5 (November 2006): 92–109.

Taylor, Quintard. *In Search of the Racial Frontier: African Americans in the American West, 1528–1990.* New York: W.W. Norton & Co., 1998.

Thompson, Jerry. *Laredo: A Pictorial History.* Norfolk, VA: The Donning Company Publishers, 1986.

———.*Sabers on the Rio Grande.* Austin: Presidential Press, 1974.

———. *Tejano Tiger: Jose de los Santos Benavides and the Texas–Mexico Borderlands, 1823–1891.* College Station: Texas A&M University Press, 2017.

Tompkins, Jane. *West of Everything: The Inner Life of Westerns,* 1st ed. Oxford: Oxford University Press, 1992.

Treviño, Javier A. "Remembering George Washington on the Rio Grande." In *Storytelling Sociology: Narrative as Social Inquiry,* edited by Ronald J. Berger and Richard Quinney, 35–48. Boulder, CO: Lynne Rienner Publishers, 2004.

Tsing, Anna, Heather Swanson, Elaine Gan, and Nils Bubandt, eds. *Arts of Living on a Damaged Planet: Ghosts and Monsters of the Anthropocene,* Minneapolis: University of Minnesota Press, 2017.

Tuan, Yi-Fu. *Space and Place: The Perspective of Experience.* Minneapolis: University of Minnesota Press, 1977.

Turner, Frederick Jackson. *The Frontier in American History.* New York: Holt, Rinehart & Winston, 1962.

———. "The Significance of the Frontier in American History." Ann Arbor: University Microfilms, 1966[1893].

Turner, Mark. *The Literary Mind: The Origins of Thought and Language.* Oxford: Oxford University Press, 1998.

Urrea, Luis Alberto. *The Devil's Highway.* New York: Little, Brown and Co., 2004.

Vega, Manuel de Jesús. "Chicano, Gay, and Doomed: AIDS in Arturo Islas' *The Rain God.*" *Confluencia* 11, no. 2 (Spring 1996): 112–18.

Villa, Raúl Homero. *Barrio-Logos: Space and Place in Urban Chicano Literature and Culture.* Austin: University of Texas Press, 2000.

Vizenor, Gerald. *Manifest Manners: Narratives on Postindian Survivance.* Lincoln, NE: Bison Books, 1999.

———,ed. *Survivance: Narratives of Native Presence*. Lincoln: University of Nebraska Press, 2008.

Webb, Walter Prescott. *The Great Plains*. Boston: Ginn and Company, 1931.

Weber, David J. *Myth and the History of the Hispanic Southwest*. Albuquerque: University of New Mexico Press, 1998.

West, Dennis, and Joan M. West. "Borders and Boundaries: An Interview with John Sayles." *Cineaste* 22, no. 3 (1996): 14–17.

White, Hayden. "The Burden of History." *History and Theory* 5, no. 2 (1966): 111–34.

White, Richard. *It's Your Misfortune and None of My Own*. Norman: University of Oklahoma Press, 1991.

———. *The Middle Ground: Indians, Empires, and Republics in the Great Lakes Region, 1650–1815*. New York: Cambridge University Press, 1991.

Whitehouse, Glenn. "Remember to Forget the Alamo: The Dynamics of Cultural Memory in John Sayles' *Lone Star*." *Literature and Theology* 16, no. 3 (2002): 291–310.

Wickelson, Paul. "Shaking Awake the Memory: The Gothic Quest for Place in Sandra Cisneros's *Caramelo*." *Young Scholars*, special issue, *Western American Literature* 48, no.1/2 (2013): 90–114.

Wilcox, Seb. S. "Laredo During the Texas Republic." *The Southwestern Historical Quarterly* 42, no. 2 (1938): 83–107.

———. "Started in 1897 by Red Men." *The Laredo Times*, February 17, 1942. Laredo Public Library Historical Collection, Laredo, TX.

Williams, Raymond. *Marxism and Literature*. Oxford: Oxford University Press, 1977.

Yoder, Michael S., and Renée LaPerrière de Gutiérrez. "Social Geography of Laredo, Texas Neighborhoods." In *Hispanic Places, Latino Spaces: Community and Cultural Diversity in Contemporary America*, edited by Daniel D. Arreola, 55–76. Austin: University of Texas Press, 2004.

Young, Elliott. "Red Men, Princess Pocahontas, and George Washington: Harmonizing Race Relations in Laredo at the Turn of the Century." *The Western Historical Quarterly* 29, no. 1 (1988): 48–85.

INDEX

ABOUT THE AUTHOR

Cordelia E. Barrera is an associate professor of English at Texas Tech University, where she co-directs the Literature of Social Justice and Environment (LSJE) initiative. She specializes in Latinx literatures, the American Southwest, and multiethnic speculative fiction. Her work concentrates on the literature of social justice and the environment.

AUTHOR PHOTO BY J. CARLTON